Western Self-Contempt

Western Self-Contempt

Oikophobia in the Decline of Civilizations

Benedict Beckeld

Northern Illinois University Press
An imprint of Cornell University Press
Ithaca and London

First published 2022 by Cornell University Press

Printed in the United States of America

Library of Congress Cataloging-in-Publication Data

Names: Beckeld, Benedict, author.
Title: Western self-contempt : oikophobia in the decline of civilizations /
    Benedict Beckeld.
Description : Ithaca [New York] : Northern Illinois University Press, an
    imprint of Cornell University Press, 2022. | Includes bibliographical
    references and index.
Identifiers: LCCN 2021036968 (print) | LCCN 2021036969 (ebook) |
    ISBN 9781501763182 (hardcover) | ISBN 9781501763205 (pdf) |
    ISBN 9781501763199 (epub)
Subjects: LCSH: Political culture—Western countries—History. |
    Civilization, Western—Political aspects—History. | Social values—
    Western countries—History. | Western countries—Politics and govern-
    ment. | Western countries—Intellectual life.
Classification: LCC JA75.7 .B434 2022 (print) | LCC JA75.7 (ebook) |
    DDC 306.209182/1—dc23
LC record available at https://lccn.loc.gov/2021036968
LC ebook record available at https://lccn.loc.gov/2021036969

In memoriam

Baltsar Beckeld

1975–2018

fratris amantissimi.

Spem in alium nunquam habui praeter in te.

And when Fashion hath once Established, what Folly or craft began, Custom makes it Sacred, and 'twill be thought impudence or madness, to contradict or question it.
JOHN LOCKE, FIRST TREATISE OF GOVERNMENT

Si Sparte et Rome ont péri, quel état peut espérer de durer toujours ? Si nous voulons former un établissement durable, ne songeons donc point à le rendre éternel.
JEAN-JACQUES ROUSSEAU, *DU CONTRAT SOCIAL*

If the cultivation of the understanding consists in one thing more than in another, it is surely in learning the grounds of one's own opinions.
JOHN STUART MILL, *ON LIBERTY*

Contents

ACKNOWLEDGMENTS

It is indicative of the resistance this book has faced that many of the specific persons I wish to thank for supporting me during its creation and promotion have since died. I wrote this text in 2016 and 2017, with only editorial alterations and the occasional update since then, and the best efforts of a number of individuals to suppress it has meant that those who would most have rejoiced at its publication will not experience it.

Very special thanks go to Professor Roger Scruton (1944–2020), *vir ille spectabilis*, who coined the term "oikophobia" and who, as a truly disinterested pursuer of truth, lent his support to my book even though it went far beyond his own exposition of this cultural phenomenon; and to Professor Ursula Schönheim (1929–2020), my erstwhile Latin professor and subsequently very dear friend, who read and commented on the first draft. I am also deeply grateful and indebted to the editorial team at Cornell University Press, and in particular to Amy Farranto, who worked tirelessly, and always with the utmost kindness and professionalism, in ushering the manuscript to publication. My gratitude is also for those oikophobes, far too numerous to list by name, both young and old, who have littered my life's path, especially within the halls of academia but also without. These people—old professors jaded by years of groupthink isolation, semiliterate youngsters unwittingly repeating the already tired prejudices of the narrow time and place in which they were born—have all strongly provoked me with their lofty assumptions, with the innocent sweetness of their most precious convictions, and they have offered me more material than would have been available in even the best of libraries. I thank them all.

For unfailing love and support during the darkest hours I thank my mother, Simonne Beckeld Hirschhorn, as well as the encouraging Morde-chai Hirschhorn and the lovely Chana Sahler.

The dedicatee of this book, Baltsar Beckeld, is my brother (1975–2018), the person I loved more than any other, and whom cancer suddenly snatched away at the apex of life. He and I shared a home while I was writing this book, unsuspecting of the horrific, excruciating calamity that was soon to bear down upon us, and he supported me continuously with the same proud love with which he had taught me to walk. In this work I shall discuss whole civilizations, but I cannot bring myself to comprehend the minute event of his death, which will baffle me—a baby brother for whom his big brother was the world and without whom he had never known life—until I die. May your name live with mine, brother, and *in perpetuum, frater, ave atque vale.*

NOTE ON TRANSLATION

All English translations of foreign-language material in this book are by me and therefore receive no further citation. I also translate some titles into English, but many of these already have traditional translations, which I adopt. Only when citing foreign-language scholarly works or secondary literature, in the endnotes, have I left the original title along with my translation of it.

WESTERN SELF-CONTEMPT

INTRODUCTION

We in the West continually come across oikophobia. We see it when a schoolteacher tells the students that Western civilization has been uniquely evil in its pursuit of colonization and slavery, with the implication that other civilizations have not engaged in such things; when a school named after Thomas Jefferson seeks to change its name because of concerns about racism; when a commercial for a Scandinavian airline insists that nothing is truly Scandinavian; when Western universities "decolonize" their departments to make them even less Eurocentric than they have already become; when the waving of one's own national flag is decried as xenophobic while other nations are encouraged to display pride in their cultures; when wild crowds tear down statues of their country's founders. These instances reveal a civilization that has stopped believing in itself, that hates itself, and that is therefore unwilling to defend the values of freedom, democracy, and scientific and scholarly skepticism that have been handed down to us since antiquity.

This book will address the question of how it could have come to this. We shall head back to the beginnings of the West and travel together through time and space up to the present day. During our journey we shall witness the cyclicality of societies through history and philosophical trends, among which oikophobia appears and reappears. At the end of this journey, we shall better see where we are and why we are there.

I was once having dinner in Rome, outside in the shade of the Colosseum, the emblem of a decadent empire whose ruins were everywhere to be seen. As the conversation topic turned toward globalization, one of my companions, a fellow academic, insisted that oppression and imperialism were the core contributions of the West to the world. This was a perfect expression of oikophobia. I looked up at the Colosseum, whose dark and gaping ruin reminds us that all things will perish. "Our own civilization is heading your way," I whispered to it. And I realized that I needed to write this book.

The simplest way of defining "oikophobia" is to state that it is the opposite extreme of xenophobia. As xenophobia means the fear or hatred of strangers or foreigners, so oikophobia means the fear or hatred of home or one's own society, *oikos* being the ancient Greek word for home, house, household. Since oikophobia is the opposite of xenophobia, it is also a corollary of xenophilia, the love of strangers and foreign cultures, and of allophilia, the love of the Other, a group not one's own. But these are not perfect synonyms, because it is possible to love the exotic and the foreign while also being loyal to one's own civilization—it depends, to some extent, on how strong and fanatical that love is or is not.

The term "oikophobia" has existed for some time in psychiatric literature in the sense of an abnormal fear of a literal home and the household appliances found therein, sometimes also known as "ecophobia," which has the same etymology. But I do not mean to suggest that oikophobes and xenophobes suffer from an actual psychiatric or medical disorder. Rather, oikophobia and xenophobia are pathologies of a cultural sort, which develop in particular sociohistorical circumstances. In this book I translate "phobia" more often as "hatred" than as "fear," which it actually means. I thereby merely acknowledge that, as we shall see, many manifestations of oikophobia display hatred, contempt, or dislike. This does not exclude the possibility that oikophobia can also express itself as fear of one's own culture or of its members, or that fear can coexist with hatred or dislike, just as it is possible for a xenophobe to both hate and fear foreigners.[1]

"Oikophobia" was used in a fictitious letter in the early nineteenth century in a less literal sense by the poet Robert Southey, to indicate the English desire for traveling abroad, a bit like the German notion of Wanderlust or even *Fernweh*, a yearning for the faraway.[2] Its more political and philosophical application, however, is not old, and although it is not my coinage, it is my intention to make it more familiar. Roger Scruton, in an article in 1993 called "Oikophobia," established the term in the sense I am employing here, namely as the fear or hatred of the familiar and of one's home culture.[3] This article was followed in 2004 by another treatment in his book *England and the Need for Nations*. In this latter work, Scruton calls oikophobia "the felt need to denigrate the customs, culture and institutions that are identifiably 'ours.'" He continues, referring to the oikophobes as "oiks" (which also happens to be British slang for obnoxious or dim-witted people): "Oikophobia is a stage through which the adolescent mind normally passes. But it is a stage in which some people—intellectuals especially—tend to become arrested. . . . The oik repudiates national loyalties and defines his goals and ideals *against* the nation [Scruton's emphasis] . . . defining his political vision in terms of universal values that have been purified of all reference to the particular attachments of a real historical community."

The oikophobe thus seeks to uproot himself, though he still tends to recognize the rootedness of others. Scruton continues: "The oik is, in his own eyes, a defender of enlightened universalism against local chauvinism. And it is the rise of the oik that has led to the growing crisis of legitimacy in the nation states of Europe. . . . The explosive effect of this has already been felt in Holland and France. It will be felt soon everywhere, and the result may not be what the oiks expect."[4] Scruton is more concerned with England, the United Kingdom, and to some extent Europe, and so within this framework he places the rise of oikophobia after World War II. There is much truth to this, because oikophobia has in fact been stimulated by the depravities to which the West and Europe subjected itself and others in the major conflicts of the previous century. These depravities have made the oikophobe forget the redeeming features of the West, just as he is often only dimly aware of the just as terrible depravities of the non-West. Much of history is often unfamiliar to the oikophobe, who, for example, knows little of the centuries of enslavement in Africa before a European ever set foot there, or of the wars of annihilation waged by Native Americans against one another. When oikophobes do know about these things, they nonetheless choose to concentrate their ire against a West that has improved more than many other civilizations in this regard. But to go beyond Scruton, it is also true that the oikophobe occurs and recurs cyclically throughout history, as I shall explain. The oikophobia that developed after World War II is therefore only the latest manifestation of the phenomenon, and nothing truly new.

The next significant treatment of the term "oikophobia" was in a 2010 Best of the Web column for the *Wall Street Journal* by James Taranto.[5] He applied the concern that Scruton had felt for England and Europe to the United States, in the context of the mosque that was proposed, at that time, to be built near the destroyed World Trade Center (dubbed "Park51"). Taranto identifies oikophobia as a sort of cultural snobbery, as well as a light Marxism by which contrary values and opinions are explained away as due to economic insecurity. And Taranto's analysis is also quite correct. It is in fact common within the halls of academia, especially, to ascribe contrary opinions to external factors, while holding one's own views to be based on reason alone. This is a type of selectively applied historicism that I shall discuss in chapter 11.

A few years later, in 2013, Thierry Baudet published a Dutch book called *Oikofobie: De angst voor het eigene* ("Oikophobia: The Fear of One's Own"). This text, however, does not really deal much with oikophobia itself, but is a rather motley collection of pieces on various sociocultural and even aesthetic subjects. Most of it has a different scope than my own work, as it is mainly concerned with Dutch politics and that country's relationship with the European Union. Somewhat closer to my own concerns in this book, Baudet also takes aim at the new class of Western transnational jet-setters who consider themselves too good for countries, and discusses how multiculturalism weakens the state.[6] There have in the last several years been increasing mentions of oikophobia both online and in print, but most of these, as far as I have seen, have not added anything significant to our understanding of the concept.[7]

Oikophobia can indeed be expressed through all these things: light Marxism, cultural snobbery, transnationalism, and multiculturalism. But as I have already intimated, oikophobia is not only a modern phenomenon. It is, rather, a natural outgrowth of the way cultures, and certainly Western cultures, develop.

Because of this broad range of considerations, I must unite several disparate strands of thought in order to increase our overall understanding of oikophobia and of our Western culture that gives rise to it. A risk with such an expansive, bird's-eye view is that academic specialists have been trained—as

I was—to fix their view on as tiny an object as possible. Such a view in and of itself is not objectionable, but if it is the only one ever held, then it makes us miss all the larger patterns. It is precisely by taking a broader view of many times and places all at once, by looking at the whole, that the phenomenon of oikophobia will become clearer. So for the civilizations that are to be observed here, only an outline of the oikophobic development will be possible, lest this text grow to an impossible length, but this will be sufficient for understanding the social phenomenon that is the object of this book.

Oikophobia is the expression of a type of cultural decadence. Those who are decadent in this way—oikophobes—believe that their own communities and backgrounds are inferior to the rest. They prostrate themselves to all the world, except for that part of it that lies just behind them, in their own backyard.[8] Oikophobia tends to be relativist (though there is also what I shall call positivist oikophobia), while xenophobia tends to be absolutist.

The absolutism of xenophobia dictates that one's own culture is superior to the rest, while the oikophobe often embraces the relativity of truth in the quest to let other cultures predominate. The xenophobe is not, however, quite as decadent as the oikophobe, in a strictly etymological sense. The word "decadent" comes from the Latin *de-cadere*, which means to fall off or away, and the xenophobe, as we shall see, is closer to the original posture of a people in an early society than is the oikophobe. (I mostly use the adjective "decadent" in this book to mean not that something is necessarily "morally bad," but that it is far removed from an earlier sociohistorical condition.) Each type, the xenophobe and the oikophobe, represents an exaggeration of what would otherwise be a healthy mental state: a wholesome promotion of one's own larger community and culture, and at the same time a recognition of and desire to improve upon its faults. But since a society's original posture is closer to the xenophobic than the oikophobic position, oikophobia is the more extreme falling off. When I subject oikophobic decadence to particular analysis in this work, it is not because I think it is worse in itself than xenophobia, but only because at this juncture in time it causes more damage to our social fabric and intellectual life than its counterpart, which, at least in polite society, has been much more marginalized.

The dynamic between oikophobia and xenophobia can be illustrated by casting a glance at Aristotle's *Nicomachean Ethics*. In that work, Aristotle famously distinguishes virtue as occupying the middle ground between two extremes, the extremes being vices that constitute a lack and an excess, respectively (book 2, with examples through book 5). So courage, for instance, is the middle between cowardliness, the lack of courage, and foolhardiness, the excess of courage; friendliness is between surliness and obsequiousness; wittiness between boorishness and buffoonery; and so on. A particularly pertinent example is honesty about oneself (the Greek *aletheia*), as between boastfulness (*alazoneia*) and self-deprecation or false modesty (*eironeia*). Here one begins to see the two types of vice I am discussing. Aristotle's *eironeia* (whence "irony") encapsulates the conceit of the oikophobe, who prides himself on the contemptuous regard in which he holds his own home, whereas *alazoneia* would be the vice of the xenophobe. Going somewhat beyond Aristotle's own specifics, if self-promotion is a virtue, then xenophobia is one extreme (an excess of it), and oikophobia is the other (a lack). And if self-critique is also a virtue, then it is oikophobia that is the excessive, xenophobia the lacking extreme. The wholesome mean would be constituted by moderate quantities of each side.

Xenophobic decadence is easier to describe and is already well known. Xenophobes believe that they and above all their culture and communities are vastly superior to others, but often without the knowledge of that culture—not to mention the culture of others—to either support or refute this claim. They simply believe it, and they demand thoughtless fealty to their own side and culture. (This is often built on insecurity, which is naturally increased during oikophobic times, which is why xenophobia will then also increase, as a reactionary force against oikophobia.) This is connected to why people of this sort of vice tend to be less educated than oikophobes: they have learned less about other cultures than the artistic-intellectual elite and are thus less likely to be bedazzled by them.

To be sure, not all artists and intellectuals are oikophobic, contrary to what one may believe from reading headlines about these or those particular antics from a university campus or art fair. We essentially owe our modern portrait of the quintessential artist to France and the Belle Époque, to that angry avascular and tubercular figure who hates his own civilization and acts like a swine in the name of his art, who imposes his own person by the putative right of his talent, all while coming across as a misunderstood victim with a thin frame and a bad cough; this character has turned immorality, dissoluteness, and cultural self-rejection into an aspiration for young artists that persists even today. It is a stereotype, certainly, but it has coalesced from various traits of artists in that era, such as Gauguin, Toulouse-Lautrec, Modigliani, and others. But anyone who knows the gentlemen artists of ancient Greece knows how trivial and obnoxious, how very bound by time, this view of the artist is. It is an image of the creative man that would have been completely alien to Aeschylus, the revolutionary poet on the decks of a trireme at Salamis; to Sophocles commanding his Athenian phalanxes at Samos; to Euripides winning boxing championships at the public games. But one certainly need not go so far back in time to debunk our current myth of the artist; one may also turn, to use some of my own favorites, to many nineteenth-century German-language lyricists, a Hölderlin or Rilke, or to the American painter Edward Hopper, to see how gentle and kind an artist can be.

The oikophobe, by contrast to the xenophobe, holds his own community and his own culture to be worse than other cultures and communities. In a typical case, an American oikophobe will consider Europe better; a Western oikophobe, the East; a white oikophobe, blacks; a Jewish or Christian oikophobe, Islam. But as opposed to the self-promotion of the xenophobe, which is merely ignorant, the self-deprecation of the oikophobe is often misleading to the extent that he will believe his disparagement of his own culture makes him individually better; we shall come across several examples of this. He is so conscious of his own persona and its cultivation that he will be convinced of that which promises to elevate him above those in his vicinity. He is thus an embodiment of vanity in many instances. His own person is his beginning and end, and he will gladly sacrifice his whole civilization for it, which would allow him to stand out all the more.

We shall be better able to understand why oikophobia is a type of decadence or "falling off" once we will have looked at the historical circumstances under which it tends to arise. Xenophobia is easy to identify in history, since there is less dishonesty in it. By insisting so strongly on himself and his own side of things, the xenophobe makes himself obvious. As a general rule, in the development of a culture or nation, the xenophobe will always emerge earlier than the oikophobe. The former tends to arise at the point where the influence and power of his culture are still rising toward their peak. This is because his realization that his culture is overcoming outside resistance will make him overconfident. He will then insist on the inferiority of those who provide or provided that resistance, as a sort of ingrained fait accompli, and he will believe that his own membership in the successful culture makes him better than those who are members of the defeated culture. The rise of this type is therefore often tied to military victories, especially those that take

place early and play a particularly formative role in the cultural consciousness—
the greater the victory, the better. Some examples are Athens after the Persian
Wars, Rome after the Second Punic War, and Germany after the Franco-
Prussian War.

But the xenophobic type can also arise as a later reaction to what is perceived as a threat to the hegemony of the culture. A pertinent example is the
present-day United States. The peak of our political and military power is
not far behind us, and culturally our influence is still completely unrivaled
in the world, but with the slow slide of our nation from world prominence,
a reaction occurs that insists that America is even greater than she actually
is, and Americans even greater than they actually are. This is the instance
of xenophobia that will generally overlap with oikophobia, which on the
whole sets in later during the development of a culture.

The oikophobe, then, will generally arise when the peak of his culture
has already been reached (Athens in Classical times, Rome in the early empire, France shortly before the Revolution, Britain in the mid-Victorian era,
the United States after World War II). He will regret the exploits of his culture and the perpetrated injustices and sufferings that will always be part of
any people's rise. The oikophobe thereby becomes filled with self-disgust—
not toward himself as an individual, but rather toward much of what belongs
to his culture, the good with the bad. Like its opposite extreme, oikophobia
is an overreaction and an exaggeration. It thereby shows many people's inability to extract themselves from the far movements of the pendulum that
so often characterize the political life of a nation. The pendulum stays for a
moment at each extreme but loses no time in the middle. This is what makes
xenophobia and oikophobia into Aristotelian vices.

The dichotomy between them is to a limited extent also similar to that
between "master" and "slave" in philosophy. The obsession with masters and
slaves is one that is found mainly among German sex-starved professors, but
it is not entirely without intellectual interest. To Nietzsche, the master is still
in an innocent state, largely unaware of the existence of the Other. He lives
in that early stage of a culture in which the ruling class has never been chal-
lenged and therefore simply and naively takes its own superiority for granted,
thereby having no reason either to especially insist on or to despise itself. The
master is not particularly self-corrective, since he sees nothing wrong with
himself and has the slaves to do his work for him and to protect him against
any hostile forces. Since the Nietzschean master assumes that he is the high-

est possible expression of the human type, he is far from being self-aware. As we shall see, self-awareness, which includes self-correction, is the starting point for a people that has passed the stage of barbarianism and become cultured, and it is awareness of the Other that pushes human beings into the direction of excessive self-promotion or excessive self-critique. The slave, on the other hand, is someone who defines himself negatively, by resentment toward the master who controls the levers of society, and by extension toward the society itself.[9]

As we begin to look together at the development of civilizations, I am not going to waste anyone's time with the original human condition and how people come to form a state. Various philosophers have attempted to answer that question already. One of them was Rousseau, for whom society finally developed out of a pristine state of nature with its noble savage. Significantly better, I believe, were the replies by the monarchical Hobbes and republican Locke. According to Hobbes, people are inherently distrustful of each other and therefore enter into a community as a restriction on their most corrosive impulses, while Locke emphasizes human reasonableness and the positive desire for fellowship. But both of them are far removed from Rousseau, who thinks that human beings would be more fulfilled in a state of anarchy than a state of statehood. All three, however, are in my view right insofar as they subscribe to the social contract, an idea that has been heavily criticized by a motley group of philosophers, who usually take it too literally.[10]

What concerns us here, rather, is what happens once a state or a full culture has been created, and what trajectory it is likely to take. If we can make an educated description of that trajectory in its broader outlines in the past, then we should be able with some degree of accuracy to divine its future. Once we do that, we might also be able to slow—not stop, but slow—our arrival at the ravine to which our culture will inevitably be led, and into which our state will eventually fall.

But although the process of oikophobic development is repetitive and has often taken place in a similar way, not everything stays the same, of course. It would be a fair statement, for example, that in the West women have more freedoms now, and are closer to being perceived as the equals of men, than at any other time in our history. (This, in fact, would be an example not merely of cyclical but of helical movement—see chapter 9—as women tend to gain more freedom in a society's waning days, but with an overall increase in freedom across societies from antiquity to the present.) So one must beware of making everything in every cultural cycle appear to be the same as in previous cycles, simply in order to fit some preconceived model. Things do change. But when they do, they follow clear and repetitive phenomena of mass psychology and human nature—and those things, on the other hand, do not change. They are as true and permanent today as in ancient times. As will also become clearer in chapter 9, I do not really speak of laws fashioned of metaphysical iron that dictate history; rather, I shall identify mere tendencies, but tendencies that are sufficiently strong to reveal tragically beautiful patterns drawn on the pages of our common past.

A salutary effect of recognizing the cyclical elements of history is an increased resistance to the temptation to live at a special historic moment. This temptation, more than any other, drives men—both king and commoner—to perversity, vanity, and cruelty. We think, for example, that the Internet is a completely new phenomenon after which communication can never be the same, and that we who lived during its creation and dissemination are specially privileged. But Gutenberg's invention of the printing press and introduction of moveable type in Europe did without any doubt cause more social and cultural change than the Internet ever has. Both the Internet and the printing press are part of the same process of the democratization of communication and knowledge that, with a few ups and downs, has been going on since antiquity. Our desire to live the crucial moment of human annals is dampened once we are able to take a broader view of the processes of which we all form a part. This realization makes us a little bit less megalomaniacal, and that, of course, is a good thing: most disasters inflicted upon humanity were the brainchildren of those who believed themselves to live in magnificent, historic times, who displayed their farcical altruism as ostentatiously as possible. When the young scream about revolution against something, anything, when the journalist frothing at the mouth announces war and death to millions of television viewers, and when for the fourth time in a couple of decades a freshly elected president announces an era of renewal and rebirth to his constituents, they are all unified by their vain desire to straddle history and reach the climax of human endeavor.

Studying cultural development will reveal why oikophobia occurs in Western civilizations, and will allow us to understand it by explaining that oikophobia is not so much the product of sensitivity and a thoughtful process as it is a vain malaise that befalls cultures at a certain point in their development. Of course, it is true that flowers can grow from dirt, and not all artistic yields of this malaise must be bad. The questionable, in the right hands, can give birth to wonderful things—much of the greatest music in the world arose out of Christianity, for example, and even though I am not a religious person, I still enjoy the sound of church bells on a Sunday morning, and the sound of the prayer call from a minaret in the desert torpor, as well as the marvelous Moorish architecture of southern Spain and the Gothic cathedrals of France. So too, oikophobia can yield the occasional fruit. Let us therefore not forget that a look at the foibles and weaknesses of the West will simultaneously be a love letter to the West, a glimpse of what makes it beautiful.

In this vein, we must also understand that there are two ways of looking at every single thing: one narrow and emotional, one broad and logical. I do not use these terms as hendiadys: something does not have to be narrow simply because it is emotional, and something need not be broad by being logical. I also do not mean to suggest that one view is intrinsically better than the other, as the adjectives "broad" and "narrow" only refer to the scope of the view, not its moral worth.[11] This division may sound like a cliché, but it is more difficult to apply in a given instance than it may seem. It is the professional obligation of the philosopher to be able to hold both views at the same time, constantly to watch over the interplay between sensible and logical knowledge. Whoever can hold only one of them—and it is usually the narrow and emotional perspective—is not a thinker. The philosophical way is to assess a particular thing for its worth, for what it does for us in the here and now—the narrow perspective—as well as to examine its causes and thereby to predict its long-term consequences—the broad perspective. Often, the latter will yield very different results from the former regarding the merits of the object in view.

The examination of the causes of things often induces a sort of melancholia, because we come to see not only why the thing happened but why, in fact, it had to happen. Virgil's statement, in his *Georgics* (2.490), that "happy is he who could know the causes of things," is rather off the mark, since to understand the causes and thereby the consequences of things gives us as much cause for pessimism as optimism. It is a pessimism that sees beauty everywhere but understands that this beauty always has a price, a pessimism that sees how the good and the bad mingle, as bundles of characteristics, in the very same phenomenon. Neither the narrow nor the broad view should completely conquer the other. It requires insight and above all strength to hold them both conjointly.

It is important to keep in mind, therefore, that although I generally position myself against oikophobia in its various manifestations, I do not primarily wish to condemn but rather to understand it. As we shall see, it is quite easy to find some manifestations of oikophobia, as they appear throughout history, to be more defensible or morally legitimate than others. If one agrees from today's point of view that, for example, the Romans had an unfortunate tendency to be rapacious brutes, then one might look sympathetically upon those Romans who felt similarly. But since such judgments are so subjective, they are not really part of what interests me in this book. My point will finally not be whether particular instances of people turning against their own cultures are "legitimate" or not, but rather that such things happen in the nexus of specific sociohistorical circumstances, that, indeed, there is a process—a development or transformation—that takes place as the culture moves from being outward-looking and self-aggrandizing to being inward-looking and self-critical. Oikophobia is the felt need to denigrate one's own culture. Perhaps some cultures or particular cultural behaviors deserve to be denigrated, so that we would not label the denigration thereof "phobic" (even though nowadays one is often labeled "phobic," as in xenophobic, the moment one criticizes some particular aspect of a foreign culture—an imbalance that is itself a result of oikophobia), but, again, this is so subjective as being capable of neither proof nor disproof. What we are looking at, rather, is how cultures develop, how they begin to turn against themselves, and what philosophical justifications are employed, all of which in turn will allow us to understand some of our own cultural predicaments today.

And so we must try to put aside our own preferences and to look at as complete a picture as possible. When one does this, the tragic Greek view presents itself. One looks both at a phenomenon's interior reality and at as many of its external causes and effects as may be discoverable. This is how the true observer must look at everything: as a thinker at causal networks and the connection between objects, and also as a poet, penetratingly, at the object itself—the philosopher must be both thinker and poet. The tragic view then presenting itself is that there is always a trade-off. This is why almost all choices we make are between bad and worse, and we are forced to say no to the positive because of its negative consequences, and yes to the negative because of its positive consequences.

The cyclicality of history means that we may welcome a particular progressive step but at the same time understand that it brings us closer to the next collapse—when we fight for freedom, we also set in motion the process that will eventually enslave us again. This is what it means to be part of a cycle: when we pull ourselves away from a bad segment of the circle, we still move closer to the beginning of that segment. People tend not to want to accept this because, obsessed with perfection as they are, they believe there can be something with only sunny sides. They are simply too emotionally exhausted and broken as individuals to commit themselves to negativity in any way. People need their particular messiah; they need to believe that salvation is possible, and so they keep striving blindly for it, often causing irreparable damage in the process, to themselves and to others. But with cyclicality comes the realization that there is no savior, and that one must resign oneself to living with negativity, with the ever unstable and ever changing and evolving. Even if within this framework one tries to reach the best solution possible, one must understand that even the best solution is temporary. When we say that an empire cannot last forever, and that as it rises, so too it must inevitably fall, it is because the process that leads to the rise is the very same as that which leads to the fall.

I shall discuss this at greater length but will take one quite illustrative example now. The gradual expansion of citizenship in the Roman Republic and subsequently Empire increased the number of fighting men and also led some of them to fight more resolutely, since they felt that now, as equal citizens, they had a personal stake in the welfare of the state. But this also led to the expansion of notions of equality, and the more people feel equal and empowered, the more they will consider themselves more important than the state itself, and more special interest groups will be created that will eventually lead to internecine conflict and the fragmentation of the state. So we consider the very same process, from the point of view of the state, to be both positive and negative, and the rise and fall to be equally inevitable. That is, though we dislike both xeno- and oikophobia, late-civilizational oikophobia is just as "natural"—just as much to be expected—as early-civilizational xenophobia. This idea that the rise and fall of a civilization are part of a unitary process, rather than representing two parts between which there is a rupture, will be useful to keep in mind as we travel together through time, space, and thought.

Finally, I wish to clarify that this is not a book within the field of history. At first glance it may appear as such, but it is in fact a work of political philosophy and the philosophy of history, even though it cuts across many academic disciplines: philosophy, philology, history, sociology, political science.

The reader should be aware that the historical expositions to be found in this book are meant only as a stepping-stone to the philosophy and sociocultural commentary that are interspersed throughout. In addition to the exigencies of the bird's-eye view, this is another reason for the brevity of my discussions of history, since history itself is not the main point. Some may wish to engage in hermeneutical battles regarding various historical events and literary figures, battles that often devolve into a competition about who knows the most, but we should not lose sight of the essential, namely the implications that such historical and literary phenomena have for the philosophy of history and for political philosophy. To put it simply, the exposition is not primarily historical, but deliberately ethical-philosophical.

Chapter 1

Oikophobia in Ancient Greece

Western civilization rests on two pillars: the Greco-Roman and the Judeo-Christian. Judaism may already have been in existence in some very primitive form when the first word of Greek was recorded in the hieroglyphic syllabary of Linear B on a clay tablet in the murky confines of a Mycenaean fortress. But Judaism became a part of the West only later, and entered it sideways, as it were, through Christianity, in the waning days of the Roman Empire. And so the West begins with Greece, and it is there that we find the first clear case of oikophobia.

With Greece we can move straight into the period of the city-states, because apart from archaeological remains, the culture of the so-called Mycenaean Greeks survives only in the tales told by Homer several centuries later, in the *Iliad* and *Odyssey,* and these are only weak reflections of that culture. Around the turn of the millennium the Greeks, along with much of the eastern Mediterranean world, descend into a Dark Age which to this day is not very clearly understood. And so Greek civilization proper—the West—begins as the Greeks emerge from this ancient Dark Age into what is known

as the Archaic Greek era (ca. 800–480 BC). A people awakens (the primordial opening bars of Bach's violin chaconne glitter all around) and, like a
child, is roused by the sudden understanding of its own influence on the
surrounding environment. Non-Greeks—the Other—do not yet feature very
strongly, and there is a general Greek mentality that is at this stage under the
influence of the mythical age as represented by Homer, where life is brief,
difficult, and heroic. There are glimmers of glory and joy only for those quick
enough to seize it. Such a mentality has no time for cultural considerations
one way or the other, and simply lives in the moment. There is little space for
metaphysics in this world, only for the exploits of the individual and his
tribelet.[1] Strictly speaking, of course, there is really no such thing as the "original" state of a people: things are always in flux, and what seems to be a beginning in fact merely follows upon something else more obscure, where various
traditions mix and wander from one culture to another. Nonetheless, there
comes a time when something approaching a civilizational awareness—of
one's own society as a cohesive, separate entity—begins to take shape.

The Archaic Greeks develop rather organically and independently, moving slowly from myth to science and rationalism through the work of the
pre-Socratic philosophers in the sixth and early fifth centuries BC. They adopt
what is useful from Egyptian, Babylonian, and subsequently Persian sources,
and leave the rest without much concern for whether those neighboring and
older civilizations are superior or not. The position of most philosophers on
the peripheries of what is then the Greek world, in Ionia (western Turkey)
and Magna Graecia (southern Italy), is certainly helpful in this regard, and
it is why, through borrowings from other cultures, the periphery develops
faster at this time than the Greek mainland, which remains more primitive
for some time.[2]

But then the late Archaic Greeks, after their Ionian cities have come under
foreign domination, clash with the Persians and, with Athens at the helm, finally emerge victorious from the absolutely crucial civilizational encounters at
Marathon (490 BC); Thermopylae, Artemisium, and Salamis (all three 480
BC); and Plataea and Mycale (both 479 BC). The battle of Marathon offers a
glimpse of two cultures at different stages of development. Herodotus, the
West's first historian, records the Persians' incredulity (*Histories* 6.112) that the
Greek hoplites simply charge at them without the support of either cavalry or
missile troops. The Athenians and other mainland Greeks are at a relatively
early stage in their culture, where each man fights with admirable naïveté

against an in many ways much more sophisticated foe; the Persians, with an older civilization, have had time to develop a much more intricate force of different departments and are not prepared to face an enemy that simply launches itself headfirst at them, with the bravado of men fighting for their families and homes. The Ionian Greeks, on the other hand, having developed culture and wealth, are less hardy and stubborn than their mainland brethren in the face of Persian aggression. The Ionians' proximity to the Babylonian, Lydian, and then Persian civilizations has had both a positive—cultural—as well as a negative—wealth and sloth—effect. For example, at a time when the Athenians are still composed mainly of yeoman farmers—people willing to die for their homesteads, for their children, and for their aging parents—the pre-Socratic philosopher Xenophanes in Ionia is already criticizing his contemporaries for having been ruined by Lydian luxury. He says of them (Fragment 3, slightly abbreviated): "Learning useless luxury from the Lydians, they went to the market wearing purple-dyed cloaks, strutting with their pretty hair and drenched and pungent with sophisticated oils."

Already here we begin to see what will be a repetitive pattern, namely that with wealth comes an unwillingness to die for one's civilization, and with that unwillingness oikophobia goes hand in hand. The fact that some pre-Socratics, such as Anaxagoras and Protagoras, are chased out of backwards, village-like Athens for their scientific or freethinking teachings, as reported by the biographer Diogenes Laertius in his *Lives and Opinions of Eminent Philosophers* (2.12 and 9.52), indicates how the Greek mainland for a long time is less advanced than the periphery. We can thus recognize little signs of proto-oikophobia or perhaps allophilia among the Ionian Greeks early on, without this meaning that Athens is anywhere close to oikophobia at that time. But I shall confine my remarks here mainly to the development of Athenian culture.

Subsequent Greek conquests, particularly that of Byzantium (478 BC), which wrests control of the Black Sea trade from the Persians and almost completely cuts off the latter from Europe, ensure the creation of a large and burgeoning Athenian empire, while the traditionalist and parochial Spartans withdraw to their own borders. At this point, xenophobia and self-love among the Greeks in general and the Athenians in particular have developed to their fullest.

Entering upon the Classical age, which by scholarly consent runs from after the Persian Wars in the 470s BC to the death of Alexander the so-called Great in 323 BC, the mainland Greeks begin to become aware of themselves.

It is because self-awareness is one of the prerequisites of oikophobia that the Greeks offer us the first clear example of this phenomenon. Once they have left their mythical past behind and scored successes against neighboring peoples, they become aware of their own power, knowledge, and uniqueness, and begin to analyze these. And self-analysis requires a distancing of the self from itself, in order to view the object of study in its entirety, so that the people becomes more objective toward itself. One of the earliest hints of this in literature is Aeschylus's play *The Persians* (472 BC), the only extant Greek tragedy based not on myth but on a historical event—and a recent one at that—namely the naval battle of Salamis eight years earlier, in which the playwright himself presumably took part. In the play, we see events from the point of view of the Other, namely the vanquished Persians, who react with shock and humanity at their lost cause. They are portrayed not as some faceless, evil horde, but as human beings with a sense of hope and tragedy. This is a remarkable achievement for a work of literature of such antiquity, especially considering the fact that it was to be presented at a dramatic competition before a judgmental audience of Athenian men, many of whom had personally fought against the Persians and had friends who had fallen in battle. The Athenians, though their cause had been just, since they had fought for their very homes against an imperialist aggressor, understand from their benches in the theater that war victimizes also those who fight unjustly, and that the suffering of losing loved ones does not distinguish between cultures. If we are pleasantly surprised that the Athenians were this open-minded, we must be astonished at the fact that they voted to award the first prize to Aeschylus. They have internalized, already at this early stage, the subsequent Jewish lesson that one should not rejoice at the demise of one's enemies. In Jewish tradition, God rebukes the angels for wanting to sing his praise as the Egyptian charioteers pursuing the Israelites are drowning in the Red Sea. To paraphrase somewhat: The enemy soldiers, too, are human beings, and my work—why should you sing in joy, when my children are drowning in the sea? (Talmud, Megillah 10b and Sanhedrin 39b).

Euripides, the third great Attic tragedian after Aeschylus and Sophocles, almost routinely questions conventional ways of thinking in his plays. For example, his in some ways sympathetic portrayal of the title character in his *Medea* (431 BC) raises the question of what a woman is supposed to do when suffering injustice in a patriarchal world where there is no higher authority to which she may turn for succor. He also shatters traditional myth. In *Heracles*

(416 BC), for instance, Euripides destroys the Greek gods, with the exception of Athena, by having them prove so evil, incapable, and spiteful, so unworthy of being worshipped, that it is only through human love and friendship, here between the kindly Theseus and the broken hero Heracles, that salvation can be found. He eventually reconstitutes the gods in a new image, through Artemis's intervention in *Iphigenia in Aulis* (staged posthumously in 405 BC). In several versions of the myth, the goddess Artemis commands that Agamemnon must sacrifice his daughter Iphigenia in order to get wind in the sails of his fleet. But Euripides does not accept that a god should require an innocent human sacrifice; he instead portrays her as a benevolent force that substitutes a deer for Iphigenia on the altar in the last moment, even though the girl had heroically taken it upon herself to die for the sake of the Greek navy sailing on to Troy. So instead of making his play about the struggle between religious or political duty and personal desire, Euripides steps out of the myth and asks his audience why on earth they should believe such a thing in the first place.[3]

Mention should also be made of the fragment from the otherwise lost play *Sisyphus*, by Euripides or perhaps Critias. In this surviving textual snippet, someone seemingly atheist is arguing that the gods were merely invented in order to frighten people into behaving morally. This is probably the first expression in history of this nowadays popular viewpoint. So in the development of Attic tragedy is found an increasing tendency to question traditional Greek attitudes, even to some extent Greek religion itself.

Drama aside, it is above all in the more or less historical and scientific treatises that we see what is properly a Greek self-study: Herodotus's historical, anthropological, and sociological comparisons between the Greeks and other peoples he visited (*Histories*, ca. 440 BC); Thucydides's perceptive observations not only of the Greek and Athenian character but also of human nature in general (*History of the Peloponnesian War*, last decade of the fifth century BC); Plato's conservative mocking of Athenian society and democracy in the *Republic* (ca. 380 BC); and Aristotle's establishment of countless scientific disciplines, perhaps most importantly, in the present context, of literary theory in his *Poetics* (ca. 335 BC), where he examines the literature of his own culture. The degree of self-examination in these works, and many others, has no parallel in any other civilization before the Greeks; it is the Greeks who invent theory.

Once external foes have been overcome and a measure of wealth and leisure established, intelligent men begin to focus on internal matters and to write about them. This is indeed similar to how Aristotle explains the rise of the pre-Socratics, in *Metaphysics* 982b: "This kind of science began to be pursued, for the purpose of leisure and pastime, when almost all necessities of life had been taken care of." Nonetheless, this heightened self-awareness, though often facilitating self-critique, is only a prerequisite for, and not identical with, oikophobia. Aeschylus wishes to be remembered more for his participation in the military defense of Greece than for his dramas: he is neither xenophobic nor oikophobic, and he does not set the Persians on any sort of pedestal or ascribe to their culture more than its due. Euripides's work is full of Athenian patriotism—it is not for naught that, in the play *Heracles* already referred to, it is Theseus, primordial king of Athens, who rescues the son of Zeus from suicide, and only Athena herself who puts an end to the carnage—even though, in the end, Euripides abandons his native city and heads north upon the invitation of the Macedonian king Archelaus I. Although Euripides is often coupled in intellectual matters with Socrates (on whom see below), he thus remains pro-Athenian, even if his patriotism knows certain bounds. Herodotus, for his part, is happy to travel but thinks the Greek world best, especially Athens, which he seems to prefer (*Histories* 5.78) to his native Halicarnassus in Asia Minor, which is under tyrannical Persian sway. Thucydides has Pericles utter some of the most patriotically beautiful words imaginable on the greatness of Athens and the indomitable Athenian spirit (*History of the Peloponnesian War* 2.35–46). Aristotle considers it quite clear, in many different passages of his works, that his Greek compatriots are culturally superior to other peoples. So these men, and others, are able to analyze and even question their own traditions without thereby slipping into oikophobia. This self-awareness, however, which eventually becomes the natural outcropping of a cultured people, will over time have both positive and negative effects.

Hand in hand with this cultural, literary-scientific development goes the legal and political development. These two will of course in some way reflect each other in every civilization. A gradual rejection of one's own traditions is accompanied by a fragmentation of the populace into smaller interest groups that will view the closer threat—other interest groups of the same people—as more urgent than the more distant Other. A conservative stubbornness holds a very protective and exclusive view of citizenship and political participation in the early Greek city-state (and this will be repeated among the Romans), but things gradually begin to change. The crushing naval victory at Salamis, won by poor and simple oarsmen rather than by comparatively wealthy, landed hoplites, leads the poor to demand more rights. This is why the conservative Plato views that battle in a negative light (*Laws* 707a–c), even though it was a Greek victory. He feels that it caused a more assertive citizenry of individuals who believe more in themselves than in the community, and he is echoed by Aristotle at *Politics* 1274a and 1304a. (Similarly, young Americans during the Vietnam War will successfully argue that if they can be asked to die for their country, they should be allowed to vote as well; this is a common phenomenon in history, another example being the enlistment of Russian serfs to fight in the Crimean War, contributing to the end of serfdom.) Increasingly, the rich and the poor, the democrats and the oligarchists, come to hate each other more than either group hates the Persians. Since the common civilizational enemy has been successfully repulsed, it can no longer serve as an effective target for and outlet of the people's wrath. Human psychology generally requires an adversary for the purpose of self-identification, and so a new adversary is crafted: other Greeks, and other Athenians.

An empowerment of the lower classes through this postwar democratization in Athens also leads to an increasing culture of dependence on the government. As the voices of regular people start to count more and more, the democratic leader Pericles and his aristocratic opponent Cimon begin to compete with each other by essentially bribing Athenian citizens voting in the Ecclesia, the Athenian Assembly. After the ostracism of his rival, Pericles's dominance in Athens (ca. 461–429) involves ever more largesse for the purpose of maintaining support from the politically strengthened populace. As governmental largesse often does, Pericles's generosity makes men ask what more they can get from the government, and makes them less willing to sacrifice themselves for the state. Late in the fifth century BC, payment to the participants in the Ecclesia is introduced, so that even the poorest citizens can afford to take off from work and partake in government there. One can look upon such a policy as equitable and fair—just as one may entirely agree with the brave trireme oarsmen at Salamis—while at the same time recognizing that it furthers the mentality of avarice, as well as the attitude that the state is simply there for one's own direct personal benefit and gain. For it should be considered an axiom of human nature that dependence leads not to gratitude but to resentment—already Thucydides knows this—and when the state provides goods at no charge, or even cash handouts, the people come to consider themselves entitled to it and develop the mentality that asks not what service one can provide to others, but how much one can get from others, primarily the state. Dependence makes people resentful and miserly, and the more they receive from the state, the less they will respect it. This is why there is often a dynamic of mutual strengthening between oikophobia and government largesse, and oikophobia and the entitlement mentality go hand in hand.

Elements of this can be seen in Thucydides (1.77), where some Athenian diplomats explain to their Spartan hosts that subjects of the Athenian empire are more resentful precisely because of Athenian generosity than they would have been if the Athenians had treated them with brutal force from the start. Another example (3.37–39) is where Cleon of Athens, in the famous debate on the fate of the rebellious Mytilenians, argues that showing kindness and mercy will not make the Athenians more liked, and that it is a general rule of human nature that people all too often despise those who treat them well and admire those who are firm. This will be echoed by the Roman commander Vocula in Tacitus's *Histories* (4.57). Once this sense of entitlement becomes the predominant outlook, the citizens of a state begin to compete more with each other, while the external enemy recedes into the background. Over time it is forgotten why the enemy, soundly defeated, was ever an enemy, and he seems harmless, even benevolent, in comparison to the ruffians at home who are competing for money and prestige. Oikophobia has begun.

The oikophobic element of these late Classical times comes creeping in well after the xenophobic phase that commences upon contact with the Other, and overlaps more with the middle, self-aware but not yet self-denigrating phase, and this pattern will generally obtain for other civilizations, too. The first very clear trace of oikophobia appears in the later Classical era, namely in the time of Socrates and his entourage. Socrates is not, as Nietzsche would have it in *The Birth of Tragedy*, so much the conspiring destroyer of Greece as part of a natural process of self-destruction that cultures in general go through, a process in which Socrates has more than enough accomplices. To understand the Greeks—and with them everyone else—we must follow them all the way to the end, something that Nietzsche is unwilling to do.

Nietzsche considers the Archaic Greeks the greatest expression of Greekdom—that is, the Greeks who were more secluded from the Other and thought themselves the best simply because they entertained no other possibility, who were naïvely closed to any other way of thinking, and who believed in their own myths—in short, Greeks as Homer portrays them. To be sure, there is much we might learn from those Greeks and from their naïveté. But Greekdom does not stop with the Archaic Greeks; it continues into Classical times, to Socrates, and beyond. The Greeks were the first of all peoples to look at themselves in the mirror, the first people who wrote about what they did and who knew that they knew. Whereas someone like the sixth-century-BC poet Theognis would have considered the Greeks to be the best simply because no other possibility was even conceivable, the fourth-century-BC Aristotle considered the Greeks to be the best because he had compared the customs and mores of various peoples and concluded that the Greeks were indeed superior. It was this latter posture that enabled them to be the first self-critical people, and that is a remarkable achievement, one that is almost entirely absent from Nietzsche's appreciation of them, and that he rejects as un-Greek.

Nietzsche's understanding of the Greeks is of a piece with his insistence that the "master" individual has such a distance from others that he, practically unaware of them and hence of other possibilities, legislates his morals without the self-consciousness that awareness of others entails. He believes that a people, to be great, must be naïve, must believe its own myths. To him, once a people becomes aware of its own history, it will become sick and enfeebled. There is much truth in this, but we must also understand that, first, this process is inevitable, and, second, until such a sickened state is reached, much good will have been accomplished along the way. Nietzsche does not understand, or refuses to acknowledge, that also the declining period of a people can produce some of its great cultural achievements, even if, as I shall discuss further, it is difficult in a way to speak of a period of decline, since it is all part of one big process. The rise itself contributes to the fall, and what was strength, namely diversity and openness in adopting new ideas, becomes weakness and fragmentation.[4]

By refusing to go past Greek Archaism, Nietzsche commits his all-too-frequent mistake of identifying the true nature of a thing only with its origin. That approach can be used effectively in attacking the genealogy of various ideas, but it also leads him to misunderstand the full bundle of Greek characteristics. An Aristotle, to take one example, the man who was perhaps not the most artistically inclined but who, when it comes to analytical intelligence, is the most brilliant ever to have lived, greater than his teacher Plato—such a man could never exist within the constraints of a great people as Nietzsche would have them. This is a bit ironic, since the ethical man as presented in Aristotle's *Nicomachean Ethics* had considerable influence on Nietzsche's conception of what a great man should be. Even Nietzsche himself, with his practically pathological hatred of his fellow Germans, at least in his later work, would have been impossible.

And so I do not reject a people's advances and heightened self-awareness simply because these will eventually lead to oikophobia. Nietzsche's hatred of Germans raises the issue of what one may call "reactionary oikophobia," which is not the genuine oikophobic article, but a too violent reaction to it. As often happens, oikophobic excesses will cause a conservative backlash, and this reactionary force will sometimes become so strong that it lapses into another kind of oikophobic hatred against what one's own civilization is perceived to have become. Nietzsche would surely qualify as an example of this; in his later years he even tried to claim Polish rather than German ancestry.[5] Other possible examples would be Plato in Greece and Juvenal in Rome.

So let us continue forward with our view of the Greeks. Socrates considers himself quite cosmopolitan and continuously questions traditional Greek moral beliefs. Due to the exigencies of his time, however, with Athens still beset by various enemies, he is a relatively mild case and not fully an oikophobic one, certainly not as compared to modern times, when oikophobes have the luxury of not having to defend their own civilization. Even the stubborn Socrates, whom no one could convince of the justice of anything, fights with distinction for his city of Athens at the battles of Potidaea and Delium (432 and 424 BC, respectively, just before and during the Peloponnesian War). And when given the opportunity to escape from prison before his execution, he steadfastly and patriotically chooses to obey the laws and remain, as recounted in Plato's *Crito*. Such actions moderate some of his words, as when in a snide jab at his fellow citizens he tells his student Antisthenes that the latter would have been less brave if both his parents had been Athenian, rather than only one of them (Diogenes Laertius 6.1, though this is also a nod to the Thracians' warlike reputation, as Antisthenes was part Thracian).

During the Persian Wars too there had been medizing Greeks—those who preferred oriental ways—but these mainly Ionian Greeks were at a more advanced cultural stage during that conflict than their Athenian and other mainland brethren. Greeks in Asia Minor could show their putative superiority over their fellows by adopting Eastern accoutrements of wealth and prestige—recall Xenophanes's statement on Lydian luxury—at a time when this would have been unthinkable on the mainland. There can be no mass medizing at an early, primitive stage of Greek culture, just as there can never be oikophobia at an early stage of any culture. But in these later times, enough wealth for a leisure class has been established that the man of action and the man of thought—the soldier and the intellectual, as it were—slowly become distinct from one another, whereas in Sophocles's generation they had still been united in the same person. And if the man of thought no longer needs to act for his state, he forgets what he owes it, or deliberately disregards his debt, as when the late-fourth- and early-third-century-BC Cyrenian philosopher Theodorus, also known as "the atheist," will maintain that a wise man would never die for his country, since that would be tantamount to destroying wisdom for the sake of the people, who are unwise (Diogenes Laertius 2.98). The common people who must act remain loyal to the state, while the elite turn inward and become oikophobic, and this circumstance answers the question, posed by so many today, of why it is often the elite of a society that despises it; other answers to that question will be uncovered by and by. When Athens falls to Sparta at the end of the Peloponnesian War (404 BC), it is the simple Athenians, not the nobility, who remain hostile to the Spartans.

During and after Socrates's time there are others who constitute more striking cases than he in this social development. Antiphon the Sophist, perhaps identical with Antiphon of Rhamnus, one of the famous Attic orators and a contemporary of Socrates, offers a radical rejection of the distinction between Greek and barbarian, and seems to claim that all human beings are equal.[6] This may sound harmless and sensible enough to a modern reader, but it is a new and unusual notion for the ancient world. The idea of equality appears precisely in that ancient civilization that could plausibly claim to be superior to all the others, in that civilization that has developed so far ahead that it begins to turn inward on itself. In less developed civilizations, by contrast, the idea of equality would appear ludicrous, just as, today, it is the advanced West that considers everyone equal, while less developed nations hold their heads high. Antiphon may also have rejected Greek religious practices, such as divination, but due to the fragmentary state of his extant work, this is less certain.

Another is Hippias of Elis, a younger contemporary of Socrates. He is also a champion of cosmopolitanism, and so intent on the equality of states and peoples that he is overbearingly arrogant and insufferable to those around him who do not feel the same. Hippias is, at least in theory, a grand equalizer, although traditional Greek culture always emphasized the *agon*—struggle, competition—between things, the weighing of things in the balance as of greater, equal, or lesser value, an activity that sharpens the intellect.

Alcidamas, who is in his mid-thirties when Socrates dies (399 BC), supports, as had Hippias, the new idea of a natural law to the effect that God has made everyone free. Alcidamas also shows pacifist tendencies, which is very unusual for such an early civilization as the Greek. In early society, pacifism cannot appear in any significant measure, since the community's very survival depends on all men being willing to fight, and so people's morals will coalesce around that circumstance. The selfish doctrine of pacifism can only exist where there is enough strength that the fighting can be delegated to a smaller group within the community, and so the pacifists are those who are outside of that group, or those who are in it but wish to exit it. The fact that pacifism now appears means that at least some Greek societies have developed wealth, a measure of security, and therefore self-righteous intellectuals. In Thucydides's *History of the Peloponnesian War* (1.84), the Spartan king Archidamus II, in a speech urging his city not to rush into war with Athens, says, "We are wise because we are not so educated as to look down on the laws," and his words are echoed by Cleon of Athens: "Intelligent people want to appear wiser than the laws . . . and thereby often end up overthrowing their cities" (3.37). (Just about two millennia thereafter, and thus illustrating the universality of these themes, Thomas Hobbes will write, in *Leviathan* 30.6, "Potent men digest hardly anything that setteth up a power to bridle their affections; and learned men, anything that discovereth their errors, and thereby lesseneth their authority; whereas the common people's minds . . . are like clean paper, fit to receive whatsoever by public authority shall be imprinted in them.")[7] It is not a coincidence that parochial Sparta remains loyal to herself, whereas it is the open Athens, full to the brim with intellectuals, that dismembers herself.

A fourth example is the aforementioned Antisthenes, a pupil of Socrates and an ardent philosophical opponent of that teacher's most famous student, Plato. Antisthenes founds or at least influences the Cynic school of philosophy. In addition to championing epistemological skepticism and nominalism (for which I warmly thank him), he also rejects much of Greek religion—a rejection connected to his epistemology—and seems to emphasize the ideas of cosmopolitanism at the expense of Greek exceptionalism. Antisthenes's belief in one God or higher natural force, as against the traditional Greek gods, is a corollary of his emphasis on one humanity as against the idea of Greek superiority.

Last among our examples we have Diogenes the Cynic, who is still a boy when Socrates dies. He is from Sinope in Asia Minor but moves to the mainland relatively early, to Athens and Corinth. He is no doubt the most obnoxious man Greece ever produces, someone who is desperate to express his personal sense of superiority to anyone he meets. He is famous, among other things, for despising his countrymen and for labeling himself a cosmopolitan. This word (Greek *kosmopolites*), in fact, is probably Diogenes's coinage and means literally "citizen of the world," which is what he replies when someone asks him where he is from (Diogenes Laertius 6.63). He is happy to act out foreign customs even when, or especially when, they are in contravention of Greek culture. He is in many ways the archetype of that American and European oikophobe that is so common today, the person who looks down on his compatriots and their beliefs as backward. When Diogenes the Cynic speaks with his fellow Greeks, it is almost always with an ironic air of condescension as he criticizes their traditional beliefs, and he revels in the arrogant self-loathing of his own culture. Plato reportedly speaks to him words that could be uttered to the oikophobe of any era: "How much pride you reveal by seeming not to be proud" (Diogenes Laertius 6.26). And in a different context, Plato writes (*Protagoras* 346a), "Bad men . . . seem happy to witness and disparagingly to hold up the faults of their parents or their country, and to accuse them, so that people will not call out their own neglect of them."

The overall time frame of these developments is clear. Athens has already seen her peak come and go, with various cities and islands breaking away from her imperial orbit, and she will slowly be supplanted by others (first Sparta, then Thebes), and her past depredations are well known. This oikophobia could not have arisen in any significant measure at the time when Athens, with the other allied Greeks, was fresh from her victories against the Persians at Marathon, Plataea, and Mycale, and still exulting at the heroism of her hoplites. And so we can identify something like three paradigmatic and partially overlapping phases on Greek society's oikophobic trajectory, which will obtain for future societies, too. First, one takes one's own cultural superiority for granted (e.g., Theognis). Second, one still considers one's own culture great, but based on evidence and comparative views (e.g., Aristotle). And third, one feels other cultures are just as good as one's own or that they may in fact be better (e.g., Diogenes the Cynic). Whereas last-phase instances do not occur in the first phase, there will still be first- and second-phase instances during the last.

The fact that Athens for much of the Classical era is a consensual and largely democratic society contributes to the oikophobic process. It is why the intellectuals are able to voice their grievances and why it is easier for the lower classes to become empowered. Inversely, as we shall see in the next chapter, Rome's conversion from republic to empire will set the oikophobic process back a bit, without however stopping it in the long run. If a consensual government does not do what people wish, it can be freely ridiculed. The comedic playwright Aristophanes cannot be considered oikophobic merely by dint of his craft as a comedian, which naturally includes mocking the various idiosyncrasies of his time. Such poets, full of acerbic wit, have existed before him, even in Archaic times, such as Archilochus and Hipponax. Aristophanes indeed still displays a certain patriotic pathos: for instance, he seems to blame foreign cults imported from the Orient for various societal ills (*Birds* 848ff., *Lysistrata* 387ff., *Wasps* 8ff., and presumably the very fragmentary *Hours*, as confirmed also by Cicero in his *On the Laws* 2.37). The import of Eastern religions will be a decadent feature also in Rome and in modern-era Europe and the United States, as we shall see. But there are certainly elements in Aristophanes that are indicative of Athens's consensual order and therefore of her ability to descend all the more easily into oikophobia. His plays contain important socio-philosophical themes that take a stand against his own group: in *Birds* (414 BC) he attacks Athenian democracy; in *Lysistrata* (411 BC) he attacks the Athenian war effort against the Spartans. These comic jabs at the state have a considerable influence on public opinion, as do comedians today. In an earlier conflict like the Persian Wars, such attacks would have been much fewer in number or even nonexistent, because the members of an earlier society, at the brink of extinction, would rally, tribe-like, to its defense.

Every society will have its Ephialtes—the man who betrayed the Greek positions to the Persians at the battle of Thermopylae—but traitors become far more numerous later on. Leisure, consensual government or at least an empowered middle class, and a perception of external threats as nonexistential are all results of a society's success, which is why, ironically, success is a prerequisite for the self-hatred of that society. Dissent is less widespread in the Archaic era, when precariousness and a still undefeated foreign foe weld the various elements of society together and hinder internal fragmentation. By 355 BC, however, the Athenian orator Isocrates, echoing Aristophanes, feels compelled to complain that his society's gods are ignored in favor of alien rites (*On the Areopagus* 29), as the elite abandon old traditions and flirt with foreign elements as a mark of distinction and personal exoticism (as do sometimes even the poor, if a sumptuous sacrificial meal is served during the oriental rite!). Around the same time as Isocrates's complaint, Plato considers it all too obvious that many people no longer believe in the gods (*Laws* 948b–c and passim).

As the society develops, more and more rights are granted to groups as a means of holding on to the consensually voting citizens' support. This increase in equality and rights actually contributes to even more dissent, because various interest groups begin to smell blood and try to obtain even more from their government, a pattern that shall recur time and again. This is why, in any civilization, the more laws appear whose purpose is therapeutic and designed for only a particular group of citizens, the surer will be the decline of that civilization. A law written for a particular group is usually intended to create more equality or inclusion, but in fact it often increases social fragmentation. Plato complains that in Athens, everyone has to be made to have the same rights as everyone else and to feel equal to everyone else: children to parents, students to teachers, foreigners to citizens, and even animals to humans (*Republic* 562d–563e). With such a pathological sense of equality and liberty, any sense of authority will disappear, along with all loyalty to the civilization at large.

At the very end of the Classical era, Athens, and even Greece as a whole, is finished as an independent entity. The fragmented and squabbling Athenian factions cannot agree on how to approach the Macedonian threat from the north, and once they do decide to fight, it is too late and the Macedonians have already grown too powerful. The orator Demosthenes, imitated in future centuries by Cicero and Churchill, advocates a unified aggressive policy, but for too long is ignored by the peaceniks, who do not think Philip of Macedon as great a threat as he in fact is. Greece ends in 338 BC, at the battle of Chaeronea, where a combined force of Athenians and other Greeks, mainly Thebans, is destroyed by the Macedonians under Philip, with his young son Alexander commanding one of the wings.

But what an end it is. As Philip surveys the battlefield after his victory, he comes across the bodies of the Sacred Band of Thebes, the little army of one hundred and fifty pairs of lovers, formed on the notion that one will fight most bravely if the person one loves more than anything in the world is standing right by one's side. And true it was, for Philip sees that the dead are all lying, not scattered here and there, but in pairs, each man having fought to save his beloved, and, when this proved impossible, seeking to expire in his arms. And it is only then that Philip, the rugged half-barbarian warrior, breaks down and cries (as Plutarch relates in *Life of Pelopidas* 18). As for Demosthenes, after the Macedonian conquest and after an unsuccessful rebellion against Antipater, Alexander's successor in Greece, he takes his own life rather than face arrest. He stands as the last great Athenian, and he teaches us that even when the good cause is lost, it should still be fought, as the Spartans and Thespians had done at Thermopylae and as the Jews will do in the Warsaw Ghetto.

The so-called Hellenistic era runs from the Hellenization of the Middle East through Alexander's conquests to the fall of the last Macedonian successor dynasty, the Ptolemaic dynasty in Egypt, with the deaths of its last representatives, Cleopatra and her teenage son Caesarion, fathered by Julius Caesar. (After this, at the latest, the eastern Mediterranean will have become fully Roman.) As the inauguration of that Hellenistic era we find doubtless the most destructive expression of all ancient oikophobia: Philip's son, Alexander the Great. The Macedonians speak Greek and therefore consider themselves to some extent representatives of Greekdom, although many Greeks themselves would hardly agree. With Alexander's murderous crusades against not only Persia but almost the whole then-known world, the Greeks become supranational and in that sense, strictly speaking, no longer Greek.

It may seem odd, and make one raise an eyebrow or two, to claim that someone who leads armies across continents to conquer other peoples could be oikophobic, and indeed I do not mean to say that Alexander acts like a typical oikophobe. But his purported goal has much in common with an oft-expressed oikophobic ambition insofar as he strives to establish a united world empire of different nations and cultures. This leads him to deemphasize the accomplishments of Greece and exaggerate those of the oriental world. Such universalist ambition is one reason why, for example, he has people crawl before his throne in the Persian manner, completely contrary to the Greek way of debate and argument among peers. It is true that one of the reasons Alexander wishes to incorporate Persians and other Asians into his army is that Macedonian manpower itself is limited, so that there is also a purely practical factor behind his attitude. But the fact of his limited manpower arises precisely out of his desire to unify the enormous land masses of Eurasia.

Some may interject that Alexander probably did not care much for other peoples but was simply a drunken megalomaniac interested in aggrandizing his own power and surpassing the feats of Heracles, which some considered historical and not mythical. It is no doubt true that Alexander is a drunkard whose main motivation is personal advancement, but self-aggrandizement and vanity are in fact part of the overall picture of oikophobia. The oikophobe considers himself individually superior to his countrymen by dint of believing, or thinking himself to believe, in a common humanity, with his own culture having no special claim.

Chapter 2

OIKOPHOBIA AS RELATIVISM

Such a fusion of states and cultures as desired by Alexander can only take place once the truths and values of those cultures have been diluted to a watery meaninglessness. Statements to the effect that we are all really the same and that something is true if someone believes it to be true can only be made once people have abandoned the cores of their own cultures.[1] And in Greece we find the first traces of relativism. There are many forms of relativism, of course, and here is meant moral relativism.

Around the mid-fifth century BC, Protagoras had uttered ideas that many consider at least protorelativist. He famously said that "man is the measure of all things," and "there are two opposing sides to every question" (Diogenes Laertius 9.51). But he was before his time, and the Athenians sent him packing. By the time Plato becomes active at the beginning of the fourth century, things have changed quite a bit. In *Laws* 889e–890a (see also *Theaetetus* 152a and 170d–172b, where he discusses Protagoras), Plato attacks early forms of relativism that maintain that justice is only a matter of convention and not nature. Plato believes that if justice and right are considered matters of convention only, violence will inevitably follow, since in the absence of universal reason the truth will simply belong to those with the loudest voices and strongest arms. He fears an Athens where some wish to shut down argument by outshouting their opponents, and indeed he lives at a time in which the debate between nature (*physis*) and convention (*nomos*) has become a commonplace, with relativist theories of good and right being greatly in vogue.

We have already seen relativism or latent relativism among such gentlemen as Antiphon, Hippias, and Antisthenes, roughly contemporaries of Plato. Not long after Plato's death, the influential Epicurus holds that the gods do not care about human action, and that justice is consequently a matter of what people and their laws decide it to be. Plato himself, on the other hand, is a universalist, which is to say that he believes there are universal truths, true at any time and place. To him and many other Greeks, it is the incorruptibility of reason that is a manifestation of the divine: the fact that, for instance, the syllogism is and always will be true, regardless of human agency, is the hand of God in the world. From the truth of reason, according to Plato, certain other universal truths can be derived, such as what the nature of justice is.

I define universalism here as the claim that there are certain absolute truths that apply everywhere. This posture, where people are of the conviction that the truths and virtues of their own culture can or should transcend their natural borders and be accepted everywhere, is also embodied by the earlier state of societies, before oikophobia. But the relativist also lays claim to a type of universalism. He is of the view that universalism should mean the equality of all cultural morals and truths in the world, and that none of these truths should be or can be transcendent. He holds that all sets of principles are equal or have their valid claims, and that none should or could be applicable everywhere. By rejecting the universality of any one moral set, the relativist believes that he accepts the moral universe as is.[2] These two universalisms are so different that each seems, to the opposing side, to be antiuniversal. In the former manifestation, universalism is absolutist, while in the latter it is the exact opposite, relativist. There is also something of a mixed form of universalism, which is not exactly relativist but also does not seek to impose its own ancient traditions on others. This is a more utopian universalism that does believe in a higher truth—as against relativist universalism—but does not believe that this higher truth is represented by the own domestic culture—as against absolutist universalism. Of course, the striving for such a utopia is still very much a Western phenomenon, even if it goes against earlier Western traditions, so that this utopian universalism may still be considered more absolutist than relativist. It is embodied by men like Thomas More, Jean-Jacques Rousseau, and Karl Marx, as shall be discussed.

By the absolutist definition of universalism, it should be considered an axiom of civilizational development that societies become less universalist and more relativist as they advance. Since cultures during their progress tend to absorb new people, with their own competing cultures and subcultures, the logical conclusion of this progress will eventually be multiculturalism and then cultural and moral relativism. And when sufficient numbers of people no longer believe in their own—or their adopted—civilization's moral standing, in the civilization's truths, then the power of that civilization will decay. The more a culture comes into contact with other cultures and integrates them, the more the members of the original culture will begin to doubt it and become relativists. The great conundrum is thus that the more successful a culture is at spreading itself, the more it will come into contact with others, so that the decay follows directly out of the success, and relativism follows directly out of universalism.

As shall be seen time and again, a civilization's fall is therefore not a break with its rise, but a direct result and natural continuation of it. A condition is reached where the truths of all the subsumed cultures are jostling with one another for primacy, so that the weary members of that society, tired of fighting, throw up their arms in exasperation and claim all these truths to be equal. The problem here is that whereas some members of the society surrender in this way, others do not, and so it is ultimately the truths of those who refuse to give up that will crush the truths of those who side with relativism. This is happening all over the West, but in particular in Europe, where many arriving immigrants come from more universalist cultures and thereby slowly marginalize the scraps of cultural truth remaining in a far more relativist European society. For example, in some European communities the absolutist European truth of women's equality clashes with an equally absolutist Islamic truth about gender roles. Over time, Europeans become more relativist, while at least parts of the Muslim population remain absolutist, with the result that the European absolutist truth becomes relativized and the Islamic truth, which remains absolutist, is allowed to exist within European jurisdiction. If both truths had remained absolutist, such accommodation would have been impossible.[3]

And so from Greece, where relativism first arose in the West, we learn the pattern that will repeat itself incessantly. Since both relativism and oikophobia follow from a society's success, relativism becomes the easiest hook by which oikophobia can attach itself to the Zeitgeist and become profuse. In chapter 7 we shall analyze what I call positivist oikophobia, but relativist oikophobia appears first in history. Before we travel to Rome, I should like to dissect a few features of relativism as it applies in a social context (that is, cultural and moral issues, not metaethical questions of whether there actually are such things as "absolute truth," "objective morality," and so on, which would be a different discussion).

Before getting to those cultural issues, however, I should mention briefly the most obvious and therefore oft-repeated, logical protest against relativism, since it will continue to be relevant to us. And that is that it falls by its own logic, as a sort of liar's paradox. In this paradox, famous since antiquity, a person says "I am lying": so if he speaks the truth, then he is not speaking the truth, and if he is lying, then he is not lying. So too, if relativism entails that there are no higher truths, and that anything goes, then the truth of relativism itself also falls (this argument goes back to the second *Theaetetus* passage cited above). We end up with a sort of moral nihilism that no one but the insane or the teenager would ever want. Related is the idea that even though relativism claims the truths of all cultures to be of equal value, relativism is itself a Western idea. Relativism must thus reject itself as merely a Western notion with no necessary validity beyond the West, at least if the oikophobes wish to remain consistent in their view that other cultures' norms are as good as those of the West, if not better.

Because of this very specific cultural and philosophical background, relativism must itself be labeled as a sort of ethnocentrism, precisely that which the relativists purport to be rejecting. An example of how this plays itself out is when a Western apologist of Islam accuses its Western critics of ethnocentrism, even when the apologist's defense of Islam is based on Western relativism and on a Christian—especially Lutheran—understanding of what religion properly is, namely personal communion between individual and God where faith and politics do not mix, whereas in fact the mainstream Islamic conception of religion is much broader. The idea that Islamic religion should not be conflated with political action is a distinction that presumes a Western viewpoint.

Some relativists would reply to the liar's paradox conundrum that we can say something like "There are no absolute truths, except this one." But this is the same arbitrariness with which they charge the absolutist. This arbitrariness also has a whiff of Cartesianism and its "I think, therefore I am," since it is about the equivalent of saying, "Nothing is certain but me and what I legislate"—a solipsistic attempt to establish genuine knowledge.[4] Some skeptics who are too generous to the relativists maintain that we can never know universal truth even if we admit that there is such a thing. But I believe this is incorrect and that the skeptics thereby surrender to relativism through a paradox of their own, because if they were right that we can never know universal truth, then we would have to admit that the proposition "universal truth exists" might be false, in which case we would fall back into relativism. And with the statement "We can never know universal truth," skeptics express that they think they know a universal truth. But here, admittedly, we are moving beyond the scope of moral (and cultural) relativism and into other forms thereof, which is not my present purpose.

So to turn to our context, there are many facets of relativism that make it tempting and attractive as a society moves toward oikophobia. One of these is related to laziness. Relativism liberates people from having to think about right and wrong. There is a very strong tendency in the relativist segments of civilizational cycles of wanting to have it both ways and to give each side of the argument its due, even when this is a logical impossibility. This way, those who refuse to rank various moral systems need not give themselves the trouble of defending any, which is always more intellectually demanding than claiming equality. Although it is very difficult to arrive at higher moral principles, we must still recognize that these can potentially be created. And so each and every one of us is called upon, in any given instance, to decide between the morality of one course of action, and that of another. For indeed we must dare to judge. But one of the prejudices of our age is that it is arrogant to judge, although those who speak against judging always judge those who are forthright about the necessity of judgment. By refusing to put things in rank and degree, many relativists gradually lose their intellects.

A second facet—and related to the first—concerns narcissism and cowardice. Although there may be certain moral difficulties with absolutist universalism, such as the risk of its decaying into an all too positivist or overly confident self-reliance, relativism as arising from narcissism and cowardice has just as great a penchant for feelings of superiority. (And absolutist uni-

versalism is still preferable to relativism, since the former insists on the existence of higher truths, which as a practical matter must be recognized in a
globalized world where different value systems interact with each other ever
more frequently.) When the feelings of superiority over the defeated Other
have been historically exhausted, one turns to superiority over oneself and
turns the own into the Other: our set of principles is beneath me, one will
say, and others are just as good, if not better. By claiming that all moral systems are essentially equal, one aggrandizes oneself as just, magnanimous,
and above petty conflict, and in this we recognize a Hippias, a Cynic Diogenes, as well as future figures we shall come across. This narcissist relativism tends to hold sway in intellectual circles—we have all heard statements
to the effect that cultures are different but equal, and that we may not criticize a particular behavior if it is embedded in a culture. The cognoscenti are
particularly prone to relativism as narcissism, so as to bestow worth upon all
sides, and this will gain them plaudits for their great capacity for nuance.[5]
They may not realize that, in many cases, admitting the error of one way
makes it impossible to fault the other. To be for something also requires a
person to be against something, which can be dangerous, and this is where
cowardice comes into play. If you are not against anything, being for something is only going to be a nominal matter.

Relativist oikophobes are fairly easy to recognize because they are the ones
who will instinctively react against any distinction of superiority or nobility
between different entities. They set up contradictory poles and then claim
that each pole is right in a way, or that each is wrong, as for instance when they
condemn Hamas's rocket attacks while maintaining that Israel's counterat-
tacks are also wrong—an impossible position and a sort of fallacious "argument to moderation" that is styled to be just and objective. It is a watered-down
attempt at moral democracy, and the ironic thing is of course that the relativists reject the superiority of any one moral set or system while suggesting that
their own position is superior. It is indeed indicative of this relativist oikophobe that his desire for superiority is oftentimes greater than that of those
who freely admit the superiority of one system over another. The former is in
a certain sense a more nefarious kind of superiority than that posed by moral
absolutism, because whereas the recognition of one moral system above
others only claims the superiority of a particular idea, the rejection of all
systems as being equal or relative seems to seek the superiority of the relativist person himself, at least if we look at the behavior of our aforementioned

Greek gentlemen and of others we shall meet. This sort of oikophobe seeks to be above "ideology," which in recent times has become a dirty word (chapter 11 will look at postmodern times). By detaching himself from anything larger, the oikophobe may stand alone in the spotlight, in unadulterated glory.

A third facet of cultural and moral relativism concerns proper terminology. The relativist often confuses convention with arbitrariness. If a particular behavior is conventional or arises from convention, many relativists assume that such behavior, or the value it represents, is completely arbitrary. And if something can be labeled as arbitrary, the relativists will reject it. In fact, however, whereas all norms are conventional, within the arena of convention there are varying degrees of arbitrariness. Some norms, for example, are related to life and death, and it is a natural, entirely non-arbitrary inclination of living organisms to strive for life and self-propagation and to avoid death. The convention of burial, to take an obvious instance, may thus be said to be less arbitrary—since it arose in part from a desire to protect the living from the unsanitary conditions of decomposing cadavers—than the convention that the right hand should be extended when one meets a new person. But relativists tend to obfuscate this distinction and to use the terms "conventional" and "arbitrary" practically as synonyms, which very clearly they are not.[6] Such an obfuscation makes it easier for the oikophobe to reject his society's norms and conventions.

Since relativism first arose in Greece, we learn more about that philosophy by looking at some of the historical circumstances that made it possible. And when we do this, we find that the development of relativism is intimately wound up with the rise of oikophobia and with the weakening of more traditional culture. By stretching Greek culture to foreign lands, Alexander the Great dilutes it, since the incorporation of new cultures leaves neither the old nor the new ones the same. An influx of Middle Eastern thought, for example, will stimulate the rise of the Hellenistic schools of philosophy, which in turn will move Greek thought and mentalities yet farther away from their sources in Homeric polytheism. This reinforces the point that cultures simply cannot coexist without losing many of their core characteristics, as we shall see for other civilizations as well, and that pluralism is thus an oikophobic manifestation. Indeed the historical trajectories of our civilizations will reveal how multiculturalism and pluralism—an extended contact with and ultimate absorption of the Other—play an integral part in the development of oikophobia.[7]

It is Alexander and his father Philip who, by uniting the Greek city-states, ruin the competition that makes them thrive. It is similar to how Bismarck's unification of Germany in 1871 will spell out the decline of the astonishing concentration of cultural genius in the German-speaking states of the eighteenth and nineteenth centuries, a concentration second in world history only to fifth-century-BC Greece.

Chapter 3

Oikophobia in Rome

Let us look at the next great Western people of culture, the Romans. Early on, as with the Greeks and any other major grouping, this is a people only naïvely aware of its own strength, but, unlike the Greeks who were more isolated, both from non-Greeks and even from each other, the Romans quickly enter into contact with the Other. In the rise of their monarchy and subsequently of their republic, surrounded everywhere by other nations and tribes, with whom they soon come into conflict and shifting alliances, the Romans gain a sense of their own power.

Not even in Latium itself do the Romans become dominant until the early fourth century BC, and they become a rugged and hardened people in the process, toughened even further by their loss, and even the temporary fall of the city of Rome, to the Gauls under Brennus around 390 BC. These difficult birth pangs make the people warlike, and the Romans remain for many hundreds of years almost constantly at war. By the mid-third century BC they have established control of most of the Italian peninsula, including the colonial Greek cities in the south. Surprising feats of tactical ineptitude—the battle of the Allia against the Gauls and the total surrender at the Caudine Forks to the Samnites are particularly egregious examples—have brought them humiliation and almost extinction on several occasions, so that the thought of not fighting for the collective would scarcely occur to anyone. These failures contribute to the facetious saying that the Romans never won a battle, but never lost a war: their grit and endurance would always carry them through in the end.

Control of the peninsula does not entail the end of fighting, however. If anything, it only makes Rome's conflicts enter upon a larger and more destructive stage. It is especially the successful resistance against Pyrrhus's invasion of the Italian peninsula (280–275 BC) and, even more so, Rome's defeat of Carthage in the First and Second Punic Wars (264–241 BC and 218–201 BC) that contribute to Roman confidence and xenophobia, because these are the first conflicts in which major Mediterranean powers, as opposed to mere Italic tribes, have been overcome. Taking their first significant territories beyond the mainland, namely Corsica, Sardinia, Sicily, and southeastern Spain in the first two Punic Wars, the Romans gain an outsize perception of their own influence.

Important in this context are also the first major contacts with the Greeks. These take place primarily through the Romans' stretch into southern Italy and Sicily, where Greek culture has been blossoming for half a millennium since the early colonial days of Magna Graecia, and especially during the Second Punic War, when the Romans stop Philip V of Macedon from coming to the Carthaginians' aid and then defeat him with the help of some allied Greek cities (First and Second Macedonian Wars, ending in 196 BC). These events are a cultural turning point in the Romans' meddling in the affairs of other peoples, and roughly mark the time when Greek culture begins to influence the Roman elite.

In fairness, Roman meddling during the early and mid-republic is not caused by expansionist ambitions as much as by the desire to enjoy peaceful borders, as evidenced by the Romans' repeatedly pulling out of Greece after each victory but being forced by renewed Greek war making to reenter it. The Romans finally have enough after the Third and Fourth Macedonian Wars (172–168 and 150–148 BC) and decide to hold Greece. This is, incidentally, usually the fate of great powers. Large-scale imperialism is generally unjust, but only rarely is it caused by a concerted and deliberate original plan to conquer the world (exceptions would be instances like Hitler, Napoleon, and Alexander the so-called Great).[1] Rather, one foreign entanglement will lead to the next, which will lead to the next, and this is true in both ancient and modern times. The British after the Napoleonic Wars, like the Americans after World War II, will find that merely preserving the status quo will require an ever-growing web of foreign alliances and conflicts.

At this stage, the Romans are well aware of their military superiority and thereby—a common leap people like to make—of their cultural superiority. But for a remarkably long time there is almost no Roman literature, that is, literature written in the Latin language. Over several centuries this still relatively barbarian people does not create much of literary interest, excepting the occasional festive inscription, whose importance nowadays is mainly archaeological. The concept of literature is, in the main, imported from the Greek culture of southern Italy, Sicily, and then mainland Greece itself. The first inscriptions attest to early Archaic Latin religious songs, especially those of the Arval and Salian priesthoods, but the first proper extant Latin work we have is by Livius Andronicus, a Greek slave who translates Greek poetic works into Latin for his Roman masters in the late third century BC. Particularly his *Odusia*, a translation of Homer's *Odyssey* and which survives in fragments, comes across as an ancestral history of the Romans, since Odysseus travels to Italy, and since in Roman myth the fall of Troy and Aeneas's escape therefrom will lead to the beginnings of the Roman people. Andronicus's work thus supplies a sense of cultural rootedness and dignity to a group that has overcome external enemies and wishes to pat itself on the back. The fact that Greekdom is a catalyst in the awakening of Roman literature, and that Latin writing is therefore not entirely self-made, as it were, can be seen in the fact that the first writers produce all kinds of genres at once—epic, tragedy, and comedy. A more "organic" process, such as had taken place among the Greeks, grows from tentative beginnings and aristocratic tradition that finally coalesce into a literary product of an opening genre, usually epic.

Once the idea of literature has taken hold, it acquires, in spite of the plethora of genres, a rather proto-Hegelian flavor, which is to say that it concerns itself mainly with the excellence of the Roman state, and considers virtue to be political virtue. The Greek influence remains, such as through the Roman adoption of Homer's dactylic hexameter and through further Latin adaptations of Greek works, most notably by comedic dramatists Plautus and Terence—and what in Greek literature comes later, namely comedy, thus lies early in Latin—but as Roman literature comes into its own, it begins to glorify its own civilization. Gnaeus Naevius produces an epic on the First Punic War (late third century BC) and Quintus Ennius a text of *Annals* on Roman history and *Scipio* (early second century BC) on the deeds of Scipio Africanus, who vanquished Hannibal in the Second Punic War. There is a certain charming pugnaciousness among Latin writers early on against their own ruling classes, which is largely absent from the earliest Greek literature—the grammarian Aulus Gellius describes in his *Attic Nights* 3.3 how Naevius had to compose some of his works in prison after having heaped vulgar abuse upon the Roman aristocrats—but this is facilitated by the fact that the mid-republican Romans are no longer a strictly discrete people, but rather composed of various tribes with different languages falling at one time or another within the Roman orbit. Naevius, for instance, is presumably Campanian, while Ennius comes from Calabria. This is another instance of the perennial fact that diversity causes disunity, although this disunity is still moderate at the early and middle stages of the republic. What will be considered "classical" Roman literature will come later than had been the case in Greece. But the general trend in the early Roman consciousness is clear and perfectly expected: Rome is great, other cultures less so. And yet it is worthwhile to remember that this glorification of Rome is facilitated by the influx of non-Roman literary treasures. A progressive adoption of foreign culture is thus sometimes a great good for a civilization, even if at other times it may cause disunity and dilution.

And indeed as the cultural influence of Greece makes itself felt, there is a conservative and even xenophobic reaction. The paradigmatic example of the conservative Roman at this time is Cato the Elder, Rome's first significant prose writer, whose terse admonitions magnify the greatness of Roman culture as vindicated by her victories. He understands the long-term danger to the state posed by an exaggerated individualism as expressed in the cult of personality—exemplified by the victorious generals of the Second Punic War, in which he himself had fought. He refuses to have his son tutored by educated Greek slaves, as is the custom among the Roman aristocracy, and informs him that the Greeks are a worthless tribe that will only corrupt. Instead, Cato writes his own didactic history of Rome, the *Origins* (second quarter of the second century BC), even though he himself in his writings is clearly influenced by Greek rhetoric. He berates the government for letting the famous Greek embassy of philosophers stay too long in Rome (155 BC), and when he visits Athens, according to Plutarch (*Cato the Elder* 12), Cato refuses to speak Greek with the locals, even though he is proficient in the language, and only communicates with them in Latin, through an interpreter. He also urges the Senate to completely destroy the already weakened Carthage once and for all, which is achieved in the Third Punic War (149–146 BC).

Important to note is that Cato's background is as a farmer, and he will remain devoted to the cause of farming throughout his life, composing also the text *On Agriculture* (ca. 150s BC). As will be true in modern times as well, oikophobia tends to develop much more strongly in the cities than among those who adhere to an earlier, simpler way of life—namely farming. Based on this latter text, as well as on Cicero's later *On Old Age*, in which Cato appears as a speaker, and also on Plutarch's aforementioned biography *Cato the Elder*, Cato believes that there is no greater joy than to walk on a Roman farm, over a Roman field, under a decidedly Roman sun, with a fistful of Roman manure in his strong and Roman hand, all while muttering incoherently about those effeminate, artistic, and quite obviously queer Greeks. The fact that the young gentlemen of the rising Roman elite are starting to take an interest in the Greek cultural encroachment, even to be fascinated by it, only makes matters worse from Cato's point of view. The rather conservative Cicero, in the century after Cato, will continue this jingoistic and self-conscious reaction, even if in a milder form, such as in the beginning of his *Tusculan Disputations* (ca. 45 BC), where he is at pains to explain to his impressionable Roman readership that Rome has superseded Greece in almost all fields, and shall presumably overtake it in philosophy too one day.

A prerequisite for strengthening the Roman state is the further granting of citizenship, since more men will be needed to fight the numerous hostile forces by which Rome finds herself surrounded. But this increase in equality will lead to more internal conflict. It is no wonder that, eventually, as everyone comes to partake actively in the state, they start to feel that the state owes something to them rather than they to the state, and this will come to mark a point at which legionaries become more loyal to their commanding officers than to the Senate in Rome. The politician and general Marius's military recruitment of the poor in exchange for land in the early first century BC, which effectively converts an army of citizen soldiers into mercenaries to be had for the biggest bribe, serves as a catalyst in this process. In 41 AD, Claudius will be the first emperor to feel obliged to offer the soldiery a bribe for their loyalty, which will set a tragic precedent for the remaining history of the empire. As had happened in Greece, and as will happen in modern times, the spreading of greater rights and therefore expectations to all parts of the populace leads to increasing competition among various interest groups within that populace.

There are several milestones in this development during the Roman Republic. Many of these are part of the perennial conflict between the noble patricians and the rest of the people, the plebeians. Perhaps the first is the patricians' granting of the plebeians' demands to elect tribunes, after the plebeians secede to the hill Mons Sacer in the early fifth century BC, although the event is partly shrouded in myth. The plebeians presumably complain about debt and about not being held in proper esteem though they had fought against the Latins and Sabines, and this latter circumstance makes it similar to the poor Greek oarsmen at Salamis demanding greater powers for having saved Hellas, around this same time, as well as to the aforementioned American youth serving in Vietnam and the Russian serfs having served in the Crimea, among so many other examples from world history.

Further milestones in the development are the subsequent granting of legislative rather than just veto power to the tribunes of the plebs; the opening of the consulship to plebeians and the banning of interest on loans so as to relieve the plebeians of overwhelming debt (ca. 367 BC); the opening of the priesthood to the plebeians through the law called *Lex Ogulnia* (300 BC); the *Lex Hortensia*, which makes the laws passed by the plebeians universally binding (287 BC); the attempted land redistributions to the plebeians by the Gracchi brothers in the second half of the second century BC. Certain rights, even if not full citizenship, are granted to marginal groups in the Second Punic War upon the annihilating battle defeats incurred by the legionaries at Hannibal's hands at the Trebia (218 BC), Lake Trasimene (217 BC), and especially Cannae (216 BC), the battle with the highest one-day casualty figure of all antiquity. After these disasters, and certainly after Cannae, when caution was thrown to the wind and too many legions gathered in one place, only to be destroyed, as total a mobilization as possible is required for Rome to survive, and as a result more people come to partake in the state. (For such events, too, there are many parallels: for example Aristotle, at *Politics* 1303a, discusses the event when the city-state Argos had to absorb neighboring people in order to have enough fighters, after a serious defeat against Cleomenes I of Sparta, and Sparta herself had to promise freedom to her slaves, the helots, after the disastrous loss to the Thebans at Leuctra.) The citizenship is further extended to the tribes that had rebelled in the Social War (early first century BC). Julius Caesar spreads the citizenship beyond Italy (40s BC), and, much later, in 212 AD, Caracalla grants Roman citizenship to all freeborn men of the entire realm.

These events, even if for different reasons and in different contexts, all take place along a progressive continuum. Although many of these measures are passed for the sake of preserving unity, such as to stop the plebeians from seceding, or to placate the allies after the Social War, the measures themselves assure that, in the long run, the trajectory that in the end will lead to natural fragmentation proceeds apace. Just as there had been a conservative stubbornness in Athens as well, so too many Roman patricians take a very protective view of the privilege of Roman citizenship, but they are forced to yield to the necessities of history, and by various crises to extend it to the poor and to more recently absorbed peoples. This makes Roman power grow more quickly but also, in turn, contributes to its eventual decline. The more groups a people begins to include, the weaker its tribe-like cohesion will become, and the less outward power it will, in the long term, be able to project. This is why we say, even for peoples, that what goes up must come down.

And as the Romans rise from a primitive tribe to a cultured and worldly people, the major force of the Mediterranean, they begin to look more objectively at themselves. Gentlemen like the philologist and logographer Aelius Stilo and his students Varro and Cicero, with their works on Latin grammar and Roman religion and rhetoric in a more scientific vein, are at the forefront of a civilization that is now looking at itself in the mirror, corresponding thereby to that stage of Greek development where the people emerged from its Archaic beginnings and began to question themselves through works of philosophy and history. Varro, indeed, is probably the closest thing to Aristotle that Rome ever offers (though of course enormously inferior to him), a man of universal learning who can question the myths of the state, and interpret the gods euhemeristically—that is, as having originally been human beings who then became idealized—without letting it compromise his patriotism.

In Greek civilization, because literature or at least a strong oral tradition had existed early on, there was more time for the self-glorifying, epic stage before the scientific era was reached. In the more barbarian Roman civilization, on the other hand, the state has had time to be militarily successful and to achieve a considerable measure of wealth and leisure before much literature has been written, with the result that the self-questioning stage follows quickly upon the self-glorifying one. Thus we see quite early on the rise not only of science but also of the first—and probably only—truly Roman literary genre, namely the satire, through the able stylus of Lucilius, though already Ennius had dabbled in the genre. (And it makes sense that satire—Latin *satura*, meaning "mixture" or "medley"—would be the truly Roman genre, as also the Roman rhetorician Quintilian agrees (*Institutes of Oratory* 10.93), since literature began there as an attempt to adopt almost everything at once from Greece.) But as always, the turn to science, scholarship, and even ridicule, a result of that leisure brought on by success, is also a preparatory stage for eventual oikophobia.

Riches gained through control of the Mediterranean lead to luxury, and allow individual persons to rise to greater prominence, and to consider themselves more important than the state—precisely what Cato the Elder had feared. This fragmentation on the individual level mirrors the fragmentation on the mass level, where interest groups—the two largest being plebeians and patricians—compete against each other for prestige. There are many and complex causes for the fall of the republic during the civil wars that rage decade after decade in the first century BC, but social fragmentation and competition, among individuals and groups, made possible by wealth, by the elimination of external threats, and by overextension and consequent absorption of new peoples—that is, by demographic diversity—are major factors in the conflicts, and are an integral part of the oikophobic process that societies in general go through. Factionalism has grown so great that Rome simply cannot exist as a republic any longer.

Toward the end of the civil wars, the so-called Neoterics or "new poets," with the great Catullus at the helm, turn away with disgust from the state and from politics, and indulge their own private passions. Turning away from the state is of course in itself a political act, but it is not one that favors the state. With the establishment of empire and relatively peaceful times, a new generation of Augustan Romans arises who are too young to remember the previous turbulent years and who therefore view their state without gratitude, and their peace as a given. An attitude of urbanity and learning, which looks with disdain at more primitive rural ways, develops in Rome. The poet Ovid, who is only a boy when the civil wars wind down, emphasizes personal pleasures and leisure, a soft urbanite with little interest in the travails of the state, and without much understanding of what they have given him. His older contemporary Propertius, a fellow elegiac poet, is a similar example.

As a general rule it is easier for those who are born in privileged times to criticize the status quo. This is obviously not to say that critique of the state and the powers that be is illegitimate in and of itself, only that such critique, or such turning away from the state, falls within the expected trajectory of the oikophobic process of fragmentation and self-aggrandizement that is given a new impetus by lasting peace. Ovid is an individual who is an individualist when individualism is fashionable—and collective individualism, which may be an oxymoron in theory but repeatedly manages to exist in practice, occurs in all decadent, self-engrossed societies. He does not care much for the body politic, and brags in his poetry—*Art of Love* (ca. 2 AD)—about how the girls are clamoring for attention at the door to his study (but it was probably just his wife bringing porridge for his weak stomach). He treats foreign deities like Isis as respectfully as the Olympian or Roman gods. As opposed to the state, which views foreign mystery cults with suspicion, Ovid wants to please his female readers, among whom such cults have become popular.

In the early empire the work of the poet Lucretius, after his death in the mid-first century BC, spreads the Epicurean notion that the gods do not care about human affairs and that religious rites are therefore unnecessary, and that one should withdraw from the world of politics in order to achieve a tranquil mind. Epicureanism will never become as popular in Rome as Stoicism, which is more suited to the Roman temperament, but the fact that these notions are able to gain traction attests to how far Rome has now come. Such attitudes, especially the anticeremonial one, could never have spread early on in the culture, which simply would not have been ready for it, and this is even truer of Roman than it would have been of Greek culture. Rome had always prided herself on her piety, and for instance considered the Greek epithet "godlike" to be blasphemous—surely no human being can be like the gods!—which is why, for example, while Homer frequently refers to his heroes as "godlike" (*antitheos* and *theoeides*, among several expressions), Virgil more modestly refers to his hero as *pius* ("pious") *Aeneas*. And so the fact that Epicureanism gains a strong foothold in Rome, in such a parochial and political society, is further indicative of how the Romans are abandoning their traditions en masse, once they come to experience long-lasting peace and prosperity.

Along with success comes an increasing culture of dependency, similar to that in Periclean Athens, where large numbers of citizens were on the government dole in one capacity or other. This dependency fragments the citizenry further by making them more loyal to a generous politician or commander than to the state itself, a pattern that repeats itself incessantly from antiquity to the present day. Clodius's free grain dole for the populace during the waning days of the republic, like, later, emperor Domitian's conspicuous largesse to propitiate the people, both fall on that trajectory. As the republic goes under, a consul or usurper can often rely on his legionaries to be more loyal to him than to the Senate in Rome, not to mention to the idea of Rome as a whole.

To return to the Greek, tragic view of the world, it is possible to view an individual step in the democratizing and equalizing process as good and just, while at the same time recognizing that it contributes to the lengthy process of civilizational decline. Converting the republic to an empire is, in a manner of speaking, a reset that allows the realm to survive for another several centuries through a concentration of power in one person and consequent slowing of the fragmenting process. Nonetheless, the same trajectory of a leveling self-centeredness—as exemplified by the Neoterics, Ovid, and others—and thereby ultimately of fragmentation is carried over from the republic. And the overall process of power diffusion and its concomitant fragmentation also continues—albeit with the setback at the beginning of the empire—such as in the parallel example of citizenship expansion after the Social War of the republic and the Edict of Caracalla during the empire. After all, the emperor is not untouchable, and to hold on to power he must frequently—as had senators during the republic—bribe not only individuals but whole classes of people. And this, too, increases competition among groups and allows fragmentation. A historian like Edward Gibbon, who emphasizes Emperor Commodus's role in Rome's decline,[2] therefore states the truth only from a rather narrow point of view: things do take a clear turn for the worse during Commodus's time in power, yes, but if we wish to grasp civilizational processes in general, we must understand that the processes of decline really begin well before the peak of power has even been reached.[3]

As this peak of Roman power comes and goes, a stage of nascent oikophobia naturally sets in. As always happens among peoples, with self-observation comes a sense of shame, and as Adam saw that he was naked, peoples of culture see what they have done. Again, with the attainment of enough wealth and power to afford a large and largely permanent leisure class, and at least some leisure even for the middle classes, oikophobia slowly arrives. This is generally true of cultured societies, and it is one of the reasons why oikophobia cannot exist in any significant measure early on in the community and is a result of that community's success. This will always remain the internal contradiction of oikophobia, that it rejects that success to which it owes its existence.

An example of the Roman oikophobe during the empire is Seneca the Younger (first two-thirds of the first century AD), who harbors the regret regarding past depravities that every civilization comes to feel once it has exhausted itself. There is the foreboding in his work of a grand equalizer, in the spirit of a Hippias or an Antiphon, that all is equal and no group better than any other, that, by extension, Rome has no right to call herself the better of others. One thinks of such relativist statements of Seneca as that people love their country simply because it is their own (*Letters to Lucilius* 66, which is also a sort of historicism—ascribing people's opinions to external and historical factors; compare also the cosmopolitanism of *Letter* 28). His statement is true enough of the xenophobically conservative, but not of the many thoughtful people who may clearly recognize their own country's contributions to the world and, in Rome's case, conclude that their civilization's production of advanced jurisprudence and perennial engineering—these being the areas in which the Romans clearly surpassed the Greeks—is superior to the superstitions of Celtic druids or the human sacrifices of the Scythians.[4]

But as do oikophobes today, Seneca simply dismisses patriotism as simple-mindedness. Were he forced to live among the Britannic Celts, however, or on the desolate shores of the Black Sea, as had Ovid, he would no doubt realize Rome's virtues quite quickly. (His own temporary exile on Corsica was comparatively mild.) Seneca's emphasis on mercy and generosity, though of a piece with his Stoic philosophy, happens at a point in cultural development when enough blood has been spilled and people no longer have the will to strive for power over the external Other. That is to say, although mercy and generosity may of themselves very often be good things, they are also indicative of the natural decline and oncoming inertia of a people.

This is where someone like Nietzsche goes wrong. If something is indicative of the decline of a people, that thing, he feels, must necessarily be bad and unconditionally rejected (see chapter 1). He is unable to hold two emotions in his heart at the same time, at least on this question. But we can in fact be even more Greek thàn he was, and realize that there is no such thing as perfection, that we always have to live in a negative state by being, on the civilizational level, either strong and cruel, or weak and kind. Of course, oiko-phobic kindness toward the Other is usually vanity masquerading as open-ness, but more about that later. The Christian or proto-Christian virtue of nonviolence and kindness often works well for individuals but is suicidal on the geopolitical level, as will be further touched upon in chapter 11. Indeed Gibbon, in chapter 15 of his great work, makes a similar point. And so Seneca's proto-Christian emphasis on mercy is indicative of a weakening culture.

In the decadence of the later Roman Empire, the culture moves ever farther from its roots. Roman religion grows weaker under Nero, the younger contemporary of Seneca. For example, the epic poet Lucan removes the traditional gods from his epic *Pharsalia*—unfinished at his death in 65 AD—and restricts his narration to human agency alone. The Roman religion took shape, as religions often do, in a smaller, agrarian community. Since the living conditions in such a community are harsher, the religion imposes a certain harshness as well, which is not suited for the easy and comfortable lifestyle of a wealthy city. This is true both of late antique or early medieval Christianity, of Judaism, and even of pagan Roman religion, with its strong emphasis on ritual and obligation.[5] In a larger and more fragmented state, people develop much more individual spiritual needs—leading to the above-mentioned popularity of personalized foreign cults among urban Roman women, to whom Ovid caters—needs which earlier and more collective forms of religion cannot satisfy.

We can imagine ourselves in the late first century AD, walking in the shadow of the poet Juvenal in the vicinity of the newly built Colosseum—known then as the Flavian Amphitheater—and listening to what he will write a few years later in his *Satires* (1 and 6). A group of Syrian-looking men, speaking with each other in Greek, skip by him. Juvenal wrinkles his nose at the fancy purple cloak from Tyre that one of them is wearing—we recall Xenophanes's complaints about Lydian luxury—and he mutters that there is barely a single actual Roman to be seen in Rome these days. They remind him how the capital has been overrun by Orientals—it is not Rome who conquered them, but they Rome!—and how religious cults from the East have become so popular. He says Roman women ignore the Roman gods and instead go to Jewish soothsayers—is it for this that we took Judea?—and perform their amorous activities under the sign of Isis. He looks up at the Colosseum, which is indeed beautiful, with its elegant archways and columns in relief, and says with a wry smile: we shall see how long it lasts.

The fact that traditional religion slowly disappears in Rome, however, does not mean that superstition disappears, or that people become any more rational than they hitherto have been. Superficial individualism, pop spiritualism, astrology, physiognomy, vegetarianism—these are some of the expressions of the replacement of traditional religion with new, more customized cults. Seneca, for instance, becomes a vegetarian for a while. Similarly, in Greece, physiognomy, though first appearing early, did not gain broader credence until late in that civilization. All this should sound familiar to us. The observation in Tacitus's *Annals* 11.15, describing the mid-first century AD, that native religious rites are being ignored in favor of alien superstitions, repeats complaints we have already heard from Aristophanes and Isocrates among the Greeks. Finally, under Septimius Severus, whose reign ends in the early third century AD, oriental cults will become sanctioned by the state in an act of propitiating syncretism. The superstitious mysticist individualism of the later empire will pave the way for the rise of Neoplatonism, which in turn will compete with and influence the early Christians, but that is another story.

As opposed to the earlier and wonderfully boisterous historian Sallust (mid-first century BC) and, indeed, as opposed to the natural optimism of all earlier chroniclers, the historians Tacitus and Suetonius, contemporaries, paint bleak pictures of Rome. Their work is pervaded by the general malaise of a declining culture that has stopped believing in itself—even by a sense of collective shame and bad conscience. Tacitus's *Germania* (ca. 98 AD), about a land he never visited, in many respects sets the northern Germanic tribes above the Romans of his day. So too in his *Agricola* (also ca. 98 AD), the tribes of Britain receive a similar treatment: their virtue and self-sacrifice are contrasted with the greed, cruelty, and power lust of Rome, most famously in the speech by the Caledonian chieftain Calgacus (*Agricola* 30–32), who as Tacitus's mouthpiece decries the vice of the Romans in the oft-quoted words: "Robbery, butchery, and rapine they call by the false name of 'Empire,' and where they have wrought desolation, they call it 'peace'!" Other passages of a similar purport are his *Histories* (ca. 100 AD) 4.17, where the Batavian rebel leader Civilis says that Rome's Gallic subjects "have falsely called miserable servitude by the name of peace;" and *Annals* (ca. 115 AD) 12.37, where the captured Britannic rebel Caractacus asks of his tribunal in Rome: "If you want to rule over everyone, does it follow that everyone should accept servitude?" And see also *Annals* 14.35, with the rebel Boudicca's anti-Roman (and protofeminist) harangue.

It is noteworthy that in none of these instances are the specific charges against Rome countered in the text. Tacitus also writes almost with a sense of disgust about some of the trappings of his own culture, like porticoes, baths, and banquets (*Agricola* 21). All this sets Tacitus himself apart from his countrymen, since it signals his ability to recognize superior virtue, an ability supposedly lacking in his Roman contemporaries, to whom the Germanic and Britannic peoples are being compared.

This is an ever-recurring theme of the oikophobe: by disparaging his own kind, he places himself among those who are putatively greater than that kind, and thereby saves himself from the ruinous state of his own civilization. This can be achieved by means of the narcissist relativism mentioned in chapter 2. The price of his own culture's nobility is one he willingly pays for the purpose of stuffing his own pockets with honor and greatness, and he does so by holding up his own people's mistakes and vices for all to see. Admittedly, Tacitus, due to his intellectual complexity, can be difficult to classify: there are some passages in his work (e.g., *Annals* 4.32–33 and 14.15) where he seems to veer more in the direction of a conservative, that "reactionary oikophobia" of someone who harkens back to the good old days, more like a Plato, a Cato the Elder, or a Juvenal.

Indeed Tacitus looks down on many other surrounding peoples, too, and not only on his fellow Romans, but still he cannot rid himself, in the *Histories*, of the civilizational shame he feels about Rome's struggles. In the *Annals*, he views Roman religion as something rather old-fashioned and quaint (e.g., 4.58), while at the same time calling down the gods' wrath upon Rome (e.g., 4.1, 16.13, 16.16). (The not terribly bright Suetonius, on the other hand, still takes every seeming divine portent at face value.) Tacitus is a figure who is tossed by the liminal wave of civilizational crisis: the ingrained sense of patriarchy and hierarchy in Rome—stronger than in Greece—shields him and his fellow Romans from the most extreme excesses of oikophobia, and of all our civilizations, the Roman is where we find the least of it, but the general tendencies of the oikophobic development are clear in Rome, too, and Tacitus senses that Rome has, in some way, come to an end. Approaching the grandeur of his spiritual ancestor Thucydides, Tacitus understands the forces of group competition, caused by success, and decadent mentalities in the fall of civilizations (*Histories* 2.38), even though he himself forms a part of that decadence—the abandonment of religion, the self-glorification of the learned urbanite at the expense of his countrymen—in Rome.

As Plato had described the excessive egalitarianism and fragmented group mentality of latter-day Athens, Tacitus and those of his era, like the novelist Petronius in his *Satyricon* (second half of the first century AD), witness how, for example, the increasing freedoms of women and the feminization of men slowly break down the patriarchy that is the final bulwark against oikophobia. (And it is possible to recognize that patriarchal forces served as such a bulwark while one is at the same time strongly in favor of increasing freedoms for women; only to simple minds are things purely good or purely evil.) The virtue of the farmer who loves the land he tills is abandoned and mocked by the urbanites, who are the makers of manners and mores.

There are many reasons why Rome fell, and even more reasons than those have been offered. It is a subject about which more has been written than thought. But regardless of all the specific explanations, it is important to remember that Rome fell because she had to fall. And she had to fall because she went through the predictable trajectory of cultural development where the seeds that sowed her greatness were exactly the same as the ones that grew and aged into her rotten malaise. Expansion led to too many competing interest groups; by 200 AD there are so many Greek-speaking senators from the eastern part of the empire that the sense of national solidarity in Roman government has collapsed. Further, the abandonment of traditional religion leads to identity crises and self-hate. The late Romans, just as today's Western society, struggle with their religious heritage and the putative offensiveness of traditional religious symbols. The altar of Victoria, the Roman goddess of victory, on which the senators used to sacrifice incense and wine, is removed by Constantius II, reinstated by emperor Julian, and then removed again by Gratian (all in the fourth century AD), before the victory of Christianity settles the question. Further yet, success made Rome slovenly, fragmented, and androgynous, which are all common phenomena on the trajectory to oikophobia.

Androgyny indeed occurs in later stages of culture. Ovid is a precursor of it in Rome, where the habit of making love and rising late replaces that of marching in a column. One also thinks of Seneca's calumny of muscle and power (*Letters to Lucilius* 15), where, in proto-Christian and anti-Greco-

Roman fashion, he establishes the modern bourgeois prejudice that a muscular physique and a strong mind cannot go together. The Roman body, especially those of the metropolitan elite, becomes weaker, just as had happened in Greece. The Greek hoplites who charged upon the Persians at Marathon, who fought and died for their very homes and families, were all strong, and all wore beards. Alexander the Great shaved his chin and started a new fashion, one which is visible among the Hellenistic Greeks two centuries after Marathon, who are effeminate and childlike. The softness of the bodies of Hellenistic sculpture, such as Leochares's *Apollo Belvedere*, an early Hellenistic example, contrasts very poorly with the sharp muscularity and manliness of Classical work like Myron's *Discus Thrower* or Polycleitus's *Spear Carrier*. The traditional male virtues of strength and risk-taking are weakened in the late Roman Empire, just as our own modern denigration of these virtues, as well as our insistence on "gender fluidity"—that is, androgyny— are a clear proof of our culture's decline.

Even the fact that I preface "male virtues" with the word "traditional" is a telling sign: it should not be necessary to call them "traditional," as if perhaps they were not really male.[6] It is an undeniable fact of history that masculinity dominates the beginning of a culture, and femininity its end. We see here, and shall see for other civilizations, how male chauvinism yields to feminine sensibilities as the civilization advances; feminine interests also become more dominant, as seen for instance in late-civilizational mystery cults in Greece and Rome whose memberships are dominated by women. A salutary mid-point—without either boorishness or effeminacy—would be what Thucydides has Pericles say of the Athenian character in *History of the Peloponnesian War* 2.40, namely that "we cultivate the mind, but without growing soft." But the human species, taken as a whole, is incapable of the golden mean, which is why the rush of cruel conquest and male brutality will fall back into feeble and effeminate self-effacement.[7]

Our own late-civilizational androgyny reveals itself not only through the idea of gender fluidity, but also through the related statement that gender identities or gender roles are social constructs. Even if social construction does condition the genders to some extent, this does not mean that there is not also an underlying sociobiological reality. In fact, if such a reality did not exist, there would have been no reason for the additional social construct to develop in the first place. Social constructs and conditioning must develop over a fundamental reality, or else they would appear *ex nihilo*, out of nothing, and there would be literally no reason for them to develop in one direction rather than another. That is to say, social constructs are actually a proof that there is in fact an underlying sociobiological reality. To deny this would be to deny cause and effect.

As the ancient world comes to a close, it is the simple and oft-maligned farmer who has the last laugh. While his urban counterparts destroy themselves and are burned by the barbarians who take Rome, the life of the farmer continues as before. Not much changes for him as he privately and calmly tills his plot, while the powers that be call him first a pagan Roman, then a Catholic Italian, Frenchman, or Spaniard.

Chapter 4

The Role of Religion

As the final dismemberment of the Western half of the Roman Empire is accomplished, no European people is able to achieve any significant measure of literacy and, therefore, advanced culture. A by-and-large cultured Mediterranean civilization is replaced by a barbaric and mainly Germanic one. Western and southern Europe become the home of various assortments of Franks, Goths, and others. It is not necessary to follow here the history of every single or even any individual medieval people. Rather, it may be established as a general rule that from the fall of the Roman Empire until the Renaissance, culture, which thus far I have used somewhat loosely but by which I now specifically mean literacy and an interest in matters beyond one's own little village, does at no point advance significantly outside of royal courts and the confines of monasteries.

Since we have just looked at oikophobia in the cultured societies of Greece and Rome, we learn more about this social pathology by understanding why it does not arise in less cultured societies, such as the kingdoms that control Western Europe for a millennium, where frequently the king himself does not know how to read. In the Middle Ages, there can be no oikophobia, because generally some limited form of a consensual social order, or at the very least a degree of intellectual freedom for a larger class, is necessary for oikophobia to arise in any significant measure. This is why a limited oikophobic phenomenon in antiquity will become an even greater mass phenomenon in modernity, through the ever-increasing democratization and egalitarianism of Western society (see chapter 9).

The statement that at least some limited form of a consensual order or a degree of intellectual freedom is necessary for oikophobia, leads me to a question I often receive, and with which we might as well deal briefly before moving on. That question is: Does oikophobia only happen in the West? Well, since democracy, consensual government, and intellectual freedom are largely Western manifestations, it stands to reason that oikophobia is a particularly Western malady. But this is not to say that oikophobia cannot occur at all in non-Western societies, only that it is a rarer occurrence in them.

Historically, traces of oikophobia can be found in those non-Western societies that managed to achieve enough wealth, security, and freedom for its leisure class to attack its own civilization, even if the measure of free intellectual exchange will usually not have equaled that in the West. This may have been the case, for example, for Chaldean Babylonia, where under the last king, Nabonidus (sixth century BC), there appears to have been a weakening of traditional religion and a certain internecine restlessness on the part of the elite; and for the Zhou dynasty in ancient China, when Chinese philosophy laid its roots and began to question the authority of the state, especially through the thoughts of Laozi (perhaps late sixth century BC, if this person actually existed), with his universalist communitarianism and latent pacifism, less through the thoughts of Confucius, who emphasized rigid social structures. But delving into any detail regarding these non-Western developments would go beyond the scope of this book.

In modern times, oikophobia can arrive in non-Western societies through Westernization. One example with which I have personal experience is that of indigenous African tribes, among many of which the gradual spread of Western technology and ideas leads a new generation to leave their villages, move into their countries' capital cities, and lead more Western lives. Upon returning to their ancestral homes, after having had the experience of working with computers and visiting movie theaters, they sometimes look with disdain upon their tribe's more traditional ways. These African oikophobes consider the West better than their own culture, while Western oikophobes reject the West and consider African cultures noble and beautiful. What these two sets of oikophobes have in common is that each set understands the Other very poorly. Western oikophobes who have not spent time studying the intricacies of African cultures cannot understand them, just as the reverse is true. Many Western oikophobes would react with horror to discover the common practice of (by Western definitions) sexual assault and rape of underaged girls in indigenous Kalahari Desert communities, for instance, while African oikophobes, who due to the legacies of colonization are obliged to live in two worlds simultaneously, often prefer those parts of the West that glitter: the individualistic pleasures of computers, cars, and Hollywood stars, which disrupt African communal life, while for Western ideas like scientific skepticism and equality of the sexes they sometimes have less patience or understanding.[1] The important difference here, however, is that this African oikophobia does not develop organically, as it were, but through direct and overpowering Western influence, whereas Western oikophobia, though stimulated by contact with the Other, develops much more as a result of domestic intellectual movements. Thus, oikophobia remains not exclusively but certainly predominantly a Western phenomenon.

To return to the Middle Ages and the West, in order to get a clearer grasp of why no oikophobia arises at this time, one would do well to examine the role of religion in society, and indeed we have seen already how oikophobia is preceded by a decreasing adherence to traditional religion. There are two considerations to keep in mind here. The first is that since a community requires sacrifice, and sometimes even self-sacrifice, a positive feeling in the individual of communal membership and togetherness is necessary for that community to function. Religion provides this feeling of membership. This is part of how religion arises, and one of the reasons why it sooner or later always returns, in one form or other, after having been banished. It is easily observable, both in the present and in the past, and for both monotheistic and pagan religions, that the sense of togetherness and community cohesion is strongest in those communities that are also the most religious, such as among the Amish, Hasidic Jews, and, to make a big jump in time, the Sacred Band of Thebes mentioned in chapter 1, whose love, blessed by religious grace, had made them fight to the death for one another.

The second consideration to bear in mind is that the beginnings of every civilization are shrouded in religion, that is, that religion is the cornerstone of every civilization. There are no exceptions to this rule.[2] This means that the farther away a civilization moves from religion, the farther it moves from the traditions of its own origins. A civilization sets out small and weak, and the more success it experiences, the less religious it becomes. This is why, inversely and logically, setbacks and failures often strengthen religion temporarily, as the civilization finds itself reduced to a more primitive state that it earlier occupied. Witness, for example, the brief but desperate reintroduction of human sacrifice in Rome immediately upon the news of the devastating defeat at Cannae, which was on the one hand a "normal" psychological reaction of a terrified people, but which therefore also corresponded to the natural process of religion's strengthening and weakening in history. A contemporary example would be the brief spike in American church attendance after the 9/11 terrorist attacks.

These two considerations, when taken together, yield a very important result. Since the membership supporting the civilization, as well as the civilization's very beginnings, are underpinned by religion, the rejection of religion is generally accompanied by the rejection of communal membership and by a declining loyalty to the civilization as a whole, and not just to its religion. The weaker the sense of membership, the stronger the pursuit of self-aggrandizement on the part of individual members, which is why oikophobia and the entitlement mentality generally go hand in hand, as we saw in Greece in the context of government largesse. The oikophobes come to feel that they are above any larger group requiring membership. It should therefore not be surprising that on the whole, the more religion there is in a society, the more sense of community and the less oikophobia we will find there.

Since the beginnings of a civilization are religious, the natural end of civilization is the rejection of religion—by losing their religion, the members lose their sense of membership that ties them to the community. They decreasingly see themselves as parts of a cohesive whole, and cease to be loyal to one another, becoming more reluctant to sacrifice themselves for the greater good. They no longer consider the greater good good, with the result that a society and its religion stand and fall together. Greece, Rome, and perhaps Israel among ancient civilizations, and France, Germany, and Russia, among modern ones, offer particularly striking examples of what happens when religion is abandoned en masse, but the phenomenon is true in general.[3] That religion is the strongest force of communal cohesion has also been known by otherwise such diverse thinkers as Machiavelli, Hobbes, Voltaire, Rousseau, Hegel, Schopenhauer, Nietzsche, and Durkheim.[4] The presence of especially Voltaire and Nietzsche in this list is noteworthy: even though they were both quite anti-religious, the importance of religion is so great that it nonetheless impressed itself upon them.

The evidence of history thus points to a nexus of civilizational weakening, religious weakening, and oikophobic rise. This is why the most radical departures from religion always coincide with a rejection of much of the traditional culture of the civilization—including its nonreligious elements—and a decreasing desire on the part of its members to defend the civilization against hostile forces. Someone might interject that it was really the Greeks' relatively early embrace of the importance of reason and democracy in human affairs, and thus the ability to self-criticize and self-correct, that made them militarily superior to the Persians in many instances.[5] There is definitely truth to this, but religion and reason are not mutually exclusive. Overall the Greeks in early Classical times were still a highly religious people. Rationalism per se does not exclude that considerable amount of spirituality and religion that was part of the Greek mentality. It is in fact a rational and clever people that, as the Spartans did, sacrifices to the god of love rather than war before marching to battle, thereby strengthening their unity and their willingness to die for each other out of religiously motivated love.

This capacity to reason and thus to self-criticize and self-correct is not anti-religious in and of itself. Civilizations become self-examining before they become oikophobic, and the ability to self-analyze and self-correct is an integral part of the process of self-promotion that appears before oikophobia sets in. And so there is no contradiction between religion contributing to communal cohesiveness, and reason helping the community overcome exterior foes. As we have also seen and will continue to see, the rejection of religious beliefs only entails an embrace of other beliefs, not of reason, and the new beliefs will often be held with just as fanatical a zeal as were the traditional religious ones. The notion, for instance, that human beings are equal has no more rational basis than the notion that Jesus is the son of God and died for our sins; both notions are mere beliefs.

With time, the rejection of religion leads to a replacement not only of the religion, but to something that is hostile to that civilization as a whole. We are thus naïve if we believe that the destruction or complete sidelining of the Judeo-Christian faith system will bring about a more civilized community in the West. Other attempts at establishing community cohesion, ones not based on religion—such as activist communities, socialist groups, and so on—will never be as successful, because religion, by dint of incorporating the supernatural, is capable of drawing together and motivating people with nearly supernatural strength, something that material-based interests cannot accomplish. Further, religion is not only belief in the supernatural; even more important, it is about the sacred, and about the division between sacred and profane.[6] It is the sacred that allows people to face battle after battle, even if only mundane battles like making it to work on time, raising children, and enduring the little humiliations that are part of human interaction, since they will have that domain of the sacred to which to return, to anchor them in the face of all odds. Certainly what is "sacred" can take many forms for different people, but one cannot dictate to them what the sacred should be; one area of the sacred cannot be replaced by another at the flick of a switch. And so one robs people of the sacred at one's own peril.

It is therefore possible to be an atheist (as I personally am) while at the same time recognizing the important and even salutary role that religion can play in a society. As thinkers and as lovers of words we are obliged to see as much of any picture as is possible to see, with the ultimate goal of viewing all the world at once. When we have opened our minds to the potential of this vision, we are ready to defend those with whom we disagree, always a useful and healthy exercise. Gentlemen like Spinoza and Nietzsche knew how to fight and win against society's godly images, whereas leading atheists today are philosophy laymen like Richard Dawkins, who make fun of the Bible because, for instance, there is a deity in it that takes an interest in human affairs, or a woman who is turned into a pillar of salt.[7] By that standard, we should make fun of the *Iliad* too, since there is a man in it who can only be injured in his heel, and a woman who pops out of the sea from time to time to give advice to confused and grumpy warriors. The truth is of course that the Bible—especially the Hebrew Bible—contains remarkable human fates and some philosophically very interesting passages. Like Greek myth and tragedy, it is the tale of a race of fallible heroes, people who have much to teach us if we delve beyond the most superficial reading of the stories.

Even when Dawkins occasionally recognizes the value of the Bible as a work of literature (but more on that in a moment), he soon scampers back and rejects any moral authority that one can find in its tales, and genuinely wonders why we cannot all just be kind and moral without any higher spiritual law. How poorly he understands the human psyche, he who thinks that science can replace religion as a mass phenomenon! As many others have known, whereas a philosopher is skeptical of religion insofar as he is seeking the truth, he is a friend of religion insofar as he understands that it is necessary for the majority of mankind to have religion as a general guide for practical behavior, as a surrogate for philosophy, as a restraint on their more corrosive impulses. Dawkins would reply to this that it is frightfully condescending to suggest that societies cannot manage without religion.[8] But if Dawkins really wants the truth, he should be less worried about whether the view that societies need religion is condescending, and more concerned with what the actual evidence of history has to say in that regard. Whether condescension is at play or not is in fact entirely irrelevant: the truth does not care if it is condescending.

As for when Dawkins says that "The good book should be read as a great work of literature—but it is not a guide to morality," this misunderstands both religion, and literature.[9] Dawkins, the ultracrepidarian king, understands neither. Literature, like religion, is something that sweeps up the participant and pervades the whole body and its mind; one cannot simply separate off moral lessons from a work of literature and still let it be literature. To get intelligent critique of religion, we need a class of intellectuals who are Renaissance men, people who understand the complexity of knowledge, who have their fields of expertise but are also thoroughly familiar with Aeolic and bucolic poetry, Hellenistic sculpture, Romanesque and Gothic architecture, Mannerist painting, Neapolitan and verismo opera, the Victorian novel, and much else—that is, we need genuine humanists, a breed that hardly exists anymore. Religion is such an all-encompassing phenomenon, and the human species so dependent on the transcendent, that it is sheer madness to think that religion can be neatly separated out from society, and that utter chaos would not ensue if it were. Because religion is a way by which people relate to themselves and to those around them, it is incorrect to suppose that prayer and ritual have no positive effects; those who mock ritual qua ritual, mock the bonds of love that draw people together. To understand this, one does not necessarily need to be religious, but one needs to be conversant in the great streams of art that humanity has produced, and one needs to know what it is like to be enraptured by them, what it is like to be completely conquered by something transcendent. To criticize religion because of its supernaturalism and the immoral surface meaning of some of its texts, is to betray an utter lack of imagination.

Dawkins feels obliged to criticize religion in his capacity as a scientist. But although religion has not always been a friend to science over the years, Dawkins, when he rightly criticizes the rise of postmodernism in science—the rejection of scientific truth as merely relative—does not understand that postmodernism could only arise because religion declined.[10] That is to say, he himself, without realizing it and contrary to his own wishes, has opened up more space for postmodernism. Militant atheists take an uncompromising view of religion because they do not appear to understand that it is possible to view an object—especially an extremely complex one like religion—in different ways: epistemologically, ethically, metaphysically, historically, and so on. Some of us, while we may for instance disagree with religion epistemologically and metaphysically, can see ethical and historical value in it. That is to say, one branch of knowledge should not be forced to conform to another—when that happens, we are dealing not with philosophy but with a political agenda. But the current militant atheist wave will not be happy until it has turned all married, hardworking, and charity-giving American Christians into narcissistic California millennials who are too busy uploading photos of themselves to believe in anything but their own pouting lips, into children caught in adult bodies. The notion of unintended consequences is lost on people like Dawkins, someone who does not realize that his anti-Christian campaign is rather like a crusade, that there are pockets of Christianity everywhere in his thinking.[11]

Now, in the Middle Ages, although there is still cultural, technological, and economic progress, European states are not able to advance as far as had, relatively speaking, been the case in the ancient world and as will be the case after the Renaissance. It is worth emphasizing that whereas religion does stifle scientific progress here and there, it is mainly the lack of economic progress that allows religion to remain dominant. That is to say, money is more powerful than anything, even God. Some think that it was religion that kept people in the Dark Ages, whereas it was in fact the Dark Ages themselves, and what they entailed in terms of economic and barbarian primitiveness, that reinforced religion, and so the dynamic worked mostly, even if not exclusively, in the opposite direction—if it did not, one would have to inquire why cultured nations, which also were deeply religious in the beginning, managed to move beyond such a state.

We must also recall that the royal elites of Western European societies are for the most part not the ancestors of the Romans; they are people who have

of the West in Christendom but is sometimes considered a bit outdated, gets the last laugh. As Western mores grow ever softer, with an increasing emphasis on nonviolence, empathy for the weak, and elevation of victims, they fulfill the Christian striving that broke the back of the ancient world. This combination of an explicit rejection of Christianity—of its priests, books, churches, and messiah—with an at least implicit embrace of Christian moral attitudes, is very common today. This implicit Christianity, because of oikophobia, explicitly rejects Christianity, but owes its emphasis on human rights, pacifism, and so much else to that precise dogma. That is, it tends to be highly ignorant of the grounds of its own opinions, not realizing how much of the everyday morality it takes for granted comes directly from that religion.[14]

It is worth emphasizing here the role that the French Enlightenment has played in bringing about this state of affairs. To a considerable extent the French Enlightenment was, much like religion, based on belief, not reason, because reason cannot establish that, for instance, we are all equal—just like it cannot establish that we are all unequal—or that there should be such a concept as human rights, ideas which come from the Enlightenment. These notions, rather, are drawn from an arbitrary interpretation of science and reason, *à la Kantienne*, with Christianity as a foundation. The claims of actual science are far more modest. Real science will only state, for instance, that human beings share about 96 percent of their DNA with chimpanzees, and between 99.0 and 99.9 percent with each other. On whether this means that we are not very different from the apes or not, or that we are all equal to each other or not, science has absolutely nothing to say, even though Enlightenment thinkers believed that these sorts of conclusions were part of what science and reason would allow. And so in my view it is not really the "Enlightenment" that deserves that name, but rather the scientific revolution of a few centuries earlier, because that movement, on the contrary, was in fact based on the Greek spirit of reason and empiricism. The harm caused partially by the Enlightenment—as we shall see later in the context of positivism in chapter 11—is that of prejudice thinking itself its opposite, of belief thinking itself reason, of people mocking religion while in fact owing it a great deal. So our heroes of enlightenment and empiricism should not be Voltaire or Diderot, but rather Copernicus and Galileo. If you think rebels and renegades are sexy, then look to your heart's content at those scientists, not at the pretentious scribblers who arbitrarily appropriated for themselves the thin varnish of objectivity.[15]

Perhaps one would think that this notion of the consummation of Christianity and the fulfillment of much of the Sermon on the Mount in modern mores contradicts the statement that civilizations with increasing advancement gradually move away from the religious sources of their founding. To this objection it must be specified that the defense of one's own civilization requires a conscious adherence to its values, a clear belief that one's civilization is in some way preferable to others. The modern realization of the Sermon on the Mount, however, is mostly subconscious. That is to say, it is in this case a "Christianity" that does not know it is Christian that contributes to oikophobia, by its instinctive urge to side with the underdog, to save the downtrodden, and to insist that we are all equal (before God, though this part is forgotten). The Enlightenment—and Kant—have rendered such virtues acceptable even as God himself is discarded.

As we saw in the last chapter, and as Gibbon had said, these Christian virtues of pacifism and meekness are impractical as a matter of state policy. When Emperor Constantine converted to Christianity in the fourth century and thereby thrust the Christian faith into the forefront of the geopolitics of the day, people realized that Christian virtue was not always very well suited to the challenges of international affairs. It was this understanding on the part of Christian philosophers like Ambrose, Augustine, and, much later, Aquinas that made them abandon pacifism and a degree of meekness on the state level and introduce and develop such concepts as just war (but for the Roman Empire the end was already much too near). It had been an individual-based Christianity that undermined traditional paganism and helped bring down the Roman Empire and launch a new civilization, and today it is a subconscious or implicit Christianity, but also on the state level, that is hurrying along the decline of the modern West, while a fully self-aware and individual-based Christianity is trying to preserve it—that is, trying to preserve what it originally started.

Much of the implicit, state-level Christianity—again, Christianity in the sense of an embrace of the moral attitudes of the Sermon on the Mount—ultimately aims toward a dominant culture, but not one that is Western. The preferred culture is generally a mishmash of various Eastern and indigenous cultures, a nebulous conception of collectivism, anti-consumerism, and egalitarianism that exists almost nowhere, save perhaps in a few nomadic tribal holdouts in sub-Saharan Africa. The implicit Christians also tend to be influenced by Buddhism. Much of what they seek in Buddhism is already present, in a more intellectually complete form, in ancient Greek philosophy, especially in the Hellenistic schools of Stoicism, Epicureanism, and, to a lesser extent, Cynicism—but since they are oikophobic, an Eastern religion will have a measure of allure that homegrown schools of thought cannot achieve, as we also saw in Greece and Rome, and will see in France. Sometimes they will grab bits and pieces of whatever seems pleasant enough from various sources: syncretism always cleans up religion for the middle class.

Chapter 5

OIKOPHOBIA IN FRANCE

The discussions of the previous eras of Western history should make the exposition of modern times fairly predictable, and so it is: The strengthening of European nation-states awakes the simple medieval peasant. He who had been concerned with little but the seasonal cycles is slowly converted into a wealthy landowner, or he moves into the city where he becomes a bourgeois businessman, and turns his eyes outward. The strength of these new nations asserts itself and thinks itself superior, in that initial phase of self-reliance and xenophobia that always recurs in the relatively early stages of civilizations.

But it is important to distinguish among various modern Western nations. While for example the Spanish Empire is already in decline, the peoples further north are just rising, as when France supersedes Spain as the dominant power on the continent after the Thirty Years' War. While there is often reason to speak of Western civilization in general, in the complicated mess that emerges from the Middle Ages there is the macroculture of the West, which, however, comprises several microcultures. Cervantes's *Don Quixote*, the story of a failed and delusional hidalgo, is written when the peak of Spanish power has already come and is slowly departing, but at a time when the English and French peoples—to say nothing of the disparate German principalities or the backward Scandinavians—are still approaching theirs.

In modern times we see among the disparate nations the same pattern that was manifest in antiquity and that because of religion and economic fragmentation lay dormant during the Dark Ages. We can summarize that pattern as follows: A people relatively uncivilized and uncultured, but possessed of great mobility and untested strength, awakens and, as it were, goes abroad in service of its deities. Initial successes against surrounding peoples lead to greater wealth and prestige, and a national identity is forged, accompanied by literary epics and other accoutrements of culture. Eventually, the people reaches its pinnacle of success, with so much wealth that a broad and permanent leisure class can be established, and this era of greatest political power will generally coincide, more or less, with the pinnacle of the nation's cultural and scientific achievements. There is finally enough wealth and power for the leisure class, and in many cases for people lower on the social ladder as well, to become more occupied with achieving higher states of wealth and prestige vis-à-vis their countrymen than they are with the health of the community itself.

This is where oikophobia sets in and the state's religion begins to be seriously weakened. Diverse interests are created that view each other as greater enemies than they do foreign threats. What Freud has called the "narcissism of small differences" (*Civilization and Its Discontents*, chapter 5)—which in the present context can be seen as, for instance, the urge to compete against others even through minor distinctions like a virtuous action or the newest gadget—becomes one motivation through which a particular interest expresses its superiority over others.[1] The fact that the most immediate antagonisms are at home makes oikophobia particularly tempting, since by rejecting one's culture as backward, one automatically sets oneself above all the other interests that are, precisely, parts of that culture. (There is an interesting remark in Aristotle's *Politics*, 1314a, that a tyrant only surrounds himself with foreigners rather than with his own countrymen, since the latter will have interests hostile to his own, and this is seen in practice in Tacitus's *Annals* 15.58.)

The opportunism afforded by the higher degree of wealth and leisure thus contributes to oikophobia. Earlier in the social development there is less room for opportunism, because the cooperation of a larger proportion of the people is essential for survival at a time when the nation is poorer and individuals more reliant on one another for basic security. But once the society has taken off and become affluent, there is greater opportunity to excel and more room, therefore, for people to start criticizing their own culture in an effort to get ahead personally. Human beings are always self-interested, of course, but the gulf between immediate self-interest and the interest of the state is smaller when the state itself is smaller and weaker. I say "immediate" self-interest, since even during a state's later days the health of the state is in the self-interest of its citizens, but since the state is stronger and outer circumstances less precarious, its failings will often have less of an immediate impact upon the various individual interests of the citizens. Conversely, because of the strength of the state in its later days, the individual's effort to get ahead at any price and to crush competing interest groups will often not be perceived as a threat to the state as a whole. As Tacitus tersely writes in *Histories* 1.19, people "pursue their private plans, with no care for the state."

Ultimately, one of a few possible things happens: the state falls through actually violent infighting; or a view on the part of individual members that their interests are more important than those of the state will lead to their unwillingness to sacrifice themselves for the state, and so the nation falls to the onslaught of a people that is in the beginning of their own cycle; or, finally, the state simply sinks into irrelevance, where internal fragmentation does not end violently but renders any projection of outward force impossible. It is easier today for a state to literally survive its fragmentation, since there are fewer roving tribes than there used to be, but it will lose effective power on the world stage. Cultural pessimists are often condescendingly dismissed as romantic or naïve for predicting a collapse that never comes.[2] But there are many expressions of decline, as I have just explained. It is those condescending dismissers themselves who are romantic and naïve, since they imagine decline and collapse to necessarily be something in the mold of the Roman Empire, with marauding barbarian tribes, a wild Hun raping a Roman matron beneath a broken pillar with its jagged remains jutting into an indifferent moonlight. But civilizational decline can take many forms, less dramatic but still very real, and these happen often enough.

In this and the next few chapters, let us look together at some salient examples of the modern era: France, Britain, and the United States. The decision of when France begins will necessarily be somewhat arbitrary. She will reach the apogee of her power at the time of Louis XIV, although serious political and military influence will not significantly decline until the defeat of Napoleon, during whose reign French power will briefly reach unprecedented heights, but this will be but a brief tyrannical flourish bound to collapse. Much earlier, the vigorous Frankish people of Clovis I—who becomes Catholic and makes Paris the capital—Charles Martel, and Charlemagne, all of whom strengthen and centralize what is to become the modern nation of France, grows, expands, and fights off a civilization, the Moors, with a considerably higher degree of culture than the Franks themselves possess. As we see in all civilizational examples, except perhaps that of the British, a rugged and relatively primitive force will defeat a more sophisticated enemy as the former sets out to construct its own identity: the Greeks against the Persians, the Romans against the Carthaginians, and the Americans against the British. But one can hardly speak of a France at this early time—the French example is more properly against the Italians than against the Moors—because the land is still divided into separate and mutually hostile kingdoms. The economic tribalism of the Middle Ages still stunts development and lies like a blanket over the entire Western world. Nonetheless, the stage begins to be set for the explosion of creativity and power that will follow upon the Renaissance.

At some point during the Capetian dynasty we become able to speak of a France proper. This is perhaps the case with the reigns of Philippe II (1180–1223) and Louis IX (1226–70), who consolidate monarchical power, expand the realm roughly to the borders we know today, and the latter of whom is also strongly supported by the church. Still, with English incursions and a relatively weak central authority, and continued shifting of the borders, it makes more sense to look at France as she emerges from the Hundred Years' War (1337–1453). French knights and soldiers originally fight not out of national pride or identity, but out of feudal obligation. Eventually, France is forced by a series of humiliating defeats to finally establish a proper army, with which she repels the English in the end, who retain only Calais.

By this time, a poetic tradition has already been established, but it is mainly local and Occitan, centered in the south of the country. But whereas earlier Capetian days saw a populace whose inhabitants considered themselves part only of their local area or at most simply Catholic, a more national identity comes creeping under the later Capetians and under the Valois, and the poetic tradition both encourages and is encouraged by that development. With a growing French identity, and with the slow overcoming and expulsion of the English enemy, the national consciousness must be supported by the arts, which is why there is a wide dissemination of *The Song of Roland*, one of the oldest French literary texts, written in the mid-eleventh century, around this time, from the twelfth to the fifteenth centuries. The work harkens back to the earlier era under Charlemagne, already perceived as a sort of heroic age that provides comfort and purpose to the struggling early civilization, just as the early Archaic Greeks had sought solace in Homer's mythical, heroic age several hundred years older. This is accompanied by the rise of courtly troubadour literature, which, however, remains more localized, and much of whose sometimes amorous, sometimes jocular themes should just as well be viewed within the context of errant Frankish and Italic-French medieval poetry as of a distinct French tradition, even if it will inspire later French writers.

It is after the Hundred Years' War that the French state comes into its own. As opposed to the haphazard and often embarrassing efforts in that conflict, the people finally presents a unified front and national character in its struggles against the various Italian states during the end of the fifteenth and about the first half of the sixteenth century. The French are able to plow through Italy offensively, which would have been unthinkable a hundred years earlier; they are now the young and restless people going abroad to test its strength, and they conquer as far south as Naples. This series of conflicts will ultimately not change much in terms of the territorial status quo, although on the other side of the country the French incorporate Brittany and finally take Calais back from the English. But it demonstrates that a defeat of the French will invariably require alliances of several other European states against them, something that will continue to be the case for a few hundred years—before being turned into something of the opposite, where it is French victories that will invariably require involvement and help from other states.

All along, French society becomes increasingly centralized and Catholic, culminating in the Edict of Nantes (1598) under Henri IV, the first of the Bourbons, which grants legal protections to the protestant Huguenots but which also establishes France as a Catholic nation. Henri's Edict does not put a permanent end to religious strife, however, which will continue under Louis XIII and Cardinal Richelieu, but the Catholics will always gain the upper hand; the Edict will be revoked by Louis XIV, through the Edict of Fontainebleau (1685), at the height of Franco-Catholic power and xenophobia, which will put a final end to the Huguenot threat.

The wars in Italy, where the rediscovery of antiquity has already been underway for a few hundred years, serve as a catalyst for the Renaissance in France, as previously the Roman conquest of Greek lands had cultivated the crude conquerors. This development is indicative of the fact that the import of new ideas and a diversification of social norms strengthen a civilization in its early, rising days, before becoming a liability later on. Through this Italian influence, the warlike French come slowly to develop a sophisticated aristocracy, and to look at themselves in the mirror.

A writer like Rabelais is still infused with medieval pathos and courtly ribaldry—even if his uncouth vulgarities and scatological humor will, alas, prove seminal for future French writing (I think of almost everything from Voltaire to Boris Vian)—but soon enough the artistic nobility of more southern lands will flush northward. A generation of French humanists arises, with a Pelletier du Mans to translate Homer, Virgil, Horace, and Petrarch into French and even to attempt a badly needed reform of French orthography, just as the poets of the so-called Pléiade, whose most famous member is Ronsard, strive to place French on an equal footing with other literary languages, especially Italian (though the Renaissance poet who does so most successfully is, in my own view, the utterly lovely Louise Labé). These early efforts pave the way for subsequent writers like a Michel de Montaigne and for, a bit later, a Blaise Pascal and of course a Descartes. These gentlemen produce the texts of a civilization that has finally matured, with works on society, poetics, language, religion, psychology, education, and philosophy. Montaigne is incidentally before his time in producing a piece of cultural relativism in his essay *Of Cannibals* (1580), with even the occasional oikophobic-sounding remark, but the main relativist phase of French civilization will predictably come later, and *Of Cannibals* is also to be seen in the tradition of exotic travel literature—like Thomas More's *Utopia* and Francis Bacon's *The New Atlantis*—that due to the discovery of the Americas is in vogue at this time.[3]

Louis XIII is another one of France's great centralizers. He continues the pacification of the Huguenots, and disciplines the pesky and rebellious nobles. Because of these efforts, he is the first French king that can properly be called an absolute monarch. This centralizing trend serves well the strengthening of the French state and a continued national tribalism that will allow France to project great outward power, and her soldiers to fight with great bravery. (France's centralized nature stands and will continue to stand as a marked contrast to the Anglo-Saxon tradition of parliamentarianism, decentralization, and regional association.) French forces teach both the Germanic and the Spanish Habsburgs a series of good lessons, and the king begins to build a colonial empire in North America. French civilization still has plenty of excess strength that needs to find an outlet, and it does so both near and far.

Even more important than these political and military advances is their natural accompaniment: Louis XIII strives to keep the best French thinkers and artists in France, and to invite new creative ideas to enter, conscious as he is of the need of soft power to strengthen the hard. As had Philip of Macedon, who was all muscle and metal but looked self-consciously at the brilliant writers and artists to his south in Greece, the ruler of a rising powerful people will always, after the battle, seek to wrap his sword in silk and velvet. Once a ruler has conquered militarily, he will seek other means to conquer in order to feed his ever-growing ego, and by inviting the trappings of luxury and splendor, by insisting on conquest also in the arts, he launches the development that will soften his people, turn them into vain oikophobic busybodies, and invite the next people to come in and conquer. But for now, all these developments—military and cultural—point in the same direction: a strong and largely united French people that believes in itself, and that insists on its superiority, in all domains, over other civilizations. Louis XIII sets the stage for what is the absolute peak of French civilization, falling as it does in the second half of the seventeenth and beginning of the eighteenth century, under his successor Louis XIV.

This monarch, Louis XIV, continues the natural trajectory that has been bequeathed him. The Spanish, the Dutch, the Holy Roman Empire, and even the English are all beaten at various times by the French, in an era characterized by millions of men with families and dreams dying so that a small group of inbred royals may settle their vain squabbles—men dying in the erroneous belief that there is a royal authority that cares about them. The French expand their borders, eradicate Huguenot remnants, and establish further colonies. Rebellions in the form of the *Fronde* are in no way oikophobic in nature. On the contrary, antigovernment sentiment is fueled in no small part by the fact that the chief minister at this time, Cardinal Mazarin, is actually Italian. France has replaced Spain as Europe's greatest power by the mid-1600s and will in her turn not be replaced by Britain until the defeats of Trafalgar at sea and Waterloo on land. The increasingly effete nobility continues to be pacified and distracted by the luxuries that the king continuously offers them in exchange for absolute rule. The Huguenots suffer terrible persecution in the latter part of the century, after the aforementioned revocation of the Edict of Nantes, with the result that they either convert or emigrate (or die). France will never again be as unified as she is after that. But in this great anti-Protestant zeal, even atheists are preferred to the Huguenots, which is one reason why the marginalization of religion slowly begins to become acceptable in polite society. That will eventually have dire consequences. As I have said, the state without religious accompaniment can generally not produce as ardent a fanaticism as God can, and whereas peasants will often be too afraid to reject their religion, they will rise and overthrow the state in due time.

The first cracks in the political centralization appear under Louis XV, who manages to alienate nobility and clergy through a series of poorly thought-out, even if well-intentioned, reforms. A few clumsily managed wars, including the loss of North American territories to the British, further hurt the monarchy. The morality of the nobility achieves new lows in this era, and the urban wastefulness and ungratefulness of the well-to-do for what they have mirror that of other civilizations in the corresponding eras of their developments. But the previous successes and increased wealth, leading to great population growth, also slowly begin to increase the wealth of the third estate, regular French citizens, who therefore come to develop a voice of their own, with dreams, ambitions, and opinions. As always happens, victory, success, wealth, and concomitant population increase lead to the slow fragmentation of society into mutually hostile interests. Oikophobia will not be far away.

As expected, literature at this time moves slowly from a sober self-regard to a more robust self-questioning. The absolute dictatorial powers of the monarch are not used overzealously (at least not by twentieth-century totalitarian standards) to silence unruly voices, of which the French produce more than their fair share. And so the self-questioning phase takes place in a relatively open space alongside more conventional French literature which draws heavily on Italian models and their ancient paradigms. The excessive arrogance and xenophobia of France's ruling classes provoke a proto-oikophobic and even fully oikophobic response among intellectuals. After victory over external enemies is as complete as can be in the constantly fragmented and refragmenting Europe of the time, with ever-shifting alliances and renewed war-making, the self-observing French bring on their Enlightenment around the mid-eighteenth century, just as the generation of Socrates and Euripides in Athens, after her victories over the Persians, is sometimes referred to retroactively by scholars as the Greek enlightenment.

Many French names deserve mention in this context, and a brief discussion must necessarily be very selective, especially for a tradition as rich as the French. Denis Diderot edits the enormously influential Enlightenment *Encyclopedia* (first appearance in 1751), which is at the forefront in moving French civilization away from religion. Diderot and other editors are so dogmatic and zealous in their anti-religiousness, in fact, that this becomes one reason why the editor Jean Le Rond d'Alembert finally withdraws from the project. The Marquis de Condorcet is a strong egalitarian and advocates the cause of blacks and of women, but also thinks that a class of cognoscenti should explain to the public what its best interests are. The republican Montesquieu, one of the greatest men France has ever produced, argues for the separation of powers, engages in anthropological study, and shows, especially in the *Persian Letters* (1721), that French mores may not be as great as they appear. In a very different vein, Laclos's novel *Dangerous Liaisons* (1782), which should be required reading for every young girl, since it will teach her some useful things about men, exposes the sexual filth of French aristocrat sybarites. Indeed the attitude to sexuality has changed radically over time: like the later kings, an earlier monarch such as Henri IV also had mistresses, but while his peccadilloes were considered a relatively embarrassing matter to be kept discreet, Louis XV's mistresses are common knowledge and little attempt is made to hide them. This says something about the relative states of the two phases of the civilization. In the context of national cohesion and projection of outward power and political authority, hypocrisy and dishonesty are indeed better than public degeneracy.

Rousseau—although from Geneva he falls within the French cultural ambit—is influenced by the mystique and exoticism of newly colonized lands, whose lush landscapes and seemingly innocent inhabitants seduce impressionable Europeans living on crowded and unsanitary streets. He undermines the entire raison d'être of the state and is disgusted by anything termed culture and order. As seen especially in his *Discourse on the Origin and Basis of Inequality* (1755) and to some extent *Emile, or On Education* (1762), Rousseau considers private property to be the source of inequality and therefore bad.[4] And precisely because the institution of private property lies at the beginning of society, society itself is bad in many ways, an attitude that renders Rousseau hostile to most Greek political thinking, which views the community as that which can bring out the best in us. Rousseau's natural man, or "noble savage," is calm, dispassionate, and happy, with no sense of competition toward other men—which is to say that he is a total figment of Rousseau's imagination. Rousseau's explanation of how the state of nature can be so lovely and pristine, in the *Discourse*, is shockingly bad: one man's subjugation by another cannot take place in the state of nature, because this would mean that a society has been formed, and the state of society is not the state of nature. That is to say, Rousseau's reasoning is entirely circular: X cannot happen in the state of nature, because if X happens, that is not the state of nature. (The No True Scotsman fallacy also comes to mind.) In other words, many of the problems that Rousseau ascribes to society also exist in the state of nature, but since they are problems, Rousseau maintains that this cannot be the state of nature.

Indeed reality has already refuted Rousseau, because the fact that men did move on to a state of society means that there were never any natural men to begin with. That is, the fact that societies did arise is ipso facto a negation of Rousseau's view of human nature. Rousseau himself acknowledges that he does not know exactly how the state of nature ended—or if it ever even fully existed—though he offers a few half-hearted suggestions here and there. Rousseau's care in preserving the "natural" inclinations in his protégé Emile is so incredibly meticulous that it is itself anti-natural and an artificial imposition. Rousseau so completely separates "nature" from all of actual human experience that it becomes just another meaningless idol. But in spite of these and other shortcomings, his work is immediately influential, for he lives at a time that has grown ready to throw off its old traditions. (He is also, admittedly, quite a good writer.) Rousseau says that he loves his native state of Geneva, but, in an oikophobic spirit, he wants to save the world but cannot be bothered even to treat his own family properly—and if each person could only do that, the world would be in no need of salvation in the first place.

Especially crucial is Voltaire, who in many respects is already an oikophobe, and that of a more modern type than the ancient civilizations could have produced. He attacks both the state, with its institutions, and religion. He is fairly consistently hostile to Christianity and Judaism, but has more mixed words for Islam, and kind words for Hinduism, in spite of its extreme misogyny. He chooses to befriend the faraway—although or because he understands it very poorly—so as to rise above his targets nearby. In his *Essay on the Manners and Spirit of Nations* (1756), Voltaire considers Western ways prejudicial and compares them unfavorably with Eastern traditions. Also like a typical oikophobe, albeit not quite as pathologically as Rousseau, who was probably a paranoiac, Voltaire wants to save humanity—and vanity is always the reason for that—but holds a very denigrating view of the lower classes, which is to say, of most regular Frenchmen. Like Lucan and his *Pharsalia* in a corresponding stage of the Roman Empire, Voltaire discards all theological elements in his historical works. He feels disgust at anything professing Christian religion or fealty to a higher order, such as when he mocks Blaise Pascal's religiously rapturous words as "sickly talk" in the *Notes on Pascal's Pensées* (1778; the *Pensées* had been published posthumously in 1669). The *Notes*, cowritten with Condorcet, is in fact a brilliant mosaic of anti-religious, oikophobic, and narcissistic snarkiness. We meet in Voltaire that self-important narcissism we had come across in Hippias, Diogenes the Cynic, and perhaps Seneca.

Undeniably, Voltaire contributes significantly to literary progress, such as through his emphasis on cultural history as against the contemporary tendency to equate history with the actions of politicians and war-makers only, and many of his accusations against the church and the monarchy are just. But one can pay one's respects to these advances while at the same time understanding that his hatred of his own society leads him to the other extreme, and to praising the foreign qua foreign, which he understands but poorly. Indeed, even Rousseau, who himself displays some oikophobic tendencies, in book 1 of his *Emile*, written at a time when he and Voltaire were openly hostile to one another, describes an oikophobe who could easily be Voltaire: "Beware of these cosmopolitans who will search far and wide in their books for duties that they neglect to fulfill close by. Such a philosopher loves the Tartars so as not to have to love his neighbors."

Ultimately, Voltaire is very much a child of his time, and he embodies, in especially striking and pointed form, an antitraditional, self-flagellating, self-absorbed, coquettish, and gynocratic era, which deep down knows that it has nothing more to live for. Voltaire is also a vegetarian, and his vegetarianism becomes an attempt to distinguish himself morally from his countrymen. It interacts with his other oikophobic leanings, as for instance in the *Treatise of Tolerance* 12 (1763), where Voltaire holds up the superiority of Indians to his own people because the former are vegetarians. And so his vegetarianism is of a piece with his hatred of the Western and Judeo-Christian tradition.

The role that vegetarianism sometimes plays on the oikophobic trajectory is worth dwelling upon for a moment. While in and of itself vegetarianism is of course unobjectionable, when it is undertaken for moral reasons it can represent a certain powerlessness that seeks an area of control, it becomes a mode of self-elevation, vanity coupled with compassion, yet another way in the declining days of civilizations for an oikophobic individual to express contempt for his fellow citizens. To find a way to rise above his culture, that individual will reject meat-eating as immoral and backward. Early in a civilization, most people are farmers, for whom eating the meat of their cattle or other farm animals is a simple matter of survival and common sense. As will soon be discussed, oikophobia occurs more in cities. Cities are places in which the progressed state of the declining civilization is more strongly felt than in the countryside, where life is necessarily closer to how it was in the civilization's earlier times. And so an urban oikophobe's vegetarianism becomes related to a disdain—often subconscious—of the earlier days of his civilization. By regretting and hating his civilization for having victimized other peoples, and by searching for ever newer victims as playing cards in his self-despising game, it is only natural that he will eventually individuate animals as the next set of victims that his society has treated poorly. Vegetarianism for moral reasons thus appears to him.[5]

The most famous example of vegetarianism in antiquity is that of the Pythagoreans. Pythagoras, who appears to have traveled widely and been in frequent contact with the Other, perhaps even learning the Egyptian language, in the late 500s BC established his school in the city of Croton in Magna Graecia. As we have seen, the periphery of the Greek world—today southern Italy and western Turkey—were for a long time culturally far ahead of mainland Greece. While Athens was still a village-like backwater, Croton and Magna Graecia had been blooming for centuries, with the local culture having developed many of the trappings of well-progressed civilizations. Although the Pythagoreans constituted a distinct movement and were by no means representative of the whole population, it is not a coincidence that they were able to establish themselves and their vegetarianism in a more advanced part of Greek civilization, something that would have been more difficult in the Athens of their day (vegetarianism only appears broadly in Athens in the fourth century BC, especially among the Cynic philosophers, and indeed we have seen proto-oikophobia and oikophobia with Cynics like

Antisthenes and Diogenes). The average Classical Greek did have a fairly vegetarian diet in general, but this was not for moral reasons: meat was a festive
food that was mostly consumed at religious celebrations when animals were
sacrificed.

The Pythagoreans emphasize equality, including between the sexes, and,
according to several ancient authorities, vegetarianism. Their mystic attitudes
are to an extent similar to the more personalized religious feelings that appear in a declining civilization, like the oriental and mostly female mystery
cults of the Roman Empire to whose members Ovid appeals, and the Buddhism or pseudo-Buddhism in modern American cities, along with an (again,
mainly female) interest in astrology.[6] And it is not a coincidence that Ovid
himself may well have been a vegetarian, though that question is up for debate. Another salient example of late-civilizational vegetarianism already
mentioned is Seneca in Rome, who is influenced by the neo-Pythagorean philosopher Sotion. Even though Seneca criticizes what he considers superstitious oriental cults—such as Judaism and the cult of Isis—in *On Superstition*,
he forgets that his vegetarianism was also initiated as a superstitious cult. Only
a few decades after Seneca, in the late first century AD, Plutarch launches an
aggressive tirade for vegetarianism in *On the Eating of Meat*, which Rousseau,
like Voltaire a late-civilizational figure, quotes approvingly in book 2 of *Emile*.
All these examples are reflected in the fact that vegetarianism is increasing in
popularity in our own modern civilization as it progresses.[7]

We fly back to France. The reforms undertaken by the last absolute monarch, Louis XVI, send rushing forth a development that was already underway. The king's genuine efforts to improve the lot of the poor and of religious
nonconformists, especially the Huguenots, simply remove the lid from the
violently boiling kettle and earn him his execution. The multitude of more
immediate causes behind the French Revolution (bad harvests with rising
grain prices, debt incurred from aiding the American revolutionaries, the
king's personal indecisiveness, public disgust with Marie Antoinette, the
calling of the Estates General after the nobles refuse to be taxed, etc.) are too
complex to be discussed here, and are in any case not the object of our view,
which focuses on the trajectory of oikophobia. But that trajectory indicates,
as it always does, that the decline and fall have their origins already in the
earlier and more powerful eras of the civilization. Those eras segue naturally
into that part of the development where the people's antagonistic tendencies
turn inward.

The government's insistence on borrowing rather than on levying taxes on particular segments of society is another sign of the strength of interest groups that increases during the fragmentation of civilizational decline. And the slow concessions to the oppressed class make it realize that it has a voice. The Revolution marks the beginning of the end phase of France as a strong civilization. The brief spell of imperialistic power that follows under the revolutionary regime and then under Napoleon is at worst a death spasm, and at best a temporary dictatorial flourish from a civilization that has never managed democracy particularly well. The First "Republic," declared in 1792, by its very name self-consciously brands itself as what it is clearly not, in the same manner as in more recent and current times it is a good guess that countries with the word "democratic" in their names are nondemocratic (German Democratic Republic, Democratic People's Republic of Korea, Democratic Republic of Congo, and so on).

That the forces behind the French Revolution are given an impetus by the reforms of Louis XVI is quite relevant. Since success, wealth, and leisure serve as catalysts in the rise of oikophobia, it is no coincidence that dissidents and protesters often tend to be middle-class—not lower-class, as might appear more intuitive—or those who have recently been raised out of a lower class; progress to the downtrodden is like blood to the shark. It is the better-off who have time to ponder the world's injustices, while those of the lower social strata are too busy scraping by a living. A truly poor and oppressed people does not even know how poor and oppressed it is; it is progress that suddenly instills in it the idea that things could be better, and the explosion follows.

This is another predictable pattern that repeats itself. The French Revolution did not take place under the despotism of Louis XIV or the incompetence of Louis XV, but under the reformer—albeit also quite incompetent—Louis XVI. So too, in the twentieth century, the more successful the colonial European powers were in developing underdeveloped societies, the stronger became the indigenous reaction and yearning for freedom.[8] The Marxist theory, gleaned first from *The Communist Manifesto*, that revolutions are a result of misery is not entirely false in every instance, but must certainly be modified. And it is possible to hold two thoughts in mind at once: One may think protests justified, while nonetheless recognizing the irony in the fact that the protests are partly a result of, precisely, attempted governmental responses to widespread grievance, or are being carried out by those who are less hurt than others by the object of the protest.

Much has been said about the cultural forces of the French Revolution and their implications for politics over the last centuries, but the conflict also offers one of the most perfect examples of oikophobic excess. The total rejection of both religious and secular tradition, up to the very changing of time with the incredibly jejune and childish revolutionary and pseudo-pagan calendar, reveals a society that has thrown itself overboard and is drifting like jetsam on the surface of Europe. The French Revolution illustrates why a people needs tradition in order to survive and why a thinking individual, though he may and often ought to disagree with aspects of that tradition and work to ameliorate them, would never seek its overthrow.

Robespierre, one of the central figures of the revolutionary reign of terror, stands as a perfect example of the Thucydidean horrors of human nature that cause such great suffering. All things considered, Robespierre did not kill so many—far bigger killers have existed, although indeed most of them, like Robespierre, have been egalitarians—but he embodies many of the most corrosive impulses of basic human psychology. Robespierre and those around him constitute an impressive catalogue of human vices, almost a textbook psychological study, displaying quite perfectly the astonishing depravities that flow and always will flow directly from human nature, as well as the fact that, given the right (or, rather, wrong) circumstances, perfectly ordinary people carry a monster within. Some of these depravities are the inability to find the golden mean between extremes; the cruelty of the oppressed once they gain freedom; cruelty toward others to hide inner weakness; resentment rather than gratitude as a result of dependence; thinking one's own beliefs based on reason, while criticizing others for merely believing; critique as a mere expression of vanity; oikophobia as a form of self-aggrandizement; mass killing as a bureaucratic procedure; the reduction of human lives to a simple graph on a piece of paper; the destruction of dreams by a wave of the hand. Robespierre says, in a speech to the National Convention in 1794, that "the government of the Revolution is the despotism of liberty against tyranny." "Despotism of liberty" is of course a perfect example of totalitarian double-speak, which forebodes the worst dictators of the twentieth century. It is in writing of these things that I must pause for a moment and shake my head, wondering how it can be that we and the people we love are part of such a species.

Thucydides's *History of the Peloponnesian War* must certainly be studied by those who wish to understand conflict through the ages. It is, as someone has aptly said, the history of all wars. In the spirit of these assertions, and as a mode of persuasion regarding their veracity, I offer a list—not necessarily exhaustive—of the most typical themes of human nature and conflict that are explained in Thucydides, and many of which apply to the French Revolution. Several themes also describe parts of the oikophobic trajectory: Human nature is a constant and hence predictable (1.22, 1.76, 3.39, 3.45, 3.82, 3.84, 4.61, 4.108, 5.105, 7.69); success leads to fragmentation, and so success has destructive power (1.2, 3.39), with a return to a more fragmented tribalism (3.82); counterintuitively, consensual structures lead more easily to fragmentation than nonconsensual ones do (1.141); alliances are based more on interest than on ideals or altruism, since countries have interests and not friends, and so to expect that countries should behave like individuals is foolish (up to 1.44, 1.62, 5.22, 6.85, 8.2; the strongest expression of Realpolitik is at 5.105); people (and states) dress their own interests in universal moral garb (5.89–90, 5.105; and at 6.82–87 there is an honesty about this that is impossible today); dependence causes resentment, not gratitude (1.77, 3.39); intellectualism breeds disrespect for the laws (which can lead to oikophobia), whereas the less educated do not consider themselves too intelligent for the state (1.84, 3.37), and also because the intellectual and wealthy elite can avoid facing the consequences of certain laws (3.40); people are angered when they see something that they could not accomplish themselves, and stop believing it (2.35, 3.84); the breakdown of order and hierarchies (and religion) leads to a reappearance of animal instincts (2.53, 3.81–82), not to any natural or primordial nobility or to reason; dovish factions project their own attitudes onto the Other and refuse to accept that genuine evil exists (3.37); the erstwhile oppressed become doubly oppressive once they gain the upper hand (3.82, 3.84); ochlocracy: crowds and groups are capricious and insane more often than not (6.24); the danger of hubris (4.65, 6.11, 7.28); history will always be rewritten for ideological purposes (5.11); life is tragic and there is no final messiah (5.105); greatness is driven by conflict (6.18).

Edmund Burke, in his *Reflections on the Revolution in France* (1790), condemns the Revolution for, among other things, disregarding the weaknesses and foibles of human nature. Although Burke definitively rejects any connection between monarchy and divine favor, he also recognizes the dangers of atheism to a society, and faults the revolutionaries for jumping from one extreme to the other and not properly defining terms like "liberty" and "rights." Addressing the revolutionaries, he writes, "You began ill, because

you began by despising every thing that belonged to you."[9] This is an iden-
tification of oikophobia. The fact that many self-proclaimed defenders of
liberty—including a number of Burke's own Whig party members—break
with him, only means that he is far more perspicacious than they in how
things will turn out in France and continental Europe.

And, indeed, the poets and motley artists who initially reject Burke, such
as William Blake and Samuel Taylor Coleridge, become severely disillusioned
as the French Revolution turns to terror and then into a military dictatorship that sets out to conquer Europe at the cost of millions of lives (and while
modern Germany has thoroughly rejected Hitler, and even Russia is not
overly fond of Stalin, France still has an obscene golden cupola over the little
body of the man who caused such immeasurable suffering and death; in
France, to receive such a pompous grave one must have killed three million
human beings, at a bare minimum). It is significant that Burke was praised
by liberals in the nineteenth century but, as time wore on, came to be praised
more and more by conservatives, a fact that indicates how the political spectrum as a whole is moving, with a few backs and forths, toward the left.

We can pass quite easily through the rest of our diachronic look at France.
The Napoleonic Wars are similar in many ways to the conquests of Nazi Germany: although their respective ideologies may differ, they are both the expressions of a lost people, the anger of a society that has mortally wounded
itself and takes it out on others, the impulsive and unrealistic hope for something far better—and as such, they cannot last long. As mentioned, France
is definitively eclipsed by the British with the defeats at Trafalgar and Waterloo. She will never again rouse herself from her oikophobic malaise. Religion continues to weaken, and more revolutions, little rebellions, coups, and
assassinations take place in nineteenth-century France than in any other
European country of that time, making the place look more like a twentieth-
century Latin American state. There is no longer a unified France, but a
collection of mutually despising interest groups, whose hatred of each other
grows increasingly tribal, and who are more interested in scoring internecine triumphs than in strengthening and modernizing the nation as a whole.
Republicans and monarchists, soldiers and civilians, socialists and bourgeois
hate each other more than they do the English or the Germans.

French literature continues to produce a few masterpieces, next to the
usual rubbish heap, but these focus increasingly on the victims of French
power. A heightened obsession with victimhood and the traditionally mar-

ginalized is indicative of declining civilizations, as will also be the case for Britain and the United States. This could also be seen in antiquity, with for example Tacitus's condemnation of Roman brutality against conquered peoples, although it was weaker then since the ancients had no concept of "human rights."[10] Politicians like Hippolyte Carnot and Léon Gambetta form a part of this civilizational turn, where attention is directed inward to the injustices at home, and increasing resources are devoted to the marginalized strata of society.

Henri de Saint-Simon sets the stage for this phase in the first decades of the nineteenth century by devising an early form of socialism, whose main objective is to elevate workers above the wealthy, and which will come to inspire Marx and others, although Saint-Simon is less radical than he. Stendhal's *The Red and the Black* (1830), the younger Dumas's focus in the 1840s and '50s on social justice involving women and illegitimate children, and Émile Zola's *Germinal* (1885) reduce individual agency and view people as the products of forces beyond their control. They mourn those upon whose backs French society rests, in a heightened preoccupation with themes of the oppressed that go back to Condorcet. *The Red and the Black*, by the father or perhaps grandfather of French realism, is, in addition to a very funny comedy, an outcry by the lower classes who will never be respected by the upper. And while something like *Germinal*, the peak of realism, about exploited mine workers in northern France, must also be seen within the larger European industrial and socialist contexts of the day, socialism itself—and someone like Marx—could never have arisen during that earlier part of a civilization that is convinced of its own excellence. (Since Marx was so fond of placing things in historical straitjackets, surely he would not mind being himself placed in one.)

I do not judge negatively the merits of these literary works—on the contrary there is much in them that I like and agree with—I only observe that they make their appearance in a highly predictable phase of civilizational development. It is a phase in which those who cherish France's past and those who detest it are at such loggerheads that the country loses its vigor. In an oft-repeated type of event, the literary critic Sainte-Beuve, who supports Napoleon III's Second Empire government, in 1855 must withdraw from his professorship after students disrupt his lecturing to denounce his supposed imperialism.

An especially French version of self-flagellating social revulsion is the maxim "art for art's sake" (*l'art pour l'art*), attributed to Théophile Gautier and his novel *Mademoiselle de Maupin* (1835). This posture assumes, falsely, that it is possible to be isolated from values and socio-moral attitudes, and that only beauty, in a rather narrow sense, matters, that beauty can exist as a stand-alone consideration. But in fact, all art, whether the artist likes it or not, has an agenda and endeavors to teach something ("art for art's sake" is thus the aesthetic equivalent of the false belief that selfless acts are possible, the notion that something can exist uninfluenced by the subject whence it arises). What that teaching is can of course be interpreted differently as the case may be, but "art for art's sake" does not and cannot exist. The fact, however, that the claim that it can arises in France in this period, along with its implication of social irresponsibility and unwillingness to serve a larger cause, is indicative of France's decline.

It is also indicative of the decline of the macroculture of the West, since this claim will feed the relativism of the late twentieth century across Western culture. The false claim of "art for art's sake" can only occur in a civilization that no longer supports itself, and it thus occupies yet another predictable position on the oikophobic trajectory. Since oikophobia is predominantly a Western phenomenon, it stands to reason that "art for art's sake" is also Western. In fact, "art for art's sake" is the expression of a class that already has its basic needs taken care of, and that can therefore waste its time with the purely solipsistic and putatively nonfunctional. "Art for art's sake" is thus an expression of class privilege, something against which its practitioners generally seek to revolt. One will not find "art for art's sake" among the working class, or in developing countries. I personally think that African wicker that has been plied into a vessel and painted with geometrical shapes, and is used by a young child to carry food to his mother, is infinitely more beautiful than the self-absorbed display of most contemporary Western art galleries and their empty slogans.

France ceases to be politically relevant upon defeat in the Franco-Prussian War (1870–71), when her Second Empire is handily destroyed by the Prussians. Some individual French units fight with magnificent gallantry in that conflict, but France as a whole has reached a point where internal fragmentation makes it impossible for her to mount a plausible defense. The French can still conquer indigenous peoples in Africa and Asia in their drive not to fall too far behind the British, but every conflict against other Western powers will now require outside aid. And France is lucky: an earlier and more barbaric age would have seen her permanently overrun and disintegrated by hostile forces, but the barbarians have ceased to exist in this part of the world. Because France's enemies, as well as her friends, are other Western states rather than Visigoths or Mongols, every defeat is followed by a magnanimous permission to remain alive, and every victory is purchased with Anglo-Saxon blood.

Of course, in an ever more globalized world, where distances grow smaller and smaller, France will come to remember that there are still peoples on this planet that do not share modern Western values. In the late twentieth and early twenty-first centuries, oikophobia will complicate the question of how to remain culturally French while absorbing new peoples. If France fails to produce an answer to that question, she will cease to exist in any meaningful sense. And it is only the risk of such total defeat and destruction that can start the cycle anew, rouse a people from its oikophobic pathology, and imbue it with renewed spirit. This in fact can be seen in that part of the world from which many of these peoples come: the Muslim world rose to great heights in the Middle Ages before it collapsed; it was, in part, the total defeat and humiliation at the hands of Western colonizers that eventually caused it to re-embrace its heritage, regain a sense of pride, and try to stand up for itself once more.

We shall not follow France's development into the present, because today the microcultures of the West have so fused themselves in common malaise that it makes more sense to speak of a macrocultural Western oikophobia, even though, to be sure, French twentieth-century intellectuals like Lacan, Sartre, Foucault, and Derrida will do more than their fair share to contribute to it. For the current brief survey it is enough to establish that France ceases to be relevant in the second half of the nineteenth century, and survives only by the grace of others, in a permanent state of inertia. During my years in France I always smiled to myself when I saw a journal headline with something like the self-conscious question "Is France in decline?"—Yes, France has been in decline for well over two centuries. And furthermore, as I have previously said: the processes of decline begin before the apogee has even been reached.

A final point I should like to make regarding the French development is that we find here in greater emphasis than previously the contrast between city and countryside. In Rome, soft urbanites, among whom we have met Ovid and Propertius, would sometimes hold a condescending view of the peasants. Even in Greece there had been an aristocratic-intellectual disdain of manual labor, to which they referred pejoratively as *banausia*, a word that has survived in some modern European languages. But in France there develops an even more marked distinction between urbanites and farmers, a distinction that will continue to hold for all future manifestations of oikophobia.

This will indeed become one of the key dichotomies in the swarm of competing interests as Western societies fragment. Diversity will become a problem, as for instance we saw in Rome, which expanded enormously and incorporated new peoples of different creeds, languages, and ethnicities. One reason why a French farmer is generally less oikophobic than a Parisian literatus who spends his time in cafes and intellectual salons, and why the farmer is more willing to sacrifice himself for the greater good when the Germans or English come knocking, is that the literatus lives in a more diverse environment, while the farmer leads a life closer to that of the earlier stages of French civilization; there, religion is still practiced, while atheism becomes rampant in the city. The farmer, by sowing his own food and eating what he has grown, sees more directly the relationship between labor and reward. The urbanite, on the other hand, living in a specialized and diverse environment, eats what others have grown and is thus less thankful to the land he treads. The farmer thereby often manages to have a common good sense that the urban intellectual lacks: the former must as a matter of survival apply new ideas to the sensible world around him, and discard those that do not work, while the urbanite can be content with just turning them in his head without any real-world application, which makes it harder to discover which ideas are useful and which are useless. Further, by living in a place where new trends first appear, the urban intellectual is the first to encounter novel concepts coming from afar, and so within him begins to build a sense of responsibility for transmitting these concepts to his civilization at large, and for educating the public, and this is also why the urban intellectual becomes much more subversive than the farmer. In the beginning, diversity and openness help by facilitating the introduction of new ideas. In France's case these come mainly from Italy, just as the early Greek periphery had benefited from contacts with Persia and Egypt. But after a critical point, diversity transforms itself from mostly an asset to mostly a liability, as it hastens the neo-tribal fragmentation of society into competing groups. France becomes a nation so bent on internal squabbling that she is no longer capable of effectively projecting outward force. And of this squabble, the mutual distrust between city and countryside is one of the foremost examples.[11] Part of the legacy of this distrust is the term "populism," because what is called populism these days is most often an appeal to those who live outside the cities, as opposed to the intellectuals, who live within them. And so, as always, what is actually the competition between two diverging interests—city and countryside—is dressed up in the language of morals, virtue, and human decency.

Of course, France's decline does not completely preclude cultural achievement. The greatest triumph of French civilization is the work of Marcel Proust. He is not a particularly political writer, which in the end is probably a good thing. He stays above the squabbles and simply looks at human nature. Proust's philosophical contribution is that he succeeds by poetic means in accomplishing what philosophers strive to see in theory, namely cause and effect, the connection and interaction among all things in the world, as we also do in these pages. He looks at any apparition and sees a part of its meaning through a completely different apparition that appears in his mind, and that those less perspicacious would never connect: a row of orchids, roses, and violets are understood through a row of people waiting in line, who do not know each other and preserve their individualities through their silence; the actions of a woman we adore discombobulate us just as the pre-Socratics who, before they had developed their science or any laws of causality, looked in confusion at the unknown phenomena of nature, which appeared to be but an unstable dream. Proust connects what others would consider unrelated, and his view extends over the whole world—he continues the work commenced by Homer, who explains that when Athena rushed down from Mount Olympus, it was as when a falling star, with breakaway sparks of fire, gives a portent to sailors at sea and to glittering hosts gathered across the fields. This is the philosophical-poetic view, which penetrates the objects themselves, and also grasps their causal links to all other things, their pasts and their futures. It will shed eternal honor upon French civilization that it produced, after Greece's Homer and Britain's Shakespeare, the third greatest poet of world history.

Chapter 6

OIKOPHOBIA IN BRITAIN

Britain is and has always been an unruly hodgepodge of peoples, and we shall focus here on the as always dominant English—even if these were not always English, with some of their finest poets from Ireland, some of their finest philosophers from Scotland, and kings from France and Germany. As with France, the determination of when the people have developed enough of a unity and national consciousness to be regarded as one discrete people remains somewhat arbitrary.

One obvious watershed in that original establishment would be Alfred the Great, ruler of Wessex and called king of the Anglo-Saxons, and his unification of large stretches of England in the late ninth century, repulsion of Vikings, and use and encouragement of the Old English language. But all this is thrown into confusion by continued Viking conquests and reign over parts of England, and then by the Norman invasion in 1066, which changes the makeup of the land permanently. Like France in the Middle Ages, the land is for a long time composed of different kingdoms with different languages and constantly at war with one another. The main English kingdom in the twelfth century, under the Angevins, who in fact come from Anjou in northwestern France, even includes Normandy and all of western France, before most of these continental lands are lost in the early thirteenth century under King John, appropriately nicknamed Lackland.

Another obvious watershed is the signing of the Magna Carta in 1215 between King John and rebellious barons. It is important in our context because subsequent generations will view it as the first (although it had some precedents) setting down of liberty and rights for a common English people, with protections against arbitrary royal abuse, a development that puts the nation about half a millennium ahead of its southern French neighbor. As opposed to the case in continental realms, there will never again be absolute rule in English-speaking lands. The closest to an exception is a brief spell at the end of Richard II's reign at the close of the fourteenth century, and arguably some years of James I's reign and of Oliver Cromwell's "Protectorate" in the seventeenth, but these possible exceptions amount to little more than a decade among them.

Yet another important development, this one perhaps less obvious, contributes to a distinctly English awareness, and that is the beginning of university life in Oxford and Cambridge, in the twelfth and thirteenth centuries. These institutions are important in our context because they reflect a stimulus brought by travelers, scholars, and crusaders from the Other: at that time more civilized foreign lands, especially the Middle East, Italy, Spain, and to some extent France. Although Latin remains the language of the learned, these centers of scholarship and innovation will help fuel the British rise. As always, progressivism and openness to foreign ideas are a great asset in the early stages of a civilization, as it seeks to get ahead of others and shake off the retarding influences of conservative and tribal parochialism.

But in Britain, as elsewhere at this time, feudalism keeps stifling the development of national cohesion. Locals are loyal to the baron, and the power center constituted by his castle ensures localism and isolation. Since the baron, in turn, is often in conflict with the king, and occasionally with other barons, civil strife between commoner and commoner is a near constant. Only the eventual decline of feudalism can allow the growth of an English people proper, whose development we can then follow into modern times.

A true English national consciousness stretching from king to commoner can be more clearly discerned starting with the reign of Edward I at the close of the thirteenth century. This potentate for instance subdues Wales (early

1280s) and weakens feudalism. He also banishes the Jews (1290), which is caused by, and in turn fuels, a rising and xenophobic national cohesion. The same year witnesses the *Quia Emptores* law, through which land sales replace feudal obligations, allowing the landed gentry to increase in number vis-à-vis the barons—assisted also by the population increase that is concomitant with improved economic conditions—although the trend had started earlier. The ever-growing importance of the gentry and ultimately even of the farmer is part of that slow democratization whose early civilizational onset we see in the rising Greek laborer and the increasingly powerful Roman plebeian as well.

The year 1295 brings the beginning of a Parliament proper, and it is this increased cohesiveness and sense of belonging, stretching into the very bottom of the social hierarchy, that facilitates effective wars of conquest. The first such major war is launched against France in 1337 by Edward III. This conflict, the Hundred Years' War, also acts as a catalyst in the decline of feudalism. When the king needs more money for his armies, it is granted by Parliament in exchange for more power for itself, and so military necessity precipitates the democratization of the state, as had also happened in Greece and Rome, but less in absolutist France. Similarly, the battlefields of France prove the weakness of the landed knight, for just as the oarsmen at Salamis had shown the worth of the simple sailor and laborer, so the light-footed English commoner bowmen end the medieval knight at Crécy (1346), Poitiers (1356), and Agincourt (1415).

On the cultural side, by the end of the fourteenth century the English language has supplanted French—widespread since the Norman conquest in 1066—even among the upper classes. The Old English literature of early British civilization is "serious"—for instance epic (*Beowulf*, ca. 1000, although set mostly in Sweden and surrounding areas) and scholarly (*The Anglo-Saxon Chronicle*, into the 1100s)—as early literature usually is. Someone like Geoffrey Chaucer, whose *Canterbury Tales* (1390s) is in some ways less serious, is, like the French Rabelais over a century later, more to be seen in the context of the medieval troubadour tradition and of southern influence. Chaucer indeed travels widely in France and Italy, and models his work on Boccaccio's *Decameron* (1353), the product of a rather more advanced Italian civilization. Still, we may conclude that the "seriousness" of a civilization's early literature is more a tendency than a law set in stone. Chaucer remains important to our context, however, in that he writes in Middle English, which, unlike

Old English, is still intelligible to the nonspecialist even today and which displays the existence of a common people's language that is gaining increased traction.

All the same, the excesses of and final defeat in the Hundred Years' War, which ends in 1453, along with the Black Death epidemic in the mid-fourteenth century, set the country's development back significantly, both culturally and politically. After having shown early signs of a budding and reasonably unified civilization, it tumbles back into civil strife and internecine royal-noble conflict in the War of the Roses, which ends in 1487 with the establishment of the Tudor dynasty. It is after this date that we stand before a reborn British nation, one that increasingly sees itself as superior to the European continent. The long stretch of relative peace that is sixteenth-century Tudor Britain allows rapid population increase, greater wealth, and the beginnings of a colonial empire in the New World, as the still-young people stretches its wings and learns to fly. What will seem to be a perennial British naval superiority slowly begins at this time, and the Royal Navy will quite successfully keep the French out of the English Channel.

Although the ultimate oikophobic collapse will come in due time—and with knobs on—Britain will prove herself more tenacious and enduring than most other nations in this regard. It is rather more difficult for the English than for their French neighbors to become oikophobic, in part because the former are constantly reminded of the peskiness of the Other with the help of constant troubles from the indomitable Scots and Irish. These peoples, with whom the English are now fused, now at war, are a practically bottomless well of tension and English jingoism. While the English will subdue the most far-flung peoples of the world, they cannot manage the rude tribes in their own backyard.

An important contributor to English stalwartness on the oikophobic trajectory is the Reformation. Henry VIII is enormously significant in this regard, because he—rare among Western rulers, and more in line with Islamic fashion—fuses the head of the church with the head of state through the Act of Supremacy (1534), while in Christendom in general these two were always separate. By strengthening the state in this way, he makes it more difficult for loyalty either to religion or to the state to decline, since the one is there to reinforce the other, and religious faith takes on a nationalistic dimension. A British subject who might otherwise have been less inclined to bow before the cross will nonetheless do so, for he loves his country, and a subject less inclined to march off to war for his country will still do so, for he loves God. (Although he has misgivings about the English way, Rousseau makes a similar point in *On the Social Contract* 4.8.) Catholicism in England is thereby gradually weakened, and the risk of factionalism reduced. By the time the Catholic Spanish Armada, blessed by the pope, comes sailing (1588), the Catholics in England will not rise against their Reformed masters—in part, admittedly, because a considerable number of Catholics have already been executed.

And so the centralization of monarchical power under the Tudors will for some time prevent fragmentation, which intermittently is the case also in France, and as had been the case when Rome moved from a factional republic to a unified empire. As Machiavelli's hope for Italy had been for a strong leader to unify the disparate city-states of that constantly warring peninsula, Henry VIII and his ministers, especially Thomas Cromwell, understand that brute force—as unpleasant as it may be—is sometimes quite adept at foisting unity and preventing fragmentation, and that the total subservience of the clergy and nobility might allow Britain to reach unprecedented heights of power. But what in France and on the continent in general has always been a tendency toward extremism—now in one direction, now in the other—in Britain meets upon one of the most English of phenomena, namely the spirit of compromise. Henry VIII's Church of England is still more Catholic than Protestant; his son Edward VI makes it Protestant; and finally, after a brief and reasonably murderous Catholic interlude under Mary I, Elizabeth I finds the golden mean. The Church of England remains Catholic insofar as, for example, it places itself within the unbroken apostolic tradition, and it is Protestant insofar as, for example, it creates the specifically Anglican Thirty-nine Articles (1571) and uses English rather than Latin during service.[1]

The reign of this queen, Elizabeth I, the last of the Tudors, constitutes a steady climb toward the peak of British power which is yet to arrive. The defeat of the aforementioned Spanish Armada weakens the last of Britain's serious competitors except for France. The first colonies in India and America are established at the end of and shortly after Elizabeth's reign. Britain is rather well-off, and relatively peaceful internally, with only the occasional Catholic rumble, while most of the rest of Europe is convulsed by civil war and the struggles arising from the Protestant Reformation. The successful civilization will wish to flatter its political and military power with the sanction of culture, and Edmund Spenser and his *Faerie Queene* (1590s) happily oblige, just as Virgil had flattered Augustus and his centralization of power in Rome after a period of discord.

But in spite of the best efforts of Henry VIII, Elizabeth I, and others, a unified English awareness is reinforced most strongly of all by a commoner, whose work will continue to announce the triumph of the national and human spirit even after all else has been lost, a commoner of whose work we may fairly say that there is no human emotion, no human dilemma or constellation, that is not manifested and that does not find its farthest expression of beauty and clarity therein. It is William Shakespeare who will gather in his arms and lend impetus to the force of a nation that will take the world. (Homer is the only other poet in world history of whom all these things may also be justly said.) Shakespeare, especially in his histories, establishes a common past, a past containing both nobility and depredation, but a past that defines Englishmen as bound to one another by mutual triumphs and defeats, and who may therefore face the future with a common purpose in which all are included, be they masters or mendicants, "For he to-day that sheds his blood with me / Shall be my brother; be he ne'er so vile, / This day shall gentle his condition" (*Henry V,* act 4, scene 3).

It is in the several decades following Elizabeth's death in 1603 that English culture and literature manage to catch up with the overall quite strong political and economic developments. Shakespeare achieves his apogee, and poetry moves away from what has mostly been serious religious subjects to sensual pleasures under the aegis of such gentlemen as Ben Jonson and Richard Lovelace, with a poet like John Donne being something of a liminal figure, who combines both the intensely religious and the more fleetingly sensual in his work. At the same time, the English arrive in that phase where a cultured people begins to gain self-awareness and to look at itself in the mirror.

Francis Bacon as a philosopher (*Novum Organum,* 1620) is significant in that context because of his emphasis on empiricism and the scientific method, and empiricism is always a sign of a people that has begun its maturation by moving away from tribal and religious or quasi-religious taboos. (Inversely, in the late twentieth and early twenty-first centuries, we will recognize the decline of empiricism through an increase of taboos in both the socio-humane and even natural sciences.)[2] Bacon is more advanced than, for example, Descartes, even though the latter is almost forty years his junior, insofar as Bacon discards theology as a factor in his philosophy, whereas Descartes will use the reason at which he believes himself to have arrived for the express purpose of proving the existence of God.

Descartes had begun by (erroneously) reasoning himself to the conclusion that he himself exists—the famous "I think, therefore I am." Bacon, on the other hand, simply starts with the fact of existence as a sort of empirical fait accompli, especially in the preface and book 1. That is, by looking at himself and the world, he simply accepts that there is such a thing as existence. This might be an acceptance "for the sake of argument," so that all subsequent philosophy becomes just *arguendo*, or "for the sake of argument," but this is the best we may ever hope to get; we cannot live our lives with the assumption that everything is just an illusion, even if we cannot prove that everything is not an illusion. From this acceptance of existence, an identity of the person and exterior phenomena is established through hypotheses and empirical verification. As a philosophy of science and epistemology, this is sounder than basing oneself on a weak rationalist foundation. So already at this early stage we see a strong scientific turn in British civilization.

Of course, one might interject that Bacon's empiricism is part of a larger European trend at this time rather than a specifically British event on the British civilizational trajectory. And I do not dismiss that interjection. In fact, it is both. Ever since the slow spread of the Renaissance from Italy in the fourteenth century and onward, the microcultures of Europe begin to coalesce more and more, with civilizational progress in France or Italy spilling over into Britain or the German-speaking lands, and, from the seventeenth century, even into places farther afield like Russia. This is an acceleration of the confluence of the Western macroculture.

There are many other examples of this cultural confluence, such as a civilization's focus on its victims, with a book like Zola's *Germinal* falling on the typical oikophobic trajectory while at the same time being part of a broader pan-European reaction against industrialization and unbridled capitalism in the nineteenth century. That such phenomena as empiricism and a focus on victimhood are part of a typical independent civilizational trajectory can be seen in the fact that they took place to varying degrees in the ancient world, too. As time progresses, the borders among the oikophobic trajectories of the microcultures will grow blurrier, so that even though there are clear differences in the time frames between, say, France and Britain, there will nonetheless be a more general oikophobic collapse on the macro-level in the twentieth century, which however only reinforces the fact of the earlier micro-collapses that paved the way for the later and more general malaise.

We see many other instances of a new British self-awareness. John Selden, Thomas Hobbes, and, a bit later, John Locke study forms of English law and government and determine their strengths and weaknesses. The poet John Milton is also, to some extent, to be placed within the Anglo-Saxon tradition of political philosophy through his emphasis on free speech in the *Areopagitica* (1644). There was also, a bit earlier, the precocious Thomas More, whose work had already begun the progressivist utopian attitude of which more shall be said in the next chapter. Finally, there is the awakening again of history as a proper science and self-reflection. Before the 1600s, historical literature in Britain had been of a much more annalist nature, with events simply listed in order and without any sense of a break between eras and between the past and a defined present. But after the Tudors and under the Stuarts there is a sense of a new epoch, of a difference between the Englishmen today and those of yesteryear. Instead of offering a mere chronicle, a plain list of events, historians like Walter Raleigh (*History of the World*, 1614) and Samuel Daniel (*History of England*, 1617) suddenly become investigators and storytellers. The medieval farmer did not know of a past; he had heard of Rome, but not much else. But the Stuart and Reformed Englishman knows he stands on the back of a mighty history, one that allows him to peer all the farther into the future. The new frontier that is established through an awareness of the present qua present, and the optimism that naturally comes with such a frontier, are celebrated by Britain's wiping out of its first indigenous population (1630s), namely the Pequots in New England.

But what had been an adept grip on power by the Tudors begins to slip during the reign of this Stuart dynasty. The war that caps this period is sometimes referred to as the English Revolution, but this term reeks of the latently Marxist notion that it was a conflict of the downtrodden against a cruel monarchy—or, on the other hand, it can have a whiff of protectionist monarchism in defense of an idiot king, Charles I. There is a little bit of truth in the latently Marxist view, but more properly understood, the conflict, which should be and happily often is called the English Civil Wars, is a larger clash between different geographically based interests. It indicates the unravelling of the highly centralized authority that had been established under the Tudors, and whose decline makes it easier for diverging and competing interests to emerge. It is also, to some extent, a spillover from the wars of religion plaguing the continent but to which the English through compromise have managed to prove quite resistant, having successfully stayed out of the horrendous Thirty Years' War. In Britain, it is the hot air of dispute between Episcopalians and Presbyterians regarding the church's organization that fans the flames.

As always happens, increased wealth makes the commoners demand greater representation and more power, and Parliament becomes increasingly antagonistic toward the kings, which also makes it more difficult for the monarch to project outward force. Additionally, the Stuarts, beginning with James I, rule England and Scotland together, and the diversity of these two different political traditions cause considerable friction in England with a king who does not properly understand the tradition of English Parliamentarianism, and in Scotland with resentment toward the English-Anglican manner of religious worship. As in other civilizations, the countryside tends to be more conservative and thus Royalist, while the cities side with the Parliamentarians.

It is indicative of the measured English temperament that even the most radical Parliamentarians initially advocate only a redress of grievances and not an end to the monarchy. And after the Cromwellian dictatorship proves ineffective, the largely bloodless Restoration of the monarchy under Charles II (1660) speaks greatly to the political sagacity of Anglo-Saxon peoples. While France and other European countries will repeatedly tear themselves apart well into the twentieth century, the English Civil Wars are the last serious internecine conflict England will face during her history up to the present. Fragmentation will come in England as elsewhere, and will descend into oikophobia, but not until the nineteenth and twentieth centuries, whereas oikophobia hits France already in the eighteenth. As ever, the English settle on compromise: a continued monarchy, but with increased Parliamentary powers. The period after the Restoration sees the crucial appearance of political parties in the modern sense, with the Whigs and the Tories. Such parties will still not exist for a considerable time on much of the continent, and they are extremely important because they sublimate the frustrations of factions into more clear-headed policies and necessary compromise.

One often hears people complain about party politics, and it can of course be a dreary matter, but we must never forget that once a people has emerged from its tribal cohesion, without political parties there would be either absolutism or violent factionalism. The rise of parties in Britain helps that people to avoid for a long time the self-destruction that will plague the rest of Europe. The Bill of Rights and Declaration of Right (both in 1689), after the so-called Glorious Revolution has entrenched Protestant Anglicanism in the land, further limit monarchical power and make the regular summoning of Parliament mandatory.

One may slowly gain the impression from the purport of my comments that I am partial toward Anglo-Saxon civilization vis-à-vis the European continent, to which I would reply that indeed I am, and that it is nothing I am attempting to hide. If one looks at the history of the separate continental countries, not one of them—with the possible exception of Switzerland and perhaps the Netherlands—will emerge as having managed republicanism very well. They will have thrown themselves now in one extreme, now in another. The political philosophy produced by the British, on the other hand, is superior to that of any other nation, and offers a rare instance of superiority even to the Greeks. The train of thought that develops from the Magna Carta through Milton, Locke, Adam Smith, and Burke up to J. S. Mill, and that was bequeathed unto the United States, has ensured a framework of individualist freedom combining with a noninterfering care toward fellow citizens, a refreshing contrast to all the perfection-minded and idealist Rousseaus, Hegels, and Marxes. It is precisely because the English-speaking peoples have usually not insisted that all improvement take place at once that the system has remained relatively stable and free of bloodshed, with each conflicting side compromising and yielding a little, now and then, for society to proceed to its next phase without too many convulsions; they have preferred empirical practicality to lofty ideas about the goals of history. And for those who do not agree with this conclusion, they need but ask themselves which political tradition has been the most stable and uninterrupted through the centuries, while at the same time affording its members quite unfettered creativity and free thinking, to realize that tradition's considerable sagacity. The sixth of June, 1944, when American, British, and Canadian troops stormed ashore in Normandy, was the day when old John Locke pulled out his cane and gave the little continental upstart Hegel a goodly Anglo-Saxon thrashing.

British history now arrives at its peak, whose absolute political, economic, and military summit lies in the 1860s or thereabouts. The first fruits of oikophobia will come not long thereafter. By the early 1700s Britain is one of the wealthiest nations in the world, and the growing empire is concomitant with her rise to the world's foremost maritime power. Britain's main concern during this century is to gain control of world commerce, which is successfully achieved through the navy and through the state's encouragement of private enterprise. Militarily, her eclipse of France begins with the Seven Years' War (1756–63, a world war, in which much of the French Americas becomes British) and is complete with Trafalgar and Waterloo in 1805 and 1815, respectively. The loss of the thirteen American colonies in the American Revolution (1775–83) is a severe blow to morale, but it does not significantly hurt Britain's economic interests, for the British establish good trade relations with the United States and turn their colonial focus east- and southward instead. That conflict is more harmful, in fact, to the French, even though they are on the victorious side, since it adds greatly to French debt and plays a part in precipitating the French Revolution.

As always, the increased contact with the Other sets the stage for what will later become oikophobia. The loss of America leads to a heightened development of British India instead, and when a people has developed a sense of humanity and liberty, as the British have (a stage to which a more tribal society will not yet have passed), it will be more impressionable vis-à-vis the Other. To take a famous instance of this, Warren Hastings, who serves as governor of Bengal in the 1770s and '80s, is impeached in the House of Commons upon his return to Britain; the great Edmund Burke is part of the prosecution. Hastings stands accused, among other things, of mismanagement and of crimes toward the Indian natives. Although the prosecution fails to achieve his conviction, the mere fact that a trial takes place on such grounds is significant. Common Englishmen—at least some of them—peer across the oceans, no longer as a tribe observing enemy tribes, but as human beings recognizing the human in the Other. In a speech delivered during the trial, in 1788, Burke declares, "I charge [Hastings] with having . . . wasted the country, ruined the landed interest, cruelly harassed the peasants, burnt their houses, seized their crops, tortured and degraded their persons. . . . I impeach him in the name of the people of India, whose laws, rights, and liberties he has subverted, whose properties he has destroyed, whose country he has laid waste and desolate."[3] Although the Indian may appear most alien indeed, his English counterpart recognizes in him not a mere beast, but a man.

Domestically, the increased wealth and innovation, with its concomitant increase in agricultural output, contribute to an explosion in population growth around this time. That, in turn, expands the leisure class and creates more room—as wealth and population always do—for a greater number of diverging interest groups to emerge. Predictably, the focus on individualist themes, as opposed to religion or nation, which had begun already after the Tudors, becomes stronger than ever, through the rise of the Romanticist generation of writers and poets. Percy Bysshe Shelley, for instance, turns away radically from both the state and religion and embraces atheism; he is also a vegetarian with pacifist sympathies. Similar things can be said about many of the poets of his era. But I must keep emphasizing the idea of holding two thoughts in mind at the same time: one can appreciate the achievements of this new generation of writers while at the same time recognizing the historical and predictable role they play in a civilization's move away from group cohesion toward a more splintered condition where diverse factions will eventually run up against each other rather than against external antagonists. Only to simple and vulgar minds is it a zero-sum matter.

To take one prominent example, the British Empire was not built by men like John Keats, and the self-engrossment that his work represents is never healthy for a people that seeks to project outward power. And yet, whenever I am in Rome, his grave is the first place I visit. Not where Caesar marched, sated with triumph, or Cicero declaimed with a mighty voice, or the doors of Janus opened and closed, but the tiny plot on the outskirts of the city, with his grave in a corner, a stone lyre upon it, is the place I call sacred, the place where I kneel and grow teary-eyed, and where I place an everlasting rock on his tomb in acknowledgment of his name, which shall live longer than the Colosseum and Roman law. It was on first looking into Keats that I realized how much better it would have been, rather than to extend this fitful comedy until everyone had laughed, to die an early death, freeing oneself from petty suffering, and to live merely as a little book on a shelf.

With the nineteenth century, the Industrial Revolution, which begins in Britain to a great extent thanks to large coal deposits, comes into full swing. Industrialization creates even more interest groups by entrenching upper and working classes in their respective positions, although it must be kept in mind that increased success and wealth in preindustrial societies tend to have the same consequences, and so in that context industrialization is not anything truly new either, but a continuation of earlier processes. Nonetheless, industrialization quite naturally fosters the rise of radical fringe groups and increased resentment against the wealthier strata of society, and fuels a politics of envy.

But since the spirit of free enterprise and capitalism in Britain, along with low taxes, allows a middle class to arise that is stronger and larger than elsewhere, a class who feel that they are beneficiaries of British prosperity and success, the lower-class radicals and their questioning of old English traditions are unable to push their agendas through. The British upper class, for its part, does become more effete, but not as much as had been the case in France before the Revolution; the British have a vast empire to manage, and military training thus remains a core component for young upper-class men who will be future officers. The incubating Oxbridge culture through which most of them pass also fosters male camaraderie and derring-do, as well as a strong sense of hierarchy, and so the English prove resistant to oikophobia. While the Enlightenment makes many French intellectuals despise French culture and in allophiliac and oikophobic fashion praise the far and distant, the English remain pragmatically rooted in their own traditions and in the spirit of compromise. Although there are earlier signs thereof, to be discussed presently, true oikophobia will not destroy the English until after World War II, as the cultural forces of various states of the Western world will have been intermingling for some time. And so Roger Scruton's statement, discussed in this book's introduction, which traces oikophobia in Britain to after World War II, is indeed largely true as far as that country goes.

Britain peaks in the 1860s or so, and then goes downhill. Already in the 1870s, and especially after Germany's unification in 1871, the continuous spread of industrialization to other European countries and to the United States starts to erode British power, relatively speaking. Britain still expands her empire enormously in Asia and Africa, but the first cracks become visible in the broader but thinner spread of British might. One of the most obvious signs of this, as the Victorian era draws to a close, is the Boer War (1899–1902), which is a British victory but is bought at such a high price, against guerilla opponents, and with such questionable methods, that it causes significant internal dissension. The war is especially significant in our context in that there is a sizable minority of people at home who support the Boer cause, certainly within the Liberal Party. For British socialists, whose economic agenda will necessarily question the interests of the wealthy elite who run the empire, it is natural to start siding with the enemy and to attack their own country's exceptionalism.

Anti-war and oikophobic critique we might recognize from today—that the war was supposedly started by Jews and capitalists—becomes a significant factor. British soldiers and politicians are too stupid to see that they are being duped by the capitalists; this is according to such gentlemen as Liberal Member of Parliament John Burns (in a speech in the House of Commons in 1900) and John Hobson in his book *The War in South Africa* (also 1900). There had been dissension about war before—like during the Crimean War (1853–56), as a result of poor conditions faced by soldiers and of new media of war reporting that illustrated more vividly to those at home the horrors of war—but not this sort of anti-British sentiment.

We hear a similar and clearly oikophobic tone, one of disgust with one's own culture, from a much more famous author a few decades later, namely in the words of the British protagonist of George Orwell's *Burmese Days* (published in 1934, but set in the 1920s). We witness here the outbursts of a fictional character who represents an increasingly common type of the time: "How can you make out that we are in this country for any purpose except to steal? It's so simple. The official holds the Burman down while the business man goes through his pockets . . . The British Empire is simply a device for giving trade monopolies to the English—or rather to gangs of Jews and Scotchmen." He continues, "All this will be gone—forests, villages, monasteries, pagodas all vanished. And instead, pink villas fifty yards apart; all over those hills, as far as you can see, villa after villa, with all the gramophones playing the same tune. And all the forests shaved flat—chewed into wood-pulp for the *News of the World*, or sawn up into gramophone cases." Finally, he says, "I see them [the British] as a kind of up-to-date, hygienic, self-satisfied louse. Creeping round the world building prisons. They build a prison and call it progress."[4]

This last sentence is an allusion to Tacitus's famous line in his work *Agricola* (30), quoted above in chapter 3, that "where they have wrought desolation, they call it 'peace'!" You will recall that Tacitus was another liminal figure who lived at a time of civilizational decline and increasing oikophobia. The protagonist's hatred of home in *Burmese Days* is matched by that of his native interlocutor, who loves everything English and despises his own Burmese culture; this is an example of non-Western oikophobia.

A propos of Orwell, mention should be made of his essay *Notes on Nationalism* (1945), which contains a description of what is unmistakably oikophobia and which thus serves to underscore the point that oikophobia is increasing in the first half of the twentieth century in Britain. He calls the phenomenon "negative nationalism" and, under the subheading "anglophobia," writes,

"Within the intelligentsia, a derisive and mildly hostile attitude towards Britain is more or less compulsory, but it is an unfaked emotion in many cases . . . In foreign politics many intellectuals follow the principle that any faction backed by Britain must be in the wrong." In the same essay, specifically allophiliac oikophobia is what Orwell calls "transferred nationalism," where a correlate of cultural self-hatred is love and admiration directed toward an Other: "Among the intelligentsia, colour feeling only occurs in the transposed form, that is, as a belief in the innate superiority of the coloured races. This is now increasingly common among English intellectuals. . . . Almost any English intellectual would be scandalized by the claim that the white races are superior to the coloured, whereas the opposite claim would seem to him unexceptionable even if he disagreed with it."[5] I need add nothing further to these observations; the phenomenon is all too recognizable.

Concomitant with this development is the fetish of victimhood and marginalized groups. With a store of unused power after the elimination of enemies, human nature must spend that power somewhere and somehow, and fighting for the downtrodden at home is the easiest and closest outlet. An obvious example is Charles Dickens, whose novels are wrapped in fluff and still begin to drip with saccharin every time a member of the working class enters the room. And a focus on women's interests makes its appearance at this stage of British culture. The Brontë sisters are among the first feminist English writers, and they form the vanguard of first-wave feminism, which later, as America and the macro-West begin to totter a century and a half down the road, will be replaced by the second through fourth waves. What these varying forms of feminism have in common with each other as with, for instance, the increased literary focus on women's interests in the Roman Empire, is that they appear in the latter part of a civilization's power trajectory. Feminism or protofeminism is thus part of a nexus that also includes multiculturalism and victimhood and that appears as a civilization has already achieved its peak. The more a society progresses and grows egalitarian, the more sensitive it will become to those inequalities that remain, which plays into oikophobia.[6]

At the same time, the number of religious Nonconformists increases, people who emphasize more personal morals—which, as has already been seen, is a natural result of the nation growing so large and powerful that the more traditional and parochial religion can no longer satisfy the emotional needs of its individual members. In 1871 the Universities Tests Act abolishes religious tests at the universities, so that not only Catholics and Nonconformists but even non-Christians may enroll. And so at Oxford and Cambridge, those incubators of leaders, a new generation of students unfiltered by religion may now enter and rise through the ranks.

This can easily be considered a welcome development, since inherent intellectual ability knows neither creed nor color, and if a person of my own exact temperament and worldview had sat in Parliament in those days, he would have voted in favor of the abolition. But the Universities Tests Act, to be properly understood, must also be seen as an integral part of society's diversification which will weaken that society in the long run by making it less cohesive. It is enacted mainly as an effort by the Gladstone government to obtain the vote of Nonconformists for his Liberal Party, but since it opens the door for other groups as well, it indicates that diversification will often increase exponentially, with the success of one interest group opening up the field for others, until little remains of a cohesive and unified people ready to face common challenges. Neo-tribal groupings, putting themselves before the state and their countrymen in other groups, will incapacitate the state in the long term.

The continuous increase in the size of the electorate also leads to much higher government spending on social issues in the late nineteenth and early twentieth centuries. External enemies have been conquered or subdued, and there is less of a perceived need to project outward power, and so a new enemy must arise within (often the wealthy or the "elite"), against which politicians may measure their strength and champion their cause before the people. Liberal prime ministers Asquith and Lloyd George are two such champions in Britain in the early twentieth century, as Pericles and Cimon had been in Athens and Clodius and Domitian in Rome, to mention only a few.

It is not a coincidence that Britain's turn away from militarism and from involvement in the European continent in the first half of the twentieth century coincides with the rise of the Labour Party, helped by the socialist Fabian Society and its anti-nationalist internationalism: the more money is spent on social interest groups, the less can go to the military (disgust with the costs of World War I also plays a role, of course, but it is not the only reason for decreasing military spending). This is why there is not only a cultural but also a direct economic link between the oikophobic strengthening of interest groups and a country's reduced ability to fight external enemies. Spending on welfare and pensions is less than 1 percent of GDP in 1900, but almost 5 percent in 1933, when Hitler comes to power—and will be around 8 percent in 1960 and 15 percent in 2010—just as after Pericles's death even more Athenians went on the government dole.[7] These figures would have been incomprehensible to the British themselves at their peak in the 1860s, and they also ensure that Britain will be woefully unprepared for the new threat that arises on the horizon.[8]

Britain would not have won against Nazi Germany without Allied help, and so the culture has now arrived at that point which France reached about a century earlier: namely, the incapacity to prevail in a major conflict without foreign assistance. The inward turn comes after a society has exhausted its external strength in beating its foes. Varying forms of feminism, victimhood culture, labor laws, welfare, abandonment of the family for individual pleasure-seeking—all these, and other factors yet, are part of a society that is attacking its own institutions and traditions.

It is after World War II that oikophobia becomes full-blown in Britain; it was earlier in France, and will be later in the United States. This is the point at which Britain is definitively eclipsed by the US, which takes over directly from Britain the role of the world's guarantor of relative peace—or the role of the world's heavy-handed policeman, depending on one's point of view. Britain herself has no will left for the empire, and she turns increasingly inward. Financial ruin is accompanied by a sense of shame, and the desire to dominate the Other disappears. But the desire to dominate will always remain a part of human nature, and so the dominated has become differing domestic groups rather than the Other. Large sectors of the economy are nationalized, and the welfare dole grows ever bigger. Decolonization contributes to mass immigration from the former colonies, and English society grows very diverse indeed, vanquishing what is left of a national consciousness. The empire becomes something mentioned only *sotto voce*, and it begins to be considered impolite and cruel to express any sort of pride in Britain and her traditions. In part because of Britain's astonishing imperial successes, the backlash becomes even stronger here than elsewhere, almost to the point that oikophobia will appear to be a specifically British invention. But self-pride is a rather basic human psychological need, and British oikophobic vanity is only a particularly recent iteration of such self-pride. And so Britain, instead of charting her course between the xenophobia of old and the rising oikophobia, where one would be mindful of the errors of the past but still proud of an immensely rich political and cultural heritage, lapses into an extreme.

It is now in many quarters considered racist and ridiculous to be proud of that heritage at all.

There is no need for us to follow the culture all the way up to the present day. This, rather, shall be left for the discussion of the United States and of the confluence of the West, where the developments of the Western micro-cultures will all come to look increasingly the same. For now, we remind our-selves of what some of the major features are that Britain, on her oikophobic trajectory, has in common with the other civilizations within our purview. There is democratization as a response to crisis; success leads to wealth, which leads to a leisure class free enough to examine its own society and to self-question, and so the original tribalism is abandoned; wealth also leads to population increase, which leads to more room for diverging interest groups; the diverging interest groups, coupled with the self-questioning phase, lead to oikophobia as the groups descend into a fragmented neo-tribalism with each group trying to get ahead of the others, as the external Other is forgot-ten; the powers that be try to win the grace of politically important groups and increase social spending for them, and consequently less is spent on the military.

Thankfully, Britain in modern times will be in a period of relative peace-fulness, where an inward turn will not lead to detrimental attack from abroad. But people forget that the relative peacefulness of the Western world in which they live today is largely an American invention and was established by American force of arms. Since the point at which we set out together on our journey lies almost three thousand years in the past, we may have it all the more easily impressed upon us how very brief is our current era, how it occupies but the smallest segment of our common Western history, and how few of our securities and comforts we should feel entitled to take for granted.

Chapter 7

Oikophobia as Positivism

We saw in Greece that oikophobia began to develop as a sort of cultural relativism, an ideology that still applies to many manifestations of oikophobia today. But there is another, opposite philosophical guise in which oikophobia can appear, which I shall call positivist oikophobia. Now is a good time to discuss it, because there were British thinkers who laid part of its groundwork. If not British, these thinkers had a propensity to be of the German persuasion, but this should not be surprising: since that people more than any other, save the Greeks, has produced profound and varied thought, in looking for philosophical developments of almost anything we may expect to find them among the Germans.

As will soon become clear, the type of positivism I wish to discuss here is of an epistemological sort. Whereas epistemological positivism generally posits that all that can be known are things confirmed by the natural or hard sciences, the variety we shall examine in this chapter attempts to transfer that stance into the sociohistorical and cultural realm, turning it into a moral and cultural positivism.

For us to understand what positivist oikophobia is, we first meet Thomas More. In his work *Utopia* (appearing as early as 1516, in Latin), More sets out his vision of a society free of old English institutions, and where the supposedly natural and rational kindness of human nature replaces Christianity in producing social harmony. More is thus something of a precursor of Rousseau in this respect. There is a protocommunist possession of resources, and a somewhat multicultural universal toleration of differing creeds. Now, More was a devout anti-Protestant Catholic, and some of the work is satirical, but regardless of how seriously he meant it, the work contains the seeds of the idea that a better future will entail the erasure of national cultures and a more communal and universalist attitude.[1] This progressive idea is not only protocommunist, but in fact at its roots also somewhat Christian—and more on that soon enough—so More's devotion to it, if taken at face value, should not be all too surprising after all.

In a similar vein we have Francis Bacon's *The New Atlantis* (1627, posthumously), an unfinished novel about a utopian world. Bacon was extremely influential not only in Britain but also on the continent. His epistemology and philosophy of science we have already come across in his *Novum Organum*. But in *The New Atlantis*, which contains deliberate parallels with More's *Utopia*, Bacon seems to maintain that epistemological and scientific progress can be transferred unto the ethical and social realms also. In the fictional world he conjures up there, science has helped the people conquer nature and—more crucially—human nature, and perfect their behavior toward one another.

This philosophical tradition continued, outside of Britain, with the German Enlightenment-Romanticist philosopher Johann Gottfried Herder in the eighteenth century. ("Enlightenment-Romanticist" may appear an oxymoron to some, but our dear poets and philosophers are often complex enough to defy neat academic categorization.) As Bacon had felt that scientific methods could improve human nature ever more, so Herder was one of the first to popularize the notion that humanity progresses in a linear fashion, and he thereby set the stage for positivist oikophobia; his ideas in this regard are found mainly in *Another Philosophy of History for the Formation of Mankind* (1774) and, especially, *Ideas on the Philosophy of History of Mankind* (1784–91).

Herder himself was certainly no oikophobe, and in any case lived too early in the development of German culture for that to have been the case. He was an ardent German patriot who longed for a unified Germany worthy of the German language and spirit, although he was notable for being neither a racist nor an anti-Semite at a time when most people were both (see his *Letters for the Advancement of Humanity*, 1790s), and even warns against the racist and anti-Semitic outbursts to which an embrace of German patriotism and national spirit might and of course eventually did lead. It is also the case that the teleological nature of Herder's work has been exaggerated, and he is not as extreme in this regard as Hegel, whom to some extent he inspired; for instance, Herder tempers his positivism by focusing more on physical individuals than on metaphysical laws. Nonetheless, if one is willing to cut through his verbiage, which often reads like a Sturm und Drang parody, one finds that Herder believes that all of humanity—not just the German-speaking peoples—might progress toward an ever-better state. As a true positivist, and also under the influence of Bacon and the hopelessly humorless Goethe, he thinks that the ultimate goal of human progress can be achieved and that the unfolding of history can be linked to rational progress over human nature. But although the Enlightenment as a whole, of which Herder was a part to a limited extent, traditionally prided itself on its reason, the notion of a progressive and linear history is ultimately rather Christian, and certainly very bourgeois, because it entails the satisfied messianic comfort that one day at some future time all will be well. This is why I call it not only teleological—striving toward a goal—but will also give it the more religious appellation eschatological.

And this is how I should like to define our epistemological positivism in the present context: as a sociohistorical, moral, and cultural positivism—that is, a positivism that is confident that laws similar to those used in the natural sciences can be applied to the humane and social sciences as well. Since firm knowledge of the physical world can be gained through the natural sciences, firm knowledge of the cultural and socio-moral world becomes possible by bringing epistemological positivism into it. This positivism is the belief that social scientists may discover laws through which, over time, the total body of human knowledge and understanding grows—with each scientist adding a few grains to the heap—all to the benefit and ultimate and irrevocable moral and cultural progress of mankind.

This attitude is by no means bound to lead to oikophobia. It is most certainly true that positivism can be taken in a non-, even in a sort of anti-oikophobic direction. This is what for example Hegel does. He believes that history is ruled by divine spirit (*Phenomenology of Spirit*, 1807, and especially *Lectures on the Philosophy of History*, published posthumously in 1837). After primitive and oriental phases, the world progresses to the ancient Classical phase of Greece and Rome, and finally to the Germanic and Christian end stage—that is, Hegel's own modern Europe and especially Prussia, where everyone is free and the spirit of the world is fully developed. (To echo Nietzsche's snide comment, Hegel essentially thinks that pagan tribes in the prehistory of Asia existed in order to pave the way for his professorships in Heidelberg and Berlin.) This positivism is of course very far from being oikophobic, since on the contrary it glorifies Hegel's own civilization as a goal.

To his credit, Hegel does see a measure of cyclicality in history, because— as already Thucydides taught—human passions are always the same. But nonetheless, on the level of the unfolding of the historical spirit of freedom Hegel is unable to escape the positivist and eschatological temptation of positing an end to history toward which mankind is slowly but surely progressing. There are some textual passages where Hegel seems to recognize that history may not yet be over, but also a number of passages that are quite striking in their self-aggrandizing affirmation of his own time and place as the summit of things.[2]

Wilhelm Dilthey, who was a professor in Berlin at a time when Hegel's influence was still strong, in his *Introduction to the Humanities* (1883) and *Ideas for a Descriptive and Analytic Psychology* (1894) contributes to the codification of positivist dogma by playing a part in the creation of the term *Geisteswissenschaften*. This is normally translated as the "humanities," but literally means "sciences of the spirit," as opposed to the natural sciences (*Naturwissenschaften*). Dilthey, who conjures Francis Bacon in the very first sentence of the first chapter of the former book, develops a hermeneutical approach that considers the humanities a separate science. In typical German fashion, he believes that true understanding in the humanities can be furnished by an established methodology. To be sure, he does not believe that anemic and objective measurement can be carried out within the humanities in the same way as in the natural sciences—in fact he clearly positions himself against this—but he posits a sort of Hegelian progression of the humanities within which metaphysical understanding unfolds toward more advanced phases.

But it is ultimately a rather self-congratulatory and onanistic naïveté to believe that such progress is possible within the humanities, which is why I call Hegel's eschatological flirtation—and Dilthey's progression—a "temptation" that they were unable to resist, the temptation of believing oneself responsible for real, unquestionable human progress. Natural scientists may have a right to their attitude; in their domain there is, for the most part, such real and measurable progress, but one soon runs into trouble when applying this disposition to the humanities, even if progress has been made in some areas here and there.

In fairness to Dilthey, he does distance himself (*Introduction to the Humanities*, book 1, chapter 2, and passim) from what he also calls "positivists," those who wanted to take the methodologically scientific approach to an even greater extreme; in book 1, chapters 14–15, he even criticizes the exaggerated positivism of teleological philosophers of history, including Herder; and the German *Wissenschaft*, though meaning science, can also sometimes be used in the simpler sense of "knowledge" (*Wissen*). Nonetheless, his hermeneutics are too focused on method, which in the end is something too subjective for his purported goal. The spirit of his approach, if not its exact letter, colors German academia even today, which often displays a certain queasiness at the prospect that a particular piece of literature may have more than one "correct" reading. As I used to point out during my student days in Germany, the term *Literaturwissenschaft* (literary theory, but literally "literature-science") is an oxymoron, something that was probably easier to discover for a foreigner like me than for someone who had grown up with the word.[3]

And this is where a non-oikophobic and more conservative positivism like Hegel's connects to oikophobic positivism. For if humanity is to progress positivistically toward a higher goal, then it is an easy step—one that the Hegelian Marx and his followers take—to replace Hegel's goal of Christian-Germanic consummation with a unification of all peoples across borders, and an end to struggle among them. Once this has become the new positivist goal, which requires the oikophobic suppression of one's own nation, then the erasure of national differences and the egalitarian fusion of individual cultures—that is, a form of relativism—become not only desirable but a distinct necessity. And so the left-wing Hegelians, like Marx (as opposed to the right-wing Hegelians, like Hegel), must work to undermine their own cultures from within. In this way, positivism and relativism end up lying closer together than one might originally have suspected: oikophobia as positivism becomes the road to oikophobia as relativism. The positivist progression of humanity and humanities shall unite all humans; a new way of achieving the relativism that started in Greece has thus been discovered.

In Britain, the socialists and Liberals who around the turn of the twentieth century oikophobically criticize British culture and try to undermine the
empire draw—sometimes unwittingly, sometimes wittingly—on this twin
tradition of positivist-relativist utopianism stretching back to Thomas More,
Bacon, and Marx. They also draw to some extent on a distinctly British form
of positivism, namely the philosophy of Utilitarianism, whose foremost ex-
emplars are Jeremy Bentham and—less extreme—John Stuart Mill.

Mill maintains, in his *Utilitarianism* (1861), that most social evils and suffering can be permanently removed by a reason-based social engineering, and
that the human mind is gradually altered toward higher ends (3.10 and passim). He fails to see cyclicality in history and has little inkling of the oncoming neo-tribalism into which declining civilizations will inevitably lapse. Mill
believes that "in every age some advance is made towards a state in which it
will be impossible to live permanently on other terms [than equality] with
anybody" (again 3.10, a passage where he even heads in a quasi-religious direction by speaking somewhat well of the French positivist Auguste Comte's
mysticism, which at the end of chapter 1 of the better work *On Liberty* [1859]
he had rightly criticized as despotic).

So this positivist mindset has laid the foundation for the notion, whose
popularization goes back to the eighteenth century, that humanity is slowly
but surely proceeding toward a higher ethical state. Thus it became increasingly common for people to argue that if we would all just be ready to talk
to and reason with one another, our problems and disputes would melt away.
This sort of attitude grows from the intellectual forbears I have discussed,
but often fails to consider that this goal is itself an imposition of a particular
worldview—even though the defenders of that positivist view will sometimes
lay claim to a certain postnationalist internationalism where everyone is given
their due. Some cultures wholly alien to that view will not let themselves be
assimilated and altered so easily.

All the same, Marx defeated Hegel in the search for posterity's favor, in
that the latter's centeredness on the European and Germanic, and on Prussia, as the final end of history gave way to Marx's internationalism. And so
peace and equality among various cultures became a focus of the new eschatology. Although communism would always require plenty of violence
and innocent deaths to realize even the smallest of its goals—since in a naturally unequal world equality will always demand tyranny—the normal
antagonism between national cultures was replaced by a desired peace. The

popular consciousness thereby arrived at positivist oikophobia, not always while realizing its full force: the own culture must be attacked so that all cultures can be fused in peace. What the war of one culture against another could not accomplish, namely the extinction of the enemy culture, peace between those cultures achieves quite easily, except that when the enemy culture dies, one's own disappears as well. It is not until the oikophobic phase of a civilization comes around that the human consciousness starts to regret all previous cultural wars and, as compensation, seeks to give peace and privilege to all cultures, and in doing so defeats its own noble intentions. Whenever these previously antagonistic cultures coexist in the same space, only two outcomes are possible: either they eventually break out in conflict again, or they quietly die—that is, they become gradually weakened until neither is recognizable anymore as a distinct culture beyond some very insignificant outer signs, such as using chopsticks instead of knife and fork, or saying "*Mazel tov*" instead of "Congratulations."

So this, finally, is where both relativism and positivism reveal the weakness of their philosophical or at least historical bulwarks, because they start to flow into one another. The flirtation of relativism with positivism reveals how little thought through they are in such cases. One can observe daily in many who claim that there are no higher or absolute truths, or that all cultures are equal (relativism), that they also have a firm idea of what a better society would entail and that everyone should agree on this (positivism), thus contradicting the former position. As the twentieth century got well under way, the West as a macroculture had already begun its collapse into decadent self-contempt. Oikophobia became such a necessity for people's vanity that they would take any path at all that might lead to it—relativist or positivist— even if these paths appeared, at second glance, to lead in opposite directions.

Chapter 8

Oikophobia in the United States

The Past

As opposed to what had been the case in our other civilizations, it is easy to determine when the United States begins. Of course, while this beginning is the Declaration of Independence in 1776, we must also not forget that American culture at this stage is more advanced than other cultures in their initiation periods, since the Americans inherit a great and already advanced culture from the British. This is why a shorter time will pass between the American beginning and the descent into oikophobia than was the case with the other cultures.

In spite of this and one other unique feature, which will be discussed in due course, the United States is as much of a textbook case as any other. Pre-Revolutionary society is in the main rather parochial and patriarchal, a natural trait of an agricultural economy with lots of land and slave labor but a relatively well-educated upper class. The inhabitants or at least leaders of the original thirteen colonies are reasonably unified by their resistance to the British crown: a strong, naïve, and vigorous people is able to repel the world's most lethal military force from its land and establish a new state. Although their culture stems directly from the British, the Americans still have a considerably lower level of refinement than their overlords, as they are composed mainly of farmers who form inexperienced militias. The founding of the state is secular, but religion is at this time much stronger than it is today.[1] The weakening of Christianity in the United States will not proceed in a straight line—social developments are rarely straight—since for instance the nineteenth century is by and large more devout than the eighteenth, as is true in much of Europe as well. The so-called Great Awakenings increase religiosity in society for extended periods, just as in Britain the Puritan era under Oliver Cromwell had been more devout than the Elizabethan age. But the overall direction of religious development is nonetheless clear, and across civilizations within the West, that development bends toward decline.[2]

The history of the United States is, to a considerable extent, the history of immigrant assimilation and the history of the conflict between the federal government and the separate states. So the other aforementioned unique feature of the country is that the populace is not at all autochthonous (even if it occasionally behaves as if it were), but based on immigration. And this fact actually renders one of the historical tendencies we have established—the impact of diversity—even more striking in the American case. The founding fathers—especially those supporting a strong federal government, like Alexander Hamilton, John Adams, and, to a somewhat lesser extent, George Washington and James Madison—immediately recognize the loose federation of states and the immigrant and diverse nature of the country as challenges. And their concern is well founded, because the Anti-Federalists, led by men like Samuel Adams and Thomas Jefferson, have a point in their argument that government on a very large and diverse scale will be unable to keep the public's affection, even if this point will not become evident until later in American history.[3]

A good case can be made that each side is right in its own way: the Anti-Federalists correctly predict what we see in the Civil War and also in the twentieth century—that too large a people and government will undermine loyalty to the state—while the Federalists are right that, at their time, a strong federal government is necessary to keep the nation together and to ward off external threats. It is clear that, early on, mass immigration strengthens the state—just as expansion of civic status to new peoples had strengthened Rome during the republic and saved her from extinction—because great masses of new workers, soldiers, and experts arrive on American shores. This growing strength is reflected in the War of 1812 against the British, in which the Americans actually lose a large number of the engagements but still display that ruggedness associated with early civilizations, where sheer will and ad-mirable naïveté make up for the relative lack of resources and sophistication, allowing the people to exit the conflict with their strength and honor rea-sonably intact. But there are some signs of division already now, because the war is highly unpopular in the Northern states, who prefer friendly relations with the British because they trade with them, while there is more support for it south of New England.

Nonetheless, once peace returns, the natural growth of a still young people continues at a brisk pace, thanks in large part to growing numbers of rest-less and industrious immigrants. Initial successes against surrounding peoples—the British in Cànada and from across the sea, the native Ameri-cans everywhere, and even against the far-flung Barbary States in North Af-rica (1801–05 and 1815)—lead to greater wealth and prestige, and a national identity is forged. Thomas Jefferson's Louisiana Purchase from France (1803) almost doubles the available land of an already large country and gives more room for a young and itching people to spread its wings. The Monroe Doc-trine (1823) is very significant in that it establishes the continent as uniquely American and distances it, as a separate and self-aware entity, from Euro-pean interference. The Indian Removal Act (1830) accomplishes the same thing vis-à-vis the natives; although there are some humanitarian-based pro-tests, most think it a matter of course that a primitive civilization and eco-nomy should give way to an advanced civilization and economy. It is only natural that this strong and self-reliant people will smash into whatever happens to stand in its way. The Mexican War (1846–48) is probably the best example in the American context of how a young and growing civiliza-tion, with momentum on its side, will march abroad to test its strength and advance itself at the expense of the Other, as had the Romans and the French in Italy, and the British in France. The justifications for the war are rather flimsy, but it does not matter—a rising people will do what it can to overcome neighboring civilizations.

As a natural outcropping of this state of affairs, we have the first attempts at establishing something of a uniquely American culture. Although Amer-ican philosophers will not be able to measure themselves with their European counterparts until the twentieth century (one need read only the pop-Kantianism and postcard wisdoms of an Emerson or the sophomoric and

jejune self-indulgence of a Thoreau to get a sense of this), American fiction—
especially that of Nathaniel Hawthorne—is as elegant as any other, and
deals with themes stemming from a specifically American context, such as
the conquest of a new land, and a certain American puritanism. But since
America's beginning was built on an already developed culture, the first signs
of what will later become oikophobia come creeping already now, as the
country is still striving toward its peak.

The aforementioned Thoreau is himself a prime example; his *Walden; or,
Life in the Woods* (1854) is an early indication of the antisocial self-indulgence
that plagues later stages of declining civilizations. In a sense, *Walden* actually expresses a typical American sentiment of independence and ruggedness in the wild, but from another point of view it is also reminiscent of a
teenager who dislikes his society without understanding what he owes it, and
who convinces himself that he can manage without it. But I do like some of
Thoreau, and do not wish to be mean-spirited; I shall confine myself to observing that there is probably a reason why the work is read almost only in
US high schools and nowhere and nowhen else.

And we are reminded that self-critique is not the same as oikophobia;
there is a difference between self-critique and self-denigration. Across our
civilizations we have met many people who analyzed, criticized, or questioned some of their traditions without thereby being oikophobic. In Greece
we identified three paradigmatic phases in a society's development: one's own
culture is simply assumed to be superior; one's culture is concluded to be great
based on comparative study; one's culture is considered worse than others.
Thoreau and especially Emerson still belong in the second phase.

After a critical and largely inevitable point, what has been a source of
strength—diversity—becomes also a liability and a source of weakness. One
of the earliest signs, and certainly the most cataclysmic, of this development
is of course the American Civil War (1861–65). While it is fought over slavery,
it is more fundamentally a clash of cultural, ethnic, and economic interests:
a patriarchal, Anglo-Saxon, and agrarian South and an entrepreneurial,
mixed, and industrial North, to mention a few of the differing aspects. The
liberation of the slaves in the United States expands citizenship and leads to a
greater pool of potential soldiers—and black Americans have fought gal-
lantly in every American conflict since, and in fact even before, in more
isolated instances—but it adds yet another interest group to a nation that is

already beginning to fragment, a fragmentation whose consequences will come to the fore a century later.[4]

In spite of the war, the country as a whole is at this time still rising, and once the South has been soundly defeated, the onward march continues. The economy booms, the last wars against the natives are fought, and the frontier is finally pushed all the way to the Pacific. Although the military will lag behind for some time, the US economy is the world's strongest by the turn of the century, at a time when oikophobia has already appeared in Britain. Socialist ideas begin to spread from Europe, but they will not have a significant impact until the 1930s. Until then, American growth continues quite steadily. As in the antebellum period, although particular writers might criticize this or that facet of American society—such as Mark Twain, who probably quite rightly terms the postwar era the "gilded age"—there is no particular indication that such critique is taking on a larger oikophobic dimension.

With increasing wealth and democratization comes a greater room for competing interests to grow ever more rabid. Two legal milestones in that development for the United States may be mentioned, namely the Seventeenth Amendment to the Constitution (1913), which allows for the election of federal senators directly by the people rather than by their state legislatures, as well as the Nineteenth (1920), giving women the vote. While the latter amendment carries a strong moral significance in spite of its historical role on the civilizational trajectory, the former can easily be viewed as highly problematic even today in that it makes the senators more directly responsive to the whims of the electorate. They thus become more prone to bribing their constituents for votes, a process that will eventually make the citizens more loyal to themselves and their own group than to the state as a whole. It is not for naught that already Aristotle warns, in *Politics* 1305a, that the archons—the leaders of the city-state—should be elected by the larger sub-groupings of the city (*phylai*), and not directly by the people as a whole, lest the people elect ambitious men who put their own particular constituents above the law. This is as pertinent today as ever, when legislators will stuff so-called pork into various bills designed for their own group of supporters, at the expense of the country as a whole. Similar practices have almost always existed, of course, but they become more extreme when the legislators feel obliged to sycophantically kowtow to every popular whim in order to hold on to their seats in Washington, DC.

But none of this does as yet amount to oikophobia. The nation continues quite unabashedly to soar with its wings, as in the Spanish-American War (1898) and Philippine-American War (1899–1902), in the former of which it has the moral satisfaction of giving a European power, even if a third-rate one, a jolly good thrashing. As already during the War of 1812 and the Mexican War, there are anti-war movements during these latter two conflicts as well, composed mainly of people who do not want the United States to become a colonial power like so many European countries. But these movements are not especially oikophobic, because they do generally believe in their country's greatness, only that they think that America's greatness should lie—at least as far as foreign policy is concerned—in her economic empire rather than in a territorial one. If anything, the anti-war faction during the Philippine-American War maintains, precisely, that the United States is better than Europe and therefore does not require territories overseas.

The string of American victories continues through World Wars I and II. In the former conflict the late US intervention is enough to tip the balance in favor of the Allies. By the time of the latter conflict, American industry has already grown to be the largest and most powerful in the world by far.

Socialism does not become a significant factor in the United States until the 1930s, later than in much of Europe. The Great Depression allows major overhauls and regulation of the American economy, such as through the Social Security Act (1935), among many other examples, which will weaken it in the long run. This initial crack in American rising power and seeming economic invincibility will for the moment not be able to stop that rise, whose momentum will push on for another several decades, but a politics of envy will slowly turn the subgroups of society more strongly against one another. As generally happens, the votes of the lower classes will be bought by the government in the form of various relief packages, and by this point I should hardly need to belabor the link between someone like Franklin D. Roosevelt, who initiates many of these reforms, and forbears like Pericles, Clodius, Carnot, and Asquith.

After World War II the United States reaches her peak of power and prosperity. This peak condition will lead to a far greater number of oikophobes than an earlier and in some ways simpler time can allow. It is no coincidence, of course, that religion will soon be drastically weakened, starting in the 1960s. It is the case—again, quite paradoxically—that the lack of confidence in one's own culture arises precisely from that culture's success. The more overwhelming progress is, the greater the perceived gulf will be between the vanguard of that progress and those who feel left out. Just as the Athenians and other Greeks believed in themselves at Marathon and Salamis, so the Americans believe in themselves at Yorktown and New Orleans. For a people to thoroughly believe in itself, it helps to be close to extinction, as the Greeks were during the Persian Wars, the Romans during the Second Punic War, and the Americans during the Revolution—points that come relatively early. Once success is overwhelming and extinction is no longer as palpable a threat, belief—cultural, patriotic, and religious—withers away. And so as the Athenians no longer believed in themselves during the conflict against Philip of Macedon, so too the Americans no longer believe in themselves during the wars of the last half century.

Although one might find some oikophobic traces in the generation of American writers who become expatriates in Paris and London in the 1920s, the first very clearly oikophobic wave is the Beat Generation of the 1950s. Many Beat writers do not merely seek alternative viewpoints within the American spectrum, as someone like Thoreau had done, but specifically seek out the Other, such as Buddhism—Jack Kerouac, Allen Ginsberg, and others immerse themselves in it—which has been a staple of many disaffected Western oikophobes ever since (which is not to say, of course, that a Western Buddhist is *eo ipso* an oikophobe). This development corresponds to the embrace of oriental mystery cults in the later stages of the Greek and Roman civilizations, and to the embrace of other Eastern religions, like Hinduism and Islam, by certain figures of the French Enlightenment. By seeing and appreciating the faraway, which seemingly requires a position on a higher summit, one may express one's disdain for those who stick to the old and the close-by down below. Two and a half millennia after Darius sent forces across the Hellespont that marched into Greece, where a group of yeomen met them at Marathon, the Orient remains a menacing allure, a place from which we can learn but that also threatens our way of life.

Ginsberg is perhaps the most famous beatnik. His poem *America* (1956) contains little multipurpose tidbits like: "Go fuck yourself with your atom bomb / . . . When will you take off your clothes? / When will you look at yourself through the grave? / When will you be worthy of your million Trotskyites?/ America why are your libraries full of tears? / . . . I'm sick of your insane demands," while his later poetry collection *The Fall of America* (1973, but written mostly in the 1960s) is as perfect a summary of an oikophobic mindset as can be found anywhere.[5] The Beat emphasis on spontaneity, drugs, and sexual liberation—regardless of the worth these may have for artistic creation—goes against almost everything that established American tradition represents (spontaneity being, perhaps, a partial exception).

The role diversity plays on this trajectory merits repetition. Today, diversity has become a professed goal of politicians and anyone claiming a certain cultural savoir faire. I myself, having emigrated as a teenager from frigidly homogenous Sweden to the gorgeous variety of New York City, know the beauty of diversity as well as anyone. But those who extol diversity as a goal in itself—unless they do it cynically just to hold on to their seats in Congress—might want to look again at history and mass psychology, because the evidence across civilizations that diversity in the long run weakens the social cohesion of a people is absolutely overwhelming.

To draw a parallel to the contrast established in our discussion of France, one reason why a Kansas farm boy will generally be less oikophobic than a Massachusetts college student, and more willing to sacrifice himself for the greater good, is that the college student lives in a more diverse environment, while the farm boy leads a life closer to that of the earlier stages of American civilization, when oikophobia did not exist. In the country, things change slowly, and while the fall of Rome was catastrophic for the urbanites it did not change things all that much for the simple farmers. In the city, however, where the college student lives, the necessity of self-reliance is replaced by a dependence on the Other.

Like other civilizations, the United States gains from contact with the Other, people who bring openness, creativity, and new ideas, while they at the same time take these away from the civilizations they leave behind. But over time, this diversity becomes at least as much a liability as an asset: whereas new ideas and innovations from abroad continue to be beneficial to society, this benefit is purchased at an ever-rising price, namely the society's cohesion and ability to stand as one in the face of various threats. Diverse interests, including previously marginalized and victimized groups, jostle with one another for attention. And as every interest group seeks its own influence and growth, the American version of the late-civilizational obsession with victimhood develops naturally out of those groups' increasing strength, as they seek a way of gaining special status and getting ahead. Just as it was in the interest of nineteenth-century British and French industrial workers to emphasize their suffering so as to draw the sympathy of the upper classes, victimized American groups gain by emphasizing their victimization. And so, ironically, the stronger and less victimized a previously victimized group becomes, the more it will insist on its own victimization.

One might think that America's acceptance of vast numbers of immigrants from Europe and Asia in the nineteenth and early twentieth centuries, as the country is still rising, contradicts the notion that civilizations focus more on victims in their declining days. But it is, first, not the case that there can be no concern for victims at all as a nation is still rising; we are, again, discussing tendencies, not absolute laws. Second, the acceptance of immigrants today, as the US is declining, does in fact have a more humanitarian—that is, victimhood-focused—motivation than it did in those earlier days, when considerations were often more economic. This can be seen, for example, in the fact that the US enacted the Chinese Exclusion Act in 1882, which lasted for over half a century; the Immigration Act of 1924 is another example. Laws of such scope and duration would be much more difficult today, precisely because of humanitarian- or victimhood-centered concerns (President Trump's executive immigration orders of 2017 are far more limited in scope, and the public and legal backlash against them is one that would not have occurred in earlier days to the same extent at all, as history plainly shows). Only with the Immigration and Nationality Act of 1965 does discrimination against Asians and some other groups that were considered too eastern or southern officially cease.

The conflict during which society's decreasing ability to stand as one becomes patently obvious is the Vietnam War (1955–75, but most American fighting during 1965–73). This is also the time at which American oikophobia develops into a mass phenomenon, whereas during the Beat Generation it had still been relatively confined to society's margins. The Vietnam War is to the Americans in many ways what the Boer War had been to the British: a conflict that by proving difficult and costly lays bare the distance between society's streams that have quietly been diverging for some time. All sorts of interest groups raise their colors in the general rift that occurs over the war, a rift that is a result not merely of the putative immorality or unjustifiable nature of the war (the Mexican War, for instance, a thinly disguised land grab, was clearly more imperialistic than the war in Vietnam), but also of the fact that victory is unexpectedly difficult and casualties high: it is usually when victory is elusive that the morality of the undertaking is questioned en masse. Black Americans rebel against discrimination, second-wave feminism begins to appear, and the gay subculture grows stronger. These developments can and should be understood in other contexts as well—the civil rights struggle that had begun a bit earlier, the sexual revolution in 1967, intellectual ideas spreading mainly from France, and so on—but they also occupy their logical place on the oikophobic trajectory of American civilization. That is to say, the rightness of one viewpoint does not in and of itself negate that of the other. What these movements have in common is that they all seek the overthrow of American tradition and consider their own civilization to be, in the main, an instrument of tyranny, both domestically and in the world at large.[6]

And so once again the seemingly paradox phenomenon rears its head that people begin to hate their home as a result of the grandeur that this home has attained. The war is lost not because the North Vietnamese and Vietcong antagonists are militarily stronger—they certainly are not—but because the United States has grown too diverse and finds it increasingly difficult to unify behind a challenging cause.[7] Whereas in 1812 the US lost many battles but still pushed on determinedly in order to achieve peace with honor, in Vietnam, inversely, the US wins almost all battles but nonetheless loses the war.

At this point, oikophobia reaches the highest powers in the country. The first oikophobic president of the United States is Jimmy Carter (1977–81), and the second is Barack Obama (2009–17), but one can see tendencies of the phenomenon in all presidents since Carter, with the probable exception of Ronald Reagan and the certain exception of Donald Trump. For instance, Carter often sides—albeit especially post-presidency—with violent groups abroad, such as Hamas, against Western civilization,[8] and Obama frequently questions American exceptionalism and emphasizes everything for which his country must supposedly atone. When superiority over the Other has been established, superiority must be expressed over neighboring groups at home, who become the new Other. It is thus often the snobs—those who feel that they are better than others—who are the most oikophobic, seen in Obama's statement that "I would like to think that with my election . . . you're starting to see some restoration of America's standing in the world."[9] Obama also says, infamously, that small-town Americans "get bitter, they cling to guns or religion or antipathy toward people who aren't like them or anti-immigrant sentiment . . . as a way to explain their frustrations."[10]

Like Diogenes's sneers and sarcasms about his fellow Greeks, or Voltaire's snarkiness about French tradition and religion, little virtue-signaling asides about American faults are de rigueur for those Americans wishing to communicate how cosmopolitan and superior they are. (Of course, none of this is to suggest that narcissism is limited to oikophobes, a fact of which Trump himself is a prime example!) One might raise an eyebrow about my statement that one can see traces of the cultural turn toward oikophobia even in more unabashedly patriotic presidents. One might wonder, for instance, whether I really mean to say that someone like George W. Bush, who invades two countries and wears cowboy boots, displays any oikophobic symptoms. Well, it is not that he himself is an oikophobe, but one sees how the civilization has changed. As a politician in a democracy, he is often obliged to say things that he does not really mean, but in line with the allophiliac stream of his contemporary culture, Bush for instance after the September 11, 2001, terrorist attacks praises Islam as a religion of peace.[11] He will have said such things so as not to alienate Arab allies, but this general sentiment would have been considered out of place at an earlier stage of American civilization, when political statements about Islam were often more unabashedly hostile.[12]

The state of America at the beginning of the second decade of the twenty-first century is such that oikophobia has had a debilitating effect on many aspects of society, on its culture, politics, and military. It is a nation so fixated by internal squabbles that it is no longer capable of effectively projecting outward force. That this would happen was predicted hundreds of years ago through the trajectories of previous civilizations—in fact, it was predicted thousands of years ago, before Europeans even knew of the American hemisphere. In book 8 of his *Republic*, Plato explains that the more freedom and equality is to be found in a society, the more its members will hold themselves above the state (this includes the passage 562d–563e cited toward the end of chapter 1 above). We do not need to agree with Plato's grumpy old fascism and protocommunism to understand, nonetheless, the wisdom of his description of societies' decline. Even those things we might generally consider good end up weakening our social cohesion. This is what I mean when I refer to the Greek, tragic view of life: it is possible to be ardently in favor of freedom and some forms of equality while at the same time deploring some of their long-term results.

And so we discover, through all our civilizations, that conservatism and progressivism are both needed, but in different doses at different times, though neither should ever extinguish the other. A progressive outlook is important for an early society that needs to adopt new ideas and absorb the strength of outsiders in an effort to get ahead, while conservatism is needed in late society for it not to lose its grounding and ability to stand up for itself. The perennial doom of Western societies is that early on, many people tend to be more conservative, and later on, many people tend to be more progressive, the exact opposite of what is needed. The whole discussion about who might win the "culture wars" between conservatives and progressives is consequently quite superfluous—to anyone who knows history, the final outcome was never in doubt.

The United States enjoys geographical isolation and will not be overrun by the Other any time soon. But the decline of American power will be accompanied by the rise of new power centers around the globe, of which however none in the short or medium term will gain that absolute supremacy previously occupied by the United States. China, Russia, both very dangerous countries, and perhaps India will be powers to be reckoned with in the future—powers far less benevolent than America has been.[13] Western Europe or the European Union will not grow into a significant power bloc, as it is much too fragmented for that. For all her faults, America has used her power in a more restrained way than any other great power in history. Some object that this is because we live in a different world today than, say, a few hundred years ago, when a country could simply plant its flag somewhere and destroy anyone who protested. But the answer to this objection is that it is precisely America that changed this state of affairs, after World War II, and invented the world order to which we have all grown accustomed and that we now take for granted.

I am writing these words having just sat down, at dusk, on a bench on the High Line Park in New York City. To the west is the Hudson River, with the cliffs and trees of New Jersey behind it, and to the east, right at my feet, I see a bustle of high-rises, commercial signs and graffiti paintings floating in the sky, and pedestrians navigating the streets between the yellow cabs crowding the avenues. I fly among stories and thoughts, through nature and artifice, and see all that was necessary to bring us to today. This place is but a dream for so many around the world, and as peoples through the ages flocked to Athens, to Rome, to Paris, and to London, so they also come here in pursuit of excellence. As Classical architecture from Greece and Rome took the world, so today our skyscrapers are imitated across the planet. If you ever wanted to know what it must have been like to stand, millennia ago, before the newly erected Parthenon in Athens, or before the completed Colosseum in Rome, then go to New York and look to the heavens. Though our civilization, too, shall fall, its future demise diminishes not in the slightest—on the contrary, it raises yet higher—the grandeur of these monuments to human industry, ingenuity, and creativity.

Chapter 9

CYCLICAL AND PROGRESSIVE THEORY

Now that we have finally traveled all the way up to the present, it should be clear that history in some respects moves in a cyclical fashion. Although philosophical considerations have been important all along, it is time, for the rest of this book, to delve more deeply into them. But lest one accuse me of, first, suggesting that history is all about oikophobia, or, second, trying to render the falsifiability of my claims impossible by conforming every event to them or leaving out those that do not let themselves be thus conformed, I must first make a few preliminary assertions. There are some who are most eager to display their learning to anyone who might lend them a reluctant ear, and who will point at any event or statement they can find that would seem to fall outside of the oikophobic trajectory as I have described it.

As to the first matter, I say that we are only looking here at one particular aspect of history, or only viewing history from one particular point of view, namely the development of oikophobia. Other aspects and other points of view may reveal a different pattern or follow a different trajectory, or reveal that there is in fact no discoverable pattern at all for those aspects. So I am not attempting in any way to establish a sort of "total history," as do the communists and Marx when they say that all history is the history of class struggle or of power structures. There is, thankfully, much more to history than that, and much more to it than the development of oikophobia, than the rise and fall of civilizations.

Even seemingly random events like natural disasters and pestilence can play a large part in bringing down civilizations—but this misleads some political philosophers, like Karl Popper, into believing that the rise and fall of civilizations can only be due to one type of cause, and not several. Such an attitude is typical of Popper's Manichaean thinking, by which he labels everything as open or closed, good or evil, light or darkness, democratic or tyrannical. He and others forget the much more complex, Greek view, which as I have said is tragic: the good and the bad mix in the very same object, depending on the context within which one views it. For example, in *The Open Society and Its Enemies*, Popper pooh-poohs the notion that intrinsic human nature has something to do with how history develops; the dynamism of peoples, or moral degeneration, or the cultural effect of success, is unrelated to civilizational trajectories, in his view.[1] Instead, he maintains, in for instance the Roman case, that mainly such factors as epidemics and exhaustion of the soil are to be considered. Similarly, he believes, it can often happen that the continued growth of empire forces the state to allocate too many resources to the military, with the result that investment in other sectors of the economy lags behind, causing in turn a shrinking economy and hence a reduced ability to meet continued challenges at the frontier. But Popper's view is too black-and-white to include the evident fact that none of these factors has to exclude cultural ones, and that they can all interact to produce civilizational decline.

The fact that my book is mainly about cultural and not biological or ecological developments does not mean that I consider the latter insignificant. And if, as Popper says, civilizations decline only because of such exogenous issues, then it is a curious coincidence that every civilization nonetheless does decline at some point—as if a cataclysmic epidemic or natural disaster must necessarily appear in every civilization. He also does not seem to have noticed that an example like exhaustion of the soil, or military overextension, is something that only happens once a people has grown and been sufficiently successful, and that therefore this, too, has its place on the natural civilizational trajectory, the claim of whose existence he dismisses as romantic and naïve. That is to say, Popper sets up an entirely false dichotomy.

While there are many causes behind civilizational decline, these are generally indicative of their times at large: as we saw in France, for example, Louis XV's more or less public marriage infidelities contributed to the monarchy's decline in popularity and facilitated—among a host of other factors—the French Revolution, but these public infidelities took place in a context where religion was growing weaker and the ruling class was being morally wasted by luxury, while previous kings, although they had also had dalliances, lived in an era of stronger religious awareness and thus had courtiers who made greater efforts at keeping their disgraceful behavior private. Popper emphasizes a pared-down "scientific" approach, as opposed to a psychological or moral one, but reaches just as questionable results in his description of history as do the people he criticizes. There is a rather self-righteous attitude in his work by which those with whom he disagrees are not just wrong but are dismissed as dangerous fools who wallow in prejudice. Popper is thereby able to dress his own views and prejudices in the slim robe of objectivity and science. (Funnily, he himself rightly warns against this at the end of chapter 31 of *The Poverty of Historicism*, but nonetheless slips into it.)[2] His is therefore a more deceptive prejudice than that of those who simply state based on empirical observation what they believe to be the case but without claiming to base their beliefs on the results of a scientific laboratory (see also chapter 11 below). Popper, as an Austrian member of the larger German-speaking world, is a product of his culture. While the French have always screamed their prejudices loudly from barricades, the Germans have calmly declared their prejudices to be science.

Indeed many people seem incapable of distinguishing among different fields of knowledge and consequently among different approaches. Not only are there many different causes behind decline, oikophobia being only one of these; the fact is also that one aspect may be declining while another is progressing. Technological or medicinal advancement may take place alongside cultural decline, for instance, and indeed often does. But too many want to be cheerleaders—they want everything to be either one way or the other. The recent and very popular work by Steven Pinker, *Enlightenment Now*, is paradigmatic for this absolutist way of thinking nowadays. He holds that life on a practical level has grown vastly better for the overwhelming majority of humanity.[3] But even if Pinker is right within his field—and he is—this says very little about the more cultural aspect of things.

Unfortunately, people are too busy placing themselves either in an optimistic or in a doomsday camp to notice that several things can be simultaneously possible. Pinker, like Popper, is in my view guilty of this type of partisanship, where his correct and persuasive observations in his field lead him to overextend and to dismiss different conclusions in other fields, such as philosophy.[4] It is clear from Pinker's language that he not only disagrees with what he calls "cultural pessimists," but also considers them quacks not worthy of serious consideration, often straw-manning them or attacking some of cultural pessimism's more foolish claims. But taking one's own conclusions to obtain across areas of knowledge ultimately betrays a lack of imagination.[5]

The fact that, for instance, Pinker dismisses religion as mere quackery and as clashing with reason means that he has not taken the trouble to properly understand what religion is; it is not mere belief in the supernatural, but a belief in something sacred (see my chapter 4)—and Pinker himself calls human life "sacred," which is a belief that is not necessarily wrong but has nothing to do with reason, either for or against.[6] Another good example of this lack of imagination is Pinker's perfunctory dismissal of the idea that "boredom" is a threat to the human species (p. 288: "Boredom, really?"), and he puts up a graph that shows that people think life is "exciting." But he does not understand what is meant by boredom in this context and he takes it too literally. To understand what it means, we must look in Francis Fukuyama's work *The End of History*, where it is written, "If men cannot struggle on behalf of a just cause because that just cause was victorious in an earlier generation, then they will struggle *against* the just cause. . . . They will struggle . . . out of a certain boredom: for they cannot imagine living in a world without struggle. And if the greater part of the world in which they live is characterized by peaceful and prosperous liberal democracy, then they will struggle *against* that peace and prosperity, and against democracy."[7]

This is exactly correct, and is in fact part of how oikophobia happens; and it is possible to experience this kind of boredom—or perhaps ennui—while still finding life "exciting" in a superficial sense. This lack of imagination means that Pinker is not equipped to understand more subtle, cultural issues: in his chapter 13, on terrorism, for instance, he is right that the number of deaths from terrorism is actually very low, and that one is far more likely to be killed by a host of other causes. But Pinker, by relying only on numbers, does not understand that a lot of the concern with terrorism, especially in Europe, is linked not only to large-scale attacks that make all the headlines, but also to much smaller and very incremental changes in society where people worry about the transformation of neighborhoods, safety on the streets, freedom to speak their minds, and so on, things that are not as easily measurable but that factor into people's attitudes toward terrorism. But as with religion, if something is not immediately measurable, or not as easily measurable, Pinker dismisses it as quackery; on page 403 he says that most of our claims are inherently quantitative, which is true, but in his overzealousness to have a graph as an answer to everything, he sometimes ends up quantifying the wrong thing, of which the "boredom" instance is a prime example.

So Pinker stands in the positivist tradition of Herder and J. S. Mill that we saw in chapter 7. Positivism in a general sense is fine as long as one understands to what area it can properly be applied, and I have a lot of respect for Pinker, but too often one will take a good idea and overextend it into areas where it does not belong, in this case the moral and cultural sphere.[8] And so I must emphasize that my analysis is of culture, and that inferences should not be drawn from this to technology, medicine, biology, ecology, and so on.

We should thus reject everything that seeks to reduce history or the human spirit to any one element. Often in the history of philosophy it has been the case, due to simple human nature, that when a particular thinker came upon some new idea, he was so overwhelmed with joy by his discovery that it came to dominate all his thinking. It often happens that those who have been granted a particular vision or gift have not also been granted the strength of mind and equilibrium of spirit to bear that vision properly. And so those philosophers too often descended into monomania, the obsession with one single thing, something that then tainted much of the rest of their work.

Philosophers have loved to claim that the human or social essence is one particular element, one aspect through which everything else can be explained, and of course that the particular thinker in question was, by fortuitous coincidence, the one to discover it. All these attempts, be they Hegel's spirit, Schopenhauer's will, Marx's means of production, Nietzsche's will to power, or Freud's sex drive, should be rejected—which is not to say that there is never any truth in these concepts, but simply that they must not be allowed to crowd out everything else. (Nietzsche is probably the one who comes closest to the truth, insofar as several other forces can be subsumed under the will to power.) This monomania is sometimes an expression of youth—Marx for instance tempers himself somewhat in his later work—but too often it seeks to explain everything, or most things, by reducing them to a single point. I call this macro-monomania.

This endeavor of reducing all phenomena to a core element is replicated on a smaller scale when a single phenomenon is reduced to a particular essence. This goes back in a way to Plato, who asked such questions as "What is the essence of justice?" or "What is the perfect state?" and thereby simplified and stultified by insisting that every phenomenon has a core "essence" or "idea" through which it is to be understood; this idealism of his has caused great havoc among intellectuals. It has a far greater claim to truth—and is intellectually more demanding—to approach objects and phenomena as bundles of characteristics, to use the language of David Hume in *A Treatise of Human Nature* 1.4.6, and to see how these characteristics, some of which may contradict or be in tension with others, speak toward the overall picture. To say that a phenomenon has a core essence through which alone it is to be understood, I call micro-monomania.

And so reducing all phenomena to one main element (macro-monomania), and reducing each phenomenon to one essence (micro-monomania), is harmful intellectually, because it simplifies for the sake of thinkers who want to comprehend everything, which is impossible, and it is also harmful practically, because such efforts tend toward totalitarianism, since if everything is one thing, then everything should conform to that one thing. Since the monomaniacal mindset makes it easier for people to slip into extremist ways of thinking, it must be one of the tasks of philosophy in the twenty-first century to confront modern monomaniacal manifestations. (We shall come across macro- and micro-monomania again.)

All this is why I insist that the history of oikophobia is not a total history by any measure. What I do maintain, however, is that when the rise and fall of cultured nations are studied, the appearance of oikophobia follows familiar and even unmistakable patterns. To reject for history the existence of strict Hegelian-Marxist laws set in stone does not entail, as Popper sometimes seems to feel, that we should deny the existence of these strong cultural tendencies we have witnessed.[9]

As regards the second accusation mentioned at the beginning of this chapter, that of falsifiability—that I try to conform everything to the oikophobic theory and therefore ignore those facts that might falsify it—I respond: since oikophobia is such a broad subject, with so many issues feeding into it, it is all too predictable that a series of professorial experts, with so much knowledge of the material within their own particular domain, will lash out at the larger patterns, clutching the whip of any little exception they can think of. But of course exceptions, as long as they are exceptions, do not invalidate tendencies.[10] I also agree, in a limited way, with Popper's rebellious student Paul Feyerabend's position in *Against Method*, that no interesting theory can conform to all relevant facts.[11] That book is not really as radical as its author likes to pretend, and the deliberately provocative and anti-scientific statement "anything goes," which appears repeatedly in it, is not actually what he means. In any case I find that his conclusions apply even more to the humane sciences, especially philosophy, than to the natural sciences, which is his main point of focus. Indeed Feyerabend himself would like to see it applied to philosophy.

In that light, the part of his work that I find congenial to my own purposes can be boiled down to the fact that Feyerabend actually desires more empiricism, not less. In chapter 3, for instance, he writes, "Empiricism . . . demands that the empirical content of whatever knowledge we possess be increased as much as possible. *Hence the invention of alternatives to the view at the centre of discussion constitutes an essential part of the empirical method.* Conversely the fact that the consistency condition"—that the theory be consistent with all known data—"eliminates alternatives now shows it to be in disagreement not only with scientific practice but with empiricism as well."[12]

That is to say that if every theory must conform to every available fact, then we will end up discarding even those theories that actually have a lot of truth in them, even if not the whole truth. The broader point here is that we desire a larger marketplace of ideas than can be had within the confines of those institutionalized methodologies that sometimes hinder the progress of genius, by which a good idea is rejected out of hand simply because at first glance it appears unorthodox or subjective. We must always be open to new possible approaches, and it is an exceedingly foolish academic prejudice that the subjectivity of the method must negate the objectivity of the result.

It is in fact reassuring to know that the trajectory of oikophobia is unable to explain everything, since one would rightly be suspicious if anyone came along who claimed to have all the answers: such a person is not a philosopher, but a wandering salesman. But my global outline of the historical march of oikophobia does explain much.

But here we encounter a problem. A positive thing about academic life is that it affords us the possibility of specialization. But this positive is at the same time also a negative, because the specialization of departments and the delimitation of knowledge mean that, when someone tries to understand an issue in an interdisciplinary, global way, it is in the very nature of academia to protest. Though I place this book within political philosophy and the philosophy of history, my analysis walks among many academic disciplines—philosophy, philology, history, sociology, political science. And when someone pays a visit to several departments, but then after a brief time leaves again in order to see the larger whole, it is almost inevitable that he will be accused of not being serious. An interdisciplinary approach will often, therefore, require a certain ruthlessness in tearing down, for at least a little while, the walls that keep neighboring areas apart. Members of the various departments will often resent encroachment on their turfs, since they spent so many years of hard labor to become initiates themselves.[13]

And this is the danger of specialization. To many a classical philologist, for instance, it is a mortal sin even to speak of "the Greeks," since, as they will be quick to point out, with raised index finger, the Greeks represented a multiplicity of views and ideas and could therefore never be subsumed under any one rubric. Words about a more general Greek temperament or attitude will so fully negate in their minds the years they spent in study on the glorious uniqueness and so very miniscule details of a textual fragment, that they will take as a personal affront the mere suggestion that there may have been any overall cultural tendency or larger picture with which we can associate the Greeks. But too strong an emphasis on these facts of intra-Greek diversity will obscure another fact, namely that there was a clearly discernible Greek mentality, at least before the Hellenistic era. But mental conditioning through specialization means that one will find an isolated exception to a sound generalization and then tout it too loudly, as if everything were about the exception, and nothing about the larger picture. An Aristotle, someone who frequently speaks of "the Greeks," would today be ridiculed in the universities, as would for instance a Montaigne, with his sweeping essays and comments on many facets of knowledge, not to mention a Renaissance man like Leibniz, who knew almost everything about everything. And the more things we speak about and the farther we broaden our field, the more we open ourselves up to attack from our peers, so we had better limit ourselves to the very small, to one single word in a medieval codex, about which our knowledge is so specialized, by dint of having such a small scope, that no one dare challenge us. In as broad-based a work as the present one, lots of people will find some particular area or pet peeve to be offended about. And so almost any interdisciplinary book will *eo ipso* be resisted, and any inductive inference will be met by a scandalized scream.[14]

But this book is, precisely, all about the bigger picture. If we observe a sufficiently large object, anything we say about it will inevitably be called into question, which will intimidate us into sacrificing our empiricism and not saying anything about it at all. That is to say, if I were not willing to propose a new theory even while knowing perfectly well that not every single little thing conforms to it, I would never have been able to add to our store of empirical knowledge, to propose new observations—with the lamentable consequence that our empirical view of the rise and fall of civilizations, of history itself, would have ossified. If we were concerned with all available data and had a politically correct fear of generalizations, we would remain mute, and the spirit of discovery, beyond the micrologically minute, would evaporate.

As I have endeavored to show, only when we are willing to stand back and take all the world, lovingly, in our arms—only then can we become visionaries. Only when we are willing, energized, and strong enough to hold in our spirits at the very same time such disparate things as twenty-first-century social media, American pioneers riding across the plain, British frigates cutting the wine-purple waves, French Enlightenment writing, Bach before his score, medieval Christendom, Hellenistic sculpture, the defeat of the Romans at Cannae, the soft whisper of poets in a Greek olive grove, and the erection of the Parthenon—only then do we suddenly see emerge, out of a burning mass of red light, the grand patterns whose magnificence is such that nothing less than the beauty of this whole world can account for it. Spanish explorers bending back the bushes and, dumbfounded, spotting the Pacific spread out in a newfound endlessness, Proust strolling through the Tuileries gardens mulling over the latest rejection of his novel, a Zulu warrior on a promontory seeing the redcoat cavalry and knowing he is finished, slaves dragging enormous stone blocks across the sand and dying in droves on the desert dunes, a young singer standing before the Metropolitan Opera and picturing herself on its stage, a missionary Jesuit in the jungle building himself a hut of sticks and stones, and workers climbing up the scaffolding that reaches for heaven itself—they all happen together, and the separation between them is an illusion.

And so after these answers to the two accusations, let us get to the crux of the matter in this chapter. The cyclical pattern excludes any eschatological or teleological notion of history. Teleology is the study of an end or ultimate purpose; eschatology, similarly, is the belief in a final end of things, the utmost time. In religion, eschatology is some form of judgment day or the arrival of the messiah; in history, it is the belief that history will one day come to an end, that human affairs will reach a final state of being from which little will subsequently change—and in chapter 7 I mentioned that this latter view is also, at its core, religious. Such notions have been harbored many times, and have been proven wrong just as many times. Whenever there has been a belief in a historical end among thinkers, that end has had a remarkable propensity for falling—by pure and happy coincidence, naturally—within the lifetime of the thinker in question, be it Hegel, Marx, Fukuyama, or any of the other divinely kissed end-of-times preachers.

The belief in eschatology is totalitarian. Anyone who thinks that there will be an end of history—be that ending the consummation of protestant Prussia in a glorious summit of free Germanic Christendom (Hegel), class struggle and historical materialism leading to communist control of the modes of production (Marx), liberal democracy and its comfortably bourgeois pluralism overcoming political frontiers (Fukuyama)—is in some ways totalitarian, because the end suggests an end to striving and to change and, most importantly, to dissent.[15] In fairness, we have just seen that Fukuyama expresses serious skepticism regarding the end of history and warns against a breakdown of the liberal order. But in spite of that skepticism, Fukuyama does not appear to see that it is not only possible on a practical level that the liberal order will collapse, but that this collapse is in fact ingrained in the very constellation of liberalism and its intellectual openness, as the oikophobic trajectory illustrates.[16]

The temptation of positing an end or goal of history and of human affairs is strong, because it is oftentimes an intellectual expression of either laziness or narcissism. In the first instance, laziness, it is the equivalent of lying down in bed after a long working day and saying: it is finished, we are done. It is an inability to live with the negative and to support the uncertain, the inability to bear the thought that there will never be salvation, and that people's cares and tragedies will always occur and recur. If one does have the ability to bear that thought and to live with negativity, to look at the world and see eternal suffering without outcome, then one will have a clearer, more accepting, and also a more creative view of things, tantamount to what John Keats called "negative capability."[17]

In the second instance, that of narcissism, the thinkers in question always seem to believe that they are the privileged ones who are to experience the end of history. Just as dictators, revolutionaries, and college students want to be able to say that they experienced the radical moment in history when everything changed, which makes them mindlessly want to take up arms against just about anything at all, as long as it is a proper revolution or a first-rate cataclysm, so too philosophical totalitarians want to be the embodiment of the end of history and preside over its quiet but magnificent conclusion. In the former case: *Après moi, le déluge*; in the latter case: *Après moi, rien d'important*. The former sentence is reportedly from Louis XV of France, inspired by Madame de Pompadour, although they presumably said it in a different context.[18] In the jussive mood ("After me, let the deluge come"), it summarizes the vain mindset of one who considers himself so important that it does not matter what happens after he is gone. Even if the sentence is to be understood in the indicative mood ("After me will be the deluge"), there is still a palpable self-satisfaction on the part of the speaker in placing himself as the bulwark between order and chaos. My own sentence *Après moi, rien d'important* ("After me, nothing of importance"), inspired by the first, is its opposite only on the surface, but illustrates a similarly vain mindset: everything that is important was accomplished or completed with me. Both thoughts place the thinker at the apex of a long development, and they are both to be rejected, as they have nothing to do with evidence.

On the other hand, this rejection of Hegelian-Marxist eschatology leads someone like Popper, in *The Poverty of Historicism*, to the other extreme, that of disregarding completely the predictions of history, of dismissing even the very philosophy of history as a whole, because he fears that it is the totalitarians who will be doing the predicting and the sociohistorical philosophizing. Perhaps because of the time in which he lived—World War II and its aftermath—Popper appears to think that the recognition of historical forces renders utopian social planning, such as by Nazis and communists, inevitable. But his objection should only be leveled at false prediction, and prediction for totalitarian or social engineering purposes, not against prediction in and of itself. That is to say, it is predictors who should be criticized, not prediction.

Nietzsche, as opposed to Marx, his older contemporary, was not a totalitarian, but was far more correct than Marx (albeit a low threshold) about what would happen in the twentieth century.[19] Another anti-totalitarian, many of whose predictions have come true, is Samuel Huntington (in his book *The Clash of Civilizations*; see chapter 8 above), who reacted precisely against his eschatologically inclined end-of-history student Fukuyama. And so prediction of the future is by no means necessarily linked to totalitarianism. From Popper's correct rejection of totalitarianism and utopian planning it does therefore not follow, as he thinks, that the future is a blank slate. Popper rightly views the totalitarians as the enemies of the open society, but forgets in the process that the open society is also its own enemy, as the historical development of oikophobia amply demonstrates, and that we therefore must view history cyclically in this regard—and indeed the description of history as partly cyclical necessarily involves prediction. It is Popper's ignorance of this state of affairs that allows him to view everything in such black-and-white terms.

At this point, some would put forward another but similar critique against me: They would say that my words here boil down to an embrace of that speculative philosophy of history that, through a dialectical process, attempts to reach for more than it can grasp and believes it can understand historical developments even though these involve a myriad of factors, far too numerous for any individual human mind to comprehend. The philosophy of history in general has been dismissed by many thinkers who are still reeling from the murderous calamities of the twentieth century—I always congratulate myself whenever I remember that I was born in history's most genocidal century—when hundreds of millions died in Europe, Russia, China, and elsewhere due to dictators who thought they had understood history. And these catastrophes made scholars more prone to succumb to postmodernism, which includes a rejection of all "grand narratives" of history as false and as based purely on power and coercion. Such scholars think that we cannot approach history in any holistic way, and that any attempt to do so is merely the proclamation of one truth or one narrative at the expense of others. But to dismiss the philosophy of history entirely would be—to use an expression I usually hate—to throw out the baby with the bathwater. Hegel, the dialectical thinker par excellence, and *par nausée*, and practically the founder of a dialectical philosophy of history, did his in some cases quite insightful conjectures a disservice by fusing his description of certain historical processes with an unhealthy dose of eschatological pathos: he thought that history had a goal. This serious mistake of his—which was taken up from another angle by Marx—has made it easier for philosophers to discredit the philosophy of history as a whole.

But we must remember that we are not looking here at any Hegelian "spirit" or divine law of history, only at plain flesh-and-blood human beings and their behavior. That is to say, a philosophy of history is very useful if we construct for it a proper—and more modest—framework. Such a philosophy may be achieved once we discard the progressive view that history is moving toward a goal. That notion is megalomaniacal and narcissistic, since the goal—whose exact nature people dictate according to their own personal whims—must require, qua goal, that everything conforms to it, or nearly so.

One of the very first teleologies of history was offered by Augustine in *The City of God* (early fifth century), according to which history is divided into epochs that work themselves toward a goal of ultimate pristine blessing. Augustine's Christian work, and even Thomas More's *Utopia*, make it easier to see that all later teleological-eschatological-progressivist descriptions of history lie in the shadow of the cross. In their stead I posit cycles and tendencies, the somber acknowledgment that history repeats itself, and I maintain that much of this is driven by human nature and mass psychology. In this sense, the first philosopher of history was not Hegel by any stretch, or even Augustine, but rather Thucydides. In his work we find the genuinely non-Christian view, according to which the confusion and incorrigibility of human nature and its passions exclude a lazy and narcissistic teleology. Since human nature is a constant across ages and civilizations, it stands to reason that human beings—not every individual, to be sure, but certainly the large mass—will react similarly to similar stimuli.

So while rejecting historical ends or goals, we preserve historical tendencies, forces, and cycles, whose existence is palpable across civilizations. There is, for example, some truth to Marxist economic determinism as a historical force—the notion that economics dictate ideals and morals (see Engels's preface to the English edition of *The Communist Manifesto*). But Marx drew all the wrong conclusions from it; in the first-edition preface to *Capital*, he even speaks of "natural laws" and then of "iron necessity"—though also using the word "tendencies" in the very same sentence—which means that he took his own idea to an extreme.[20] We temper this extremism by recognizing merely forces, trends, and cycles, and thereby arrive at a sort of anti-utopianism, which is a very healthy outcome, since it is always the utopians, whether communist, fascist, Nazi, religious, or secularist, who have caused the most harm in the world. If a utopia can be established—in spite of the literal meaning of the word, which is "nowhere"—then history ends. And those who want history to end have almost always been the madmen, because of course the end of history should be on their own particular terms.

Alexander the Great was the very first such madman with any real power. He was a dictator who—in foreboding the very worst totalitarians of the twentieth century—proclaimed through his actions that his massacring of literally millions of innocent human beings was necessary to establish an eternal brotherhood of man, between East and West, under one ruler (by fortuitous coincidence himself). Alexander's famous "Oath at Opis," although most modernizing translations of it should not be trusted and it is probably spurious anyway, is very typical of the attitude. At a banquet late in his career, for both his European and Asian officers, Alexander claims personal moral superiority by attempting to rise above conflicts and proclaiming the brotherhood of all, while de facto denying that brotherhood by wanting to crush anyone who disagrees. Whenever we view history teleologically, tyranny inevitably follows—again, regardless of whether it is religious, social, or economic teleology. It is not the cynical and the pessimists who kill en masse; it is always the idealists (in the common, nonphilosophical sense). Political and especially Marxist teleologists often poke fun at religious eschatologists—Christian evangelists, mainly—without realizing that they themselves are implicated in the same kind of error, which, again, is why I call all of them eschatologists.

Cyclical movements, on the other hand, are not teleological—and certainly not eschatological—because a *telos* is a "goal" or a "purpose." The mere fact that something follows from something else, as for example in a cycle, does not in and of itself imply purposes or goals; while such movements are always caused, they do not happen "for a reason," that is, they involve causality but not final causality.[21] Aristotle might have quibbled with me here, by stating that things, not just man-made objects but also natural phenomena, have some intrinsic purpose (*Physics* 198b–199a, and elsewhere). But whereas it is true that we evolved molars so as to be able to chew food—one of Aristotle's own examples—when applied to history this view of teleology, which is more Hegelian and Marxist than Aristotelian, suggests an inherent normativity that is foreign to my view of history, which is why I reject the teleological label for the cyclical movement I am describing.[22]

But although much of history moves cyclically, if one looks at history from the beginning one sees that there is also a certain forward movement overall, and in this sense people like Fukuyama make a good point. That is to say, history moves in something resembling a helical pattern: like a spiral, history moves in circles but with each circle pushing ahead of the previous one. (This bears some resemblance to the dialectical movement that permeates Hegel's philosophy—best described in the *Science of Logic*, and more concretely applied to history in the *Lectures on the Philosophy of History*—although the similarity is fairly superficial.) For example, the democratization of Western society is helical. Political power becomes more broadly diffused as society progresses, but with each civilization the end point is generally somewhat farther ahead than that of the previous civilization. The Greeks became more democratic during their history, and so have we, but our democracy is more democratic, at least in an egalitarian sense, than was theirs. So we recognize a similar democratizing phenomenon recurring in different civilizations through history, but with the phenomenon going one step further with each new manifestation. Like Bach's counterpoint, history moves back and forth, but in a particular direction, but, unlike Bach's counterpoint, it will not reach an orgasmically magnificent conclusion, but, rather, will never exit the confines of its own repetition. So Hegel is right insofar as the dialectic is true, but wrong insofar as it will ultimately not lead to any point that we can clearly define, but will only come to an end with, one day, the annihilation of our species.

Religion is another instance of helical social change. We saw briefly in the last chapter in the context of the Great Awakening that the direction of religious development "bends toward decline." Societies become less religious as they advance, but the irreligiosity of each new society is more extreme than was that of earlier ones. The development of women's liberation, yet another example of both cyclical and helical movement, tends to go hand in hand with religious decline, not very surprisingly. It is cyclical because in each civilization, women are generally freer in its declining days than they are during the rise.[23] This is true for every civilization we have looked at in this book, and it goes back to my previous remark (chapter 3) that masculinity dominates civilizations' beginnings, and femininity their ends. The helical pattern, on the other hand, is that if we look at all of the West as one block from Homer to the present, then across all those smaller cycles the overall development of women's lot has tended toward liberation.

Again, this is not to suggest that within each cycle, or from one civilization to the next, these developments occur in a straight line. Often they do not. Democratization, to take an obvious example, develops in fits and starts, and through smaller ups and downs. Britain after the Glorious Revolution of 1688 became more democratic, but over time, as the powers of the House of Commons had increased, but without electoral reform to reflect shifting demographic patterns in the boroughs, corruption became rampant and political favors bought and sold among the London elite, so that by the mid-1700s Parliament was less representative of the will of the people than it had been at the turn of the century. Significant attempts at reform did not begin until the 1780s, stimulated in part by political anger at the government's loss of the American colonies, but did not gain passage until 1832, with the Representation of the People Act, after which the democratizing trajectory could continue apace.

Another interesting issue to consider is how the progress of technology and knowledge influences the oikophobic trajectory. Advances in technology tend to produce more mobility, which in turn increases cultural uprootedness and thus contributes to oikophobia. The diffusion of knowledge that technological advances often allow turns everyone into a self-appointed expert, and thus less likely to heed the authority of his own traditions. True expertise is still a matter for the very few, something that is gained only through a lifetime of study, but the illusion of expertise is one to which, through technology, ever more people will succumb. Through wealth and access to areas that were previously the domain of elites, fragmentation and individualization in advanced societies become more extreme. And the various manifestations of this process differ only in the physical details, not in kind: the uprootedness caused by technological advances has been a fact of human civilization since prehistory and most certainly since antiquity—witness, for example, Athenian naval advances opening up the whole eastern Mediterranean for that city and strengthening its democratic faction through export and import of goods and ideas.

When the printing press in Europe made possible mass production of the Bible, which could be read in Luther's translation, it increased by enormous strides people's ability to make themselves heard and to argue with nobility and even clergy about the latter's area of expertise. The Catholic humanist Johannes Cochlaeus, in his annalistic *Commentary on the Acts and Writings of Martin Luther* (1549), describes, for the year 1522, how simple laymen would stop professional theologians to argue with them about the meaning of specific biblical passages. And so more opinions were added to a growing mass of diverging views, thereby accelerating civilizational fragmentation. Similarly, the Internet has increased people's access to sources of information, and even just a brief perusal of contemporary social media, especially Facebook and Twitter, reveals right away what already Cochlaeus had complained about, namely that ignoramuses will inveigh, with the most touching earnestness, on topics of which they have, truly, not the slightest inkling. Since access to information easily offers the illusion of expertise, we end up in a state in which the masses think that they are not part of the masses and explicitly make fun of the masses. And here we see again, *pace* Pinker, that one aspect of society can advance while another retreats, even that the progress of one aspect can be intimately connected to the regress of another.

This diffusion of knowledge will lead slowly to the arrogance of the oikophobe, because theory itself can be a great motor for vanity: Because they view themselves in the mirror, because they study or at least can access knowledge easily, the theorists place themselves above those who simply exist in a more "instinctive" way. This higher self-placement we have seen in a number of historical individuals. It eventually grows so common and taken for granted that it is ultimately the theoretic attitude that becomes the less self-reflective one. As the middle class increases its numbers in a civilization's mature days, knowledge democratizes and theory grows popular. The illusion of reflection and profound thought spreads to all and sundry. With ubiquitous education and at least a smattering of theory for almost everyone, ever larger swathes of society will fall victim to the higher self-placement that tends to go hand in hand with oikophobia. We would therefore do well to turn the in some sense laudable Horatian dictum that Kant quotes in his essay *What Is Enlightenment?* (1784), namely *sapere aude*, "dare to know," which leads to a cohort of busybodies believing that they can steer their societies teleologically by means of superficial knowledge, into an equally laudable *nescire aude*, "dare not to know," dare to admit ignorance, dare to be open to doubt and to take yourself somewhat less seriously.[24]

So the belief of the simpleton in his ability to compete with experts has been a repetitive fact of human societies. But since the pace of technological innovation and concomitant diffusion of knowledge is usually exponential, these democratizing processes take place ever more rapidly. This means that, with every passing cycle, we end up much farther ahead than at the end of the previous one, whence the helical movement, again, establishes itself. And since democratization will be farther ahead each time, it stands to reason that oikophobia, too, will be farther ahead each time. So while oikophobia is repetitive, it may be said to be more intense today than in previous eras, because democratization is also more extreme. This causes the illusion that oikophobia is a modern phenomenon, whereas it is in fact, in its contemporary manifestation, only a more extreme expression of an already ancient and ever-recurring phenomenon. Oikophobes in Greece were a relatively small class of educated elites, and the same can be said for Rome. In France, it was a somewhat broader class of people infused with Enlightenment ideals, and in Britain it seeped into parts of the lower classes, until, in many circles in America and the contemporary macro-West, it has become the sine qua non of discussion and debate. Oikophobia in history, thus, also moves in a helical fashion. All this will help us understand why we are where we are today.

In his introduction to Popper's *The Open Society and Its Enemies*, the Czech author, dissident, and politician Václav Havel asks why it is so difficult for an open society to prevail against wave after wave of tribalism. One answer that has emerged during our journey is that the long-term survival of a society requires a certain tribe-like cohesion. The open society, by replacing the tribe with reason, by substituting the blood feud with law courts—as does Aeschylus in his *Oresteia* (458 BC), the story of how a blood feud is finally resolved through arbitration and of how society thereby overcomes tribalism and becomes civil—already sows the seeds of its own destruction. Overcoming the tribal state represents civilizational progress and leads to a temporary strengthening of the culture. But it also leads to the loss of the unity that the blood of the clan offers, and thus contributes, in the long term, to the fragmentation of the culture and society's fall to the onslaught of the next tribe.

Nomadic and other early-stage peoples tend to be obsessed with genealogy, which reinforces tribalism, one of nomadism's distinct features. The subsequent invention of politics and the establishment of a state based on rationally thought-out institutions mean that the genealogical sense of union in a civilization's early stages becomes increasingly fragmented, since in an ever growing and ever stronger state a greater number of diverging attitudes develop than is possible in a smaller community where familial relationships, which often extend through the whole group, outweigh individual agendas. And so there is in turn a forward fall into a new tribalism of sorts, because people become more "tribal" in defending their particular interest group and in viewing other domestic groups as their enemies. The dependence on family is also reduced by growing wealth, and so wealth further increases the potential for oikophobia, since the family is the nucleus of the state and of civilizational loyalty.[25] So no system of government—not even democracy—is stable, because all systems are composed of human beings, who by their very nature are unstable. Even free discussion and civic openness will not be able to prevent the rise of factionalism, sectarianism, and tribalism—on the contrary, the former will often hasten the latter along.

One may thus speak of a return to tribalism in the declining stages of a civilization, just as the early advancement of the civilization had been the overcoming of tribalism. The early tribalism is "holistic," as it were, in that it gathers all of society under its umbrella, while the late tribalism is "fragmented," several tribelets existing within the overall civilization. But both these states of affairs constitute forms of tribalism. Recognizing this conundrum and acknowledging that there is no permanent solution to it—no eschatological exit of relief—is key to understanding the cyclical aspects of history, and to rejecting the eschatology of the madmen, who just want everything to end. We recognize that history constitutes a development, but without being teleological. We keep what is sensible with the Hegelian dialectic: an unfolding process, the constraints of actions within historical parameters, and self-interest rather than altruism as a driving force, but discard the foolish bits: the goal, end, or purpose, history as its own judge (that is, whatever happens is "right"), fascistic state worship, moral positivism, and the belief in inexorable laws of progress rather than just tendencies or forces. These latter bits are not just foolish, but also, as I have said, totalitarian, because they suggest that everything must conform to a certain development.

And so whenever one hears politicians say that so-and-so are on "the wrong side of history," as if history had its own right and wrong and as if things absolutely must go in a particular direction, they are actually putting forward a highly totalitarian and absolutist Hegelian-Marxist language of history. This sinister notion tries to coerce others into acting and even thinking according to prescribed norms, with the threat that the ultimate goal of history will be against them. This is on the same intellectual and moral level as the apocalyptic threats of fanatical preachers that the unrepentant shall suffer eternal damnation. The fact that our politicians are on the whole uneducated and probably unaware of the pedigree of their statement is not an excuse. It is their civic and professional duty to understand what they say.

To conclude this chapter I should like to answer a question that is often heard from various quarters: Why is it mainly the elite of a society that is the most oikophobic, that holds the most denigrating view of their own people, why are intellectuals the ones most prone to cultural self-hatred or treason? Little tentative bits of reply appear every now and then, but people seem to have a difficult time finding very concrete answers to this important question. A philosophy of history as outlined here allows us to find quite precise answers, which hold true across civilizations, both ancient and modern, and indeed most of these answers are offered or at least hinted at throughout the present text. I think it would be useful to summarize them all together. And so here is a list of ten interrelated answers:

1. In later times when there is enough wealth for an elite leisure class, and when the man of action and the man of thought have become distinct, the latter no longer needs to act for his state and therefore forgets what he owes to it. The common people, who must act, remain loyal. (See chapters 1 and 5 on wealth; chapter 1 on pacifism; note 25 of this chapter.)

2. Intellectuals are aware that they are more intelligent and educated— which of course is different from being wise or having common sense— than others, and therefore consider it a part of their raison d'être to criticize. Indeed the very spirit of intellect and of the scientific method is critique, and it is both natural and desirable for the discovering mind to challenge older ways of thinking. Intellectualism thus breeds disrespect for the laws, also because, sometimes, the elite are better able, by dint of their resources, to avoid the unpleasant consequences of certain laws. (See the Thucydides and Hobbes quotes in chapter 1; Thucydides 1.84, 3.37, and 3.40, cited in chapter 5.)

3. Human beings being what they are, personal vanity must be fed in one way or the other, and as the civilization's enemies have been defeated, superiority must be expressed over neighboring groups at home. Since intellectuals by dint of their education tend to be snobbish, oikophobia offers them the easiest outlet for their need for superiority. (Related are my remarks in this chapter on knowledge causing a higher self-placement.) It helps that the elite have more access to foreign fashions and ideas than do the common people, and so the elite abandon old traditions and use the foreign as a mark of personal distinction and exoticism. (See chapter 1.)

4. Oikophobia, by often being wound up with relativism, feeds the vanity of intellectuals, because by recognizing all kinds of truths— even mutually exclusive ones—people feel intellectual, magnanimous,

and broad-minded. (See chapter 2 and the next chapter, on the intellectual temptation of relativism.)

5. By living in a place where new trends first appear, the urban intellectual is the first to encounter novel concepts coming from afar, and so within him begins to build a sense of responsibility for transmitting these concepts to his civilization at large, and for educating the public, and this makes him more subversive. Since the elite may think of themselves as the repositories of the world's knowledge, the borders between various bodies of knowledge and their accompanying civilizations become blurrier to them than to those with less education, who only know about the home civilization. (See chapters 5 and 8 on the Paris literatus and Massachusetts college student.) Intellectuals and the wealthy also tend to be jet-setting people attending conferences all around the world, and so what they owe to a particular civilization begins to disappear in their minds; large-scale scientific advance is collaborative, and it should not matter, for the sake of that advance, where fellow scientists and intellectuals come from. The philosopher and astronomer Anaxagoras was once asked why he was not concerned with matters in his fatherland, to which he replied that in fact he cared greatly about his fatherland, and pointed to the sky; in a similar vein, the Cyrenian philosopher Theodorus, who was also an atheist or at least a freethinker, said that the world is his fatherland (Diogenes Laertius 2.7 and 2.99, respectively).

6. Intellectuals tend to live in cities, that is, in a more diverse environment, while farmers lead lives that are closer to that of earlier stages of civilizations. The farmer, by sowing his own food and then eating what he has grown, sees more directly the relationship between labor and reward. The urbanite, on the other hand, living in a specialized and diverse environment, eats what others have grown and is less thankful to the land he treads. (Again, chapters 5 and 8.)

7. In cities there is much more contact with other people than in the countryside, and the more one rubs shoulders with others, the more acerbic and jaded one's worldview tends to become. (This point has not been previously suggested in this book.)

8. It is the better off who have time to ponder their societies' injustices, while those of the lower social strata are too busy scraping by a living. (See chapter 5 on the timing of the French Revolution, etc.)

9. High and ever-increasing levels of education have a tendency to lead to ever more extreme degrees of outlandishness, where the education comes almost imperceptibly to shield the educated person from common sense, also because the higher degrees of education are accompanied by a competitive need for innovation vis-à-vis one's peers, a need that fuels ever more ridiculous positions. Peer pressure within the elite, as well as the desire for advancement, further spread oikophobia to those members of the elite who might otherwise have resisted it (as also Orwell implies; see chapter 6). In chapter 4 of *Leviathan*, Hobbes writes, "Natural sense and imagination are not subject to absurdity. Nature itself cannot err; and as men abound in copiousness of language, so they become more wise, or more mad, than ordinary. Nor is it possible without letters for any man to become either excellently wise, or, unless his memory be hurt by disease or ill constitution of organs, excellently foolish." (This is also a largely new point in the present work.)

10. Because of their education, intellectuals know more about their own culture's vices and crimes, and are able to lecture their fellow citizens about everything the civilization has done wrong, which feeds into their vanity, and they can thereby elevate themselves—which everyone tries to do one way or the other—by specifically denigrating the rest of their civilization. (See to some extent chapter 3 on Tacitus; this chapter, again, on theory and higher self-placement.)[26]

Chapter 10

OIKOPHOBIA IN THE UNITED STATES

The Present

A motley group of about a dozen volunteers from the United States were sitting outside a hostel. They had gathered their plastic chairs in the shade of a few trees in the courtyard, away from the scorching African sun. The program director, from New York City, had begun her speech about the importance of understanding foreign cultures and ideas.

"So when I was a volunteer," she explained, "having just come here from New York—this was shortly after 9/11—I met a lot of people in the village where I was working who were happy because of what Al Qaeda had done to America. Of course I was outraged."

The volunteers—many of them college-age, but some a bit older, and some a lot older—paid dutiful attention.

"But then," she continued, "I listened to my students, and they told me about how America was cruel and bombing everyone, and that Bin Laden's attack was an understandable reaction to that. And you know what? I listened to the students, and I realized they had a point. And I thanked them for having taught me something."

The volunteers—except for two, who exchanged disgruntled glances—nodded their heads concurringly.[1]

Occurrences like this take place all the time, and are indicative of how we have let foreign cultures crowd out our own, which is a shame, since it should be possible to keep loving one's own heritage while at the same time expressing interest in and learning from the Other. But many people are incapable of handling that balance, and the more oikophobic we become and the more we embrace the idea of diversity, the farther we are removed from the sources and thereby the understanding of our own culture. This is why many Americans today have only a very superficial understanding of what culture really entails.

As we saw briefly at the end of chapter 7, people tend to believe that culture is mainly a matter of such external details as whether to eat with a fork and knife or with chopsticks, or of consuming matzah ball soup on Passover or gingerbread snaps on Christmas. Americans think they are being cultural in saying "*Mazel tov*" instead of "Congratulations" when they know the addressee is Jewish, or in saying "Happy New Year" to the waiter in a Chinese restaurant in February. As a result of not only contact but of saturated mixing with the Other—with detached clumps floating around—that is, of cultural bastardization, we no longer understand what culture entails. If, however, we undertook the study of Greek and Latin, of English literature and thought, Western tonality, and much else, a study rendered easier by and in turn fostering a gratitude for our own civilization, then we would better understand how profound the idea of culture actually is. If we helped the young along the path to the beauty of Western art, to see its expression and evolution, to understand art as the most loving act in which humans can engage, to study the contrapposto, chiaroscuro, the metopes and skyscrapers, to engage with Western beauty and to cherish its ideals—for all these innovations, and many others, arose from a tradition of dissent, open debate, and the free exchange of ideas—then they would better comprehend that free speech, the equality of women with men, the ballot box, the Latin alphabet, the separation of church and state, and the sonorous synchrony of strings and woodwinds, are all unique expressions of our Western culture, and that this culture is consequently worth defending.

But since we do not, one often hears oikophobic Westerners refer with disdain to "Western values" or to those who say they treasure "Western values"—but in fact those disdainful people themselves adore Western values; they just don't know it. That is to say, they do not know that they are Western. Once during my professorial days I told the classroom that the concept of human rights is Western, and let the shock sink in among the oikophobic youngsters before me. One of my students, who had lived several years in Japan, protested that they have human rights in Japan also, to which I had to reply that this is because of American military occupation after World War II and concomitant Westernization, and I had to explain that wherever a respect for what we call human rights is found outside of the West, it is mainly because of Western influence.[2]

Since we do not understand these things, we are often surprised at the extent to which many peoples around the world—those who live at more primitive stages of development and are therefore closer to their own core cultures—are willing to fight, and die, for what they believe. We do not understand the sort of hatred and cultural identity that drive a conflict over millennia, and we believe that it is just a question of practical issues that can be practically solved, and we therefore become unwilling to stand up for our ideas. It is to the people who are still willing to do so that we shall in due time succumb in our irrelevance. (To recall chapter 2: "It is ultimately the truths of those who refuse to give up that will crush the truths of those who side with relativism.") I recall that shortly after the Islamic terrorist attack on the offices of *Charlie Hebdo* magazine in Paris in January 2015, a French Reform rabbi—and Reform Judaism is the epitome of cultural bastardization—said in an interview that her country's greatest strength is diversity. This modern prejudice has, overwhelmingly, the evidence of history against it, and this is why we may properly refer to it as a "prejudice," because it exists as a general feeling without any regard for facts.

Now, with the diachronic expositions mostly behind us, we should look a bit at the present. We have witnessed oikophobia in the forms of relativism and positivism. A little more should be said on how these branches intertwine in our culture today, and how they express themselves oikophobically.

Much of this focuses on the epistemological question: What is truth? In chapters 1 and 2 we saw the rise of relativism, or protorelativism, in antiquity. We met some of Socrates's students in this regard, and to that list may be added for example Seneca in Rome, as discussed in chapter 3, and perhaps, early on, Protagoras in Greece. The relativism that inspired the most modern variety began already in late-nineteenth-century Germany, with Nietzsche's emphasis on "perspectivism" in much of his work—that the truth depends on a person's point of view—and with the growing importance in sociological circles of mere "values" as opposed to moral truths; Max Weber was important in this last regard, although he is complex enough that I would apply the label "relativist" to him only with considerable caution. The word "value" smacks of relativism because a value is generally something that is assigned ad hoc, suggesting an appraisal. A value is thus intrinsically bound up with the subject that holds that particular value. The word has entered common parlance in this context, and since the early twentieth century we speak of "values" when we refer to such things as democracy, equality or inequality between the sexes, a progressive outlook, a traditional outlook, and so on—something is true if it is believed to be true.

Additionally, we saw in chapter 7 how a bridge was established between relativism and positivism, two philosophies that are actually opposites. I explained the role of the positivist Hegel in this process, and of Marx, who used positivism to arrive at a sort of relativism, even if this was not his express intention. Hegel himself has in fact been accused of relativism, since he argues that a particular era possesses the truth that is appropriate for it (variations of this theme appear frequently in many of his works, such as *Phenomenology of Spirit*, *Elements of the Philosophy of Right*, and *Lectures on the Philosophy of History*). Although I find this attack on Hegel to be somewhat unfair, since he argues that these phases of truth are really only stepping-stones in the ultimate unfolding of truth or spirit, his influence has contributed to the notion that the subjective—individual belief—is tied to the objective—truth.[3] This mishmash of positivism and relativism has, as a whole, influenced the minds of a great many modern American oikophobes.

As Allan Bloom points out in *The Closing of the American Mind*, talk of "values" rather than of truth and falsehood, or of good and evil, offers a great release of subjectivity from the tension that absolute opposites offer—and, as I would add, is symptomatic of tired and declining societies.[4] If there is no right and wrong, then one may do as one pleases; there is no need anymore to be grateful for one's heritage, to die for one's loved ones, or to ask oneself whether a particular act might be regretted in the morning. It should be specified, however, that in my view Bloom is incorrect when he sees the current relativist cultural development as something that has finally exploded the heritage of ancient Greece that had developed since antiquity. One of my theses is that this cultural development has recurred cyclically (or helically). Bloom writes that with the rise of mere "values" as opposed to truth, "The quest begun by Odysseus and continued over three millennia has come to an end with the observation that there is nothing to seek" (p. 143). But this simplifies the fact that a nihilistic abandonment of truth occurs repeatedly in declining civilizations in general, even if relativism is not always codified in as rigorous a way as modern thinkers have codified it. That abandonment is, of course, part and parcel of the oikophobic rejection of the standards of one's own civilization.

We thus have a situation today in which many who are relativists also believe in progress in a positivist sense: the perfection of society, step by step, toward a utopian goal. They do not realize the contradiction between relativism and the notion of progress: progress implies a higher goal, which implies a higher truth of some kind, which is antithetical to relativism. A typical manifestation of this tension is between the idea that all cultures are equal (relativism), on the one hand, and that hetero- and homosexuals must receive equal treatment before the law (positivism), on the other. When a foreign culture then kills homosexuals (for example, I happened to be staying in Uganda as that country's august parliament was debating whether to execute homosexuals or just imprison them for life), it is difficult to reconcile that culture's treatment of homosexuals with the idea that all cultures are equal.[5] But then why are so many modern oikophobes incapable of discerning this really quite obvious tension?

The answer lies in the oikophobic self-engrossment that will always plague the declining days of cultured peoples; our present state is simply its current manifestation. At the surface, relativism has become the philosophical creed: many people feel intellectual when they recognize all kinds of truths, even mutually exclusive ones. But positivism mixes with it, because in spite of their best efforts, people still do and always will need a purpose, something beyond themselves, something higher and important, of which they themselves can be part. They need something sacred. In this way, positivism proves de facto the emptiness of relativism's promises.

But if one digs a little deeper, one sees, at the same time, that both relativism and positivism stem from the self-indulgence and -engrossment of later cultural stages in that both philosophies provide an outlet for those who feel alienated from their societies. In the case of relativism, the oikophobe asks his society: Who are you to tell me what is right—cannot rightness be anything? And in the case of positivism, the oikophobe asks his society: Why must I be bound by your confines—why may I not be part of something greater and trans-cultural, something global, to whose realization I myself will contribute? Since these opposite philosophies power the same engine—oikophobic vanity—it is little wonder that such oikophobes will foist together bits and pieces of each in their efforts toward individual superiority, by distancing themselves from their civilizations by one way or the other, and preferably by both.

In the United States today, the oikophobe tends to reject patriarchality and particularity in favor of universality. There are two conflicting claims to this universality, which I have called "absolutist" and "relativist" (in chapter 2). These correspond to this mix of positivism and relativism in the modern oikophobe. Since positivism and relativism each has a separate claim to universalism, the American oikophobe uses both these outlets to lay claim to a certain internationalism (a less philosophically loaded word than universalism). Indeed the American oikophobe certainly claims or aspires to be "international." He wishes for his borders to explode, although it does not matter much where he goes thereafter. Any other place, by dint of not being America, will have its virtue. He will go to Africa because it is poor and "authentic," to Asia because it is philosophical and mystical, to Europe because it is cultural and old, and to South America because it is sexy. Only the United States itself appears to him backward and intolerant, in spite of the fact that, as the large majority of immigrants to the US, including me, will acknowledge, Americans on the whole are more open-minded and welcoming of cultural differences than any other people in the world, a legacy of our immigrant tradition.[6]

A most famous example of this oikophobic attitude to America nowadays is of course the voluminous oeuvre of Noam Chomsky. Regardless of the specific arguments, the general tenor is revealed by titles like *Terrorizing the Neighborhood: American Foreign Policy in the Post–Cold War Era*; *What Uncle Sam Really Wants*; *On Western Terrorism: From Hiroshima to Drone Warfare*; and *Requiem for the American Dream*.[7] To the question of what American values are, Gore Vidal's answer was "lying and cheating."[8] Oikophobic statements of this kind have become so commonplace that no exhaustive list could ever be compiled.

An expression of the relativist-positivist dichotomy is the postmodern-socialist dichotomy. Strictly speaking, postmodernism and socialism are mutually exclusive. The postmodern mindset rejects all grand narratives and overarching explanations, and posits truth to be subjective, simply an outcome of conflicting voices of coercion. Socialism, on the other hand, is the epitome of the grand and total narrative of history, as conceived by Marx, who was a good and obedient Hegelian boy. And yet almost all postmodernists today are also socialists. I have often heard contemporary thinkers express confusion about how the postmodern can embrace an ideology like socialism when the whole point of the former is the very abolition of grand narratives and ideologies.

But just as relativism and positivism were able to couple with one another by jointly providing fuel for oikophobia, so too both postmodernism and socialism hold out the promise of the destruction of the powerful, the upper strata of society who embody it. The oikophobe despises few things more than his own society—and when postmodernism assures him that this society has no greater claim to truth than any other society, and when socialism assures him that the keepers of his nation must fall and give way to redistribution and a socialist utopia, then he will happily incorporate both these promises into his worldview, with little thought about the deeper hostility that actually exists between the two. That is, both postmodernism and socialism have the same ultimate goal: leveling. An additional reason for the alliance between the two -isms is more historical than ideological, and is already more widely known: after the brutality and failures of Soviet and Chinese communism became apparent, Marxists were forced into a more skeptical posture—postmodernism—while still remaining socialists or communists at heart.

Related to these reasons why socialism has coupled with postmodernism is a reason why socialism tends to couple with oikophobia more generally, in addition to what we have already seen. Victimhood culture in declining civilizations often embraces the proletariat. So too, once the proletariat has become wealthier through civilizational progress and has decided not to rebel against their society, contrary to Marxist predictions, foreigners, especially those of the developing world who are poorer, become the new proletariat, so that the victimhood culture of socialism leads into oikophobia: the care and concern people had for the poor at home turns into oikophobic allophilia for the poor abroad.[9]

As has been the case in other civilizations, insofar as the political terms of "left" and "right" may have been applicable to them ("progressive" and "conservative" are more appropriate for ancient civilizations), the oikophobes dominate in left-wing areas, while non-oikophobes and, in some cases, xenophobes and anti-oikophobic reactionaries dominate in right-wing areas. The increased hostility between these two sides in the United States comes at the expected time, since the country has already slipped from her peak and is slowly descending on the other side. It is of course the oikophobic, not xenophobic, type of decadence that has asserted itself in intellectual circles and that insists on America's inferiority, or at least on her lack of superiority to the rest, which is tantamount to rendering her worse than she really is. And this, in turn, is the postmodern in a nutshell: the leveling of anything that may be called "better." The postmodern defines itself not by anything constructive, but only by the destruction of anything that dares claim a special place.

But I stop myself, and reserve the final discussion of postmodern oikophobia for the next chapter, because it makes more sense to speak of it in a larger Western than a more American context. I will say here only that the modern American psyche is especially susceptible to postmodernism, because our democratic culture that disdains old-world elitism is easier to exploit by a system that seeks to tear down those who look askance at the uncouth masses, who carry within them a sense of aristocratic privilege, and who, thanks very much, do not want to "loosen up."

America, along with our other civilizations, shows that the cultural stage at which a reasonably healthy equilibrium of self-promotion and self-critique occurs cannot be arrested. That stage, rather, falls upon a continuum, and just as the Greeks themselves were unable to halt the ongoing slide into collapse, so we in America today will remain unable to do so, a fact for which there is already plenty of evidence. Every opportunity for reasonableness, for social togetherness, is squandered in ever more bickering.

For instance, the presidential election of Donald Trump, rather than causing the oikophobes to ask themselves whether they had not been too hostile to traditional American culture, caused them to dig their trenches even deeper, which in turn caused the conservative reactionaries against them to dig further in as well, thereby only sharpening the frontier between these two American tribelets. Trump's victory was part of a natural reaction against oikophobia and against the bourgeois elite's betrayal of American ideals, an ilk among whom only the like-minded are admitted and contrary viewpoints—the essence of debate and rational exchange—are suppressed, where sneers and condescension masquerade as inclusivity, which in any case is only skin-deep.

Like Plato in Greece and Juvenal in Rome, the reactionaries hit back. But the tribalism of one side reinforces that of the other, and as the reactionaries gain influence, they too will come to scoff at critique and alternative viewpoints.

Although there are significant traces of this reactionary force on the European continent as well (e.g., the political parties Rassemblement National in France and AfD in Germany), it is no coincidence that it is making its strongest appearance in the United States and Britain, although it is weaker in the latter, since Britain is far more progressed into oikophobic collapse than the former. Brexit was, like Trump's election, a clear anti-oikophobic reaction. The Anglo-Saxon common law tradition has a much richer history of rugged democracy and independent dissent than does the continental-Napoleonic-civil tradition. Common law develops over time and therefore represents a people's collective tradition and accumulated values. In continental-Napoleonic (and EU) law, case law is far subordinate to statutory law; that is to say, what the political class ordains is supreme, and there is great respect for a superior elite that issues lofty law in the interest of the people. This attitude is quite foreign to the traditionally British and, by extension, American way of thinking, according to which it is the people, by means of the cases they bring to court, who shape legal tradition over time. The French and the Germans, whose idea of governance has a weaker democratic tradition behind it, tend to prefer proper decorum and quiet elitism in their politicians, and look with incomprehension at the rowdiness of British Parliament debate and American campaign rallies, which is, in the etymological sense of the term, thoroughly popular. In other words, and not too simplified, the continental way is the creation of law and tradition from the top down, while the Anglo-Saxon way is from the bottom up.[10]

So the result of the 2016 US election was a manifestation of the reactionary force that often develops against the concentration of Napoleonic-like power in an oikophobic elite that despises the other parts of the populace. And the elite's posture only increases the strength of the reactionaries. The more the growing number of American oikophobes isolate themselves and consider their own moral worldview of posturing platitudes to be the only acceptable one for all of society, an attitude predicted by such men as J. S. Mill and Alexis de Tocqueville—the one Frenchman who actually tried to understand American culture before criticizing it—the weaker the oikophobes in fact become.[11] It is interest, not moral superiority, that stands at the beginning of every practical and successful politics, and so the oikophobes lost the election because they sneered at the reactionaries rather than trying to engage them. The reason they did this is that they saw politics as a purely moral battle rather than as the battle of concrete diverging interests that it more typically is.

That the oikophobes would see current politics in this moral way makes perfect sense, since anything moral boosts one's vanity, and the vice of vanity is and always has been the engine of oikophobia. The US election outcome, as well as the British departure from the EU, more broadly seen, were thus victories for the Anglo-Saxon common spirit, and defeats for the continental-Napoleonic spirit. Roger Scruton was indeed prescient when he wrote that the effect of the oikophobic assault on national loyalties "will be felt soon everywhere, and the result may not be what the oiks expect."[12]

Nonetheless, despite isolated triumphs, the American reactionaries will not be able to stymie the overall direction of their nation. This can be seen in the 2020 election. They will only be able to slow, not stop, the decline of American power. If previous civilizations are any guide, which of course they are, America's trajectory will proceed overall in the same direction, with still some ups and downs to come, and so in the grand scheme of things our path will not be very different than it would have been had the oikophobes defeated the reactionaries in the 2016 election.

One way, however, in which the present American case differs from some other civilizations of the past is the fact that overwhelming American hegemony, as well as the exhaustion of Western countries with intra-Western conflict, have by now allowed two whole generations—going on three—to avoid donning the military uniform. Those who do, do so by choice rather than compulsion. It is a common trope, but one no less true for its commonness, that never having had to fight for something leads to a lack of understanding of its value, and to taking it for granted. There have been some other instances of a civilization's success sharply reducing the need to fight—one thinks for instance of the Augustan peace after the Roman civil wars of the first century BC that ended the republic, a peace that allowed writers like Ovid and Propertius to care less for the state and more about themselves. But oftentimes a civilization has continued to fight, albeit with a much-lessened sense of urgency, even during its days of saturating success (Athens, France, Britain, and others), and in this respect the American case is somewhat different. Oikophobia has expanded even more rapidly because of this lack of fight than it otherwise would have. Recent American wars like the relatively low-key conflict in Afghanistan and the two Iraq Wars are too small to have much of a moderating effect on oikophobia. But it is important to note that the current state of affairs—relative peace—only strengthens a phenomenon that would have existed anyway, for the myriad reasons that have been outlined in this book.

Within this nexus of peace and neo-tribalism, the role of young people ought to be mentioned. The younger generation is often the most oikophobic, since it naturally tends to be of a rebellious mind, and in American culture today it is young people who have gained much of the power. The rise of social media in the twenty-first century has, as technological advances often do, diffused power and influence, in this case to young people, who are the most technologically savvy. Since these media, like Facebook and Twitter, great incubators of tribalism, are dominated by the young, but since older people also partake in them to a considerable extent, there is a consequent infantilization of older people, and an unsalutary influence on them of immature ideas that should properly be confined to one's youth only.

An example of such youthful ideas or behavior that have gained broader credence in American society as a result of youth-driven media is the notion that one should never be told by others what to do and that, consequently, all ideas and sets of morals are somehow equal. Related to this is the notion, common among the young and also in popularized third-wave feminism, that no matter what one does or how one behaves, one should always stay the way one is and that if others cannot accept one's behavior, it is they who should change. This attitude is a consequence, specifically, of social media having rendered people more narcissistic and immature.[13] More generally, it results from the overwhelming success of American civilization, where the need for self-correction steadily decreases, and it is part of the self-engrossment that plagues a culture's declining days.

The dissemination of this prejudice, that one should never change for others and that one is fine just the way one is, is also a reflection of the increased purchasing power of young people. Since this prejudice happens to be expressive of a particularly infantile attitude, and since young people have more money, or at least greater access to their parents' money, than they used to (the statistic-destroying success of the film *Titanic* in 1997 did a great deal to wake up pop culture producers to this fact), the culture is going to change in order to cater to their emotional needs, and so more films will be made, more songs written, in which this prejudice is expressed. It is ultimately of course about money-making. Many of these young people will fortunately learn over time that it is in fact healthy and even essential to change in some respects every now and then, and will become less beholden to the worst elements of the extremely narrow slice of space and time that is early twenty-first-century America, but there is also a feedback loop in which the increased stress on this prejudice in popular culture influences older persons who might otherwise not have been victims of it. This prejudice attacks norm qua norm and celebrates againstness without being for anything very clearly defined, except the very own self, and it is thus the epitome of postmodernism.

It has always been common for young people to have the understanding of children but the conviction of prophets (much like actual prophets, as it happens), but it has not always been common that the broader culture will tap into this self-righteousness and disseminate it to ever broader segments of the population, and thereby to ensure that ever more people know what they hate but not what they love—that is, that they define themselves negatively, oikophobically, and not positively, such as through their being part of a special and beautiful community. This state of affairs is exacerbated by the American emphasis on "self-esteem," which contributes to a young person's individual echo chamber and to his oikophobia, because an exaggerated "self-esteem" rejects contrary opinion and insists that we are fine as we are. It thereby also rejects the tradition that offers us some basic norms of proper or gentlemanly behavior. It is in America that the gentleman's ideal is mocked more than anywhere else. Whereas individualism is important and one should listen to one's heart in the choice of work (unless one has absolutely no talent), spouse, and so forth, American oikophobes do not understand what the Greeks understood, namely that society at large should serve as a break on our worst impulses, and that action judged honorable by one's community should be embraced, if possible, except for those rare cases where it would conflict with the pursuit of genius.

Common in the American oikophobic youth block is also the combination of relativism and positivism we have already come across. Many American youngsters are too uneducated to understand that, on the one hand, historical positivism has a totalitarian streak, and that, on the other hand, relativism not only destroys the ideas they dislike but also the ideas they treasure. As I have already implied, both sides of the coin will finally lead to violence: positivism requires conformism to the given goal, and relativism, by banishing objective truth, hands the argument to those who happen to be strongest. This relativism leads to a particularly American prejudice, fueled by the oikophobic youth—and the upper limit of what constitutes youth in our society saturated with success keeps inching upward—that no one can be better than anyone else. People with manners and with education will claim that they are not better than the uncouth, the vulgar, and the criminal, and they will be praised for their humility. But this claim can be a very deceptive sort of arrogance, because insisting that one is not better than anyone else carries with it the implication that, no matter what one does or how one behaves, one is not worse than anyone else either. This is another precious gift of relativism: once everything is considered subjective and therefore inadmissible in an objective sense, it follows that everything is equally admissible, too. So a refusal to recognize superiority has as its corollary a sort of moral nihilism and an incapacity for the noble suffering and arduous self-improvement of the individual who suddenly realizes that he has erred and that he was, indeed, worse rather than better or equal. Such a moral nihilism is symptomatic of eras where cultural pride and national loyalty have disappeared. Only when an individual recognizes that people can in fact be better or worse than others, will he be ready to improve.

And, on the note of young people's education, millennials state with perfect seriousness that they are America's most educated generation. They say this because statistics show that they have more college degrees than any other American generation. What they do not understand is that the content of a college degree has changed radically across the decades, by becoming more diffused, and that, today, such a degree typically does not lead to anywhere close to the same quantity and quality of education as was the case in previous eras. The mere fact, thus, that millennials fail to grasp the very simple concept that the meaning and content of terms—in this case "college degree"—change over time, shows precisely how very poor their education has been.

So historically when a culture and its traditions are forgotten, a narcissistic attitude centered on the notion of the self often develops. Even though it really only masks the human desire of being part of something greater, of historical events, of heroism, late-civilizational self-engrossment is in our case brought to its logical continuation by the rise of social media, where no thought is thought and no feeling felt that is not broadcast to all and sundry. But there are philosophical problems with the notion of the self. It has a complicated history, but it is mainly Plato who is responsible for its creation in the West, though he appears to have adopted the idea of an immortal and separable soul from the Egyptians. Plato maintained not only that there is a soul, but also that this soul is the core or essence—the true nature—of the person. By and large, when people think of themselves, when they think about personhood and the self—insofar as they do—they think of it the Platonic way. They believe that they have an unalterable essence, a soul, that there is some aspect of their persons that would be the same through time and space. In addition to Plato, they are also beholden to the philosophy of Descartes, who believed that we have a mental, non-physical element that operates within our bodies—a "ghost in the machine," as it has come to be known by critics—and that this mental entity is our true self.[14] This is why one might hear someone say something like, "If I had lived in France during World War II, I would have joined the Resistance"; or, "If I had lived in America in the mid-nineteenth century, I would have been against slavery and joined the abolitionists." What this person is assuming is that even though he or she would have been French, lived at a different time, and so on, there is still something about him or her as a person that would have remained the same regardless of the changed circumstances.

But this is entirely false. The proper response to this person would be, "No, you would not have joined the Resistance, and no, you would not have been against slavery, because you would not have been you." When we look at a person, we see a series of characteristics and aspects. Some of them seem to be stronger than others: for example, if we look at the person against whom the Resistance resisted, Adolf Hitler, the fact that he was a genocidal maniac appears to be more significant or "dominant" than the fact that he liked dogs, was a vegetarian, or had brown hair. But the fact of the matter is that, although some aspects of a person appear more dominant than others in light of our subsequent moral judgment, they are all of a similar category: a bundle of characteristics that exist next to each other, with none of them having the claim to be the "essence" or "true nature" of that person. That is, Hitler's dislike of Jews and liking of dogs are in terms of ontological personal essence not so different; they only appear extremely different to us because one led to cataclysmic fighting and genocide while the other had no particularly discernible outcome. So it is historical hindsight that makes us call one more "essential" than the other. If Hitler had hated Jews but never been successful in his ambition of becoming a dictator and killing millions of Jews and others, the people who knew him might possibly have been justified in remembering him more for his dog-loving and vegetarianism than for his anti-Semitism.

And so the self, or the "essence" of a person, is an illusion, a piece of quasi-religious mysticism. This was seen clearly by David Hume (*A Treatise of Human Nature* 1.4.6, a passage mentioned in the last chapter), but has a precursor already in the pre-Platonic and divine Heraclitus, who saw that various aspects, and how they interact with the world, succeed one another in perpetual flux and are never quite the same from one moment to the next. That is to say, our identity, insofar as we have one, is simply the sum total of the perceptions—both our own and those by others—of all our thoughts and actions. It is true that nothing is purely nature or nurture, in the vulgar sense: we are a combination of both. But all the ways in which we define ourselves become irrelevant in another place and at another time.[15]

This is well illustrated in the famous paradox called "The Ship of Theseus," fully recorded by Plutarch (*Life of Theseus* 23) but picked up by many philosophers. As the planks of Theseus's wooden ship gradually rot, each old plank is replaced by a new one over time, one by one. But people still refer to it as "Theseus's ship," even though much of it did not exist in Theseus's time. So by calling it "Theseus's ship," we are assuming an essence of that object. We are, unwittingly, victims of our own language: referring to some entity as "Theseus's ship," or as "Mary," or as "myself," is a convenient shorthand, but it masks the fact that these things are always changing. But since we need to use words or names to designate objects, the static nature of the words themselves leads us, erroneously, to deduce a static essence in the objects to which those words refer. Through our own words we thus become victims of Plato's metaphysical essentialism or idealism. And we can indeed apply this notion to human beings.[16] The concept of a "person" is anchored, as so many other notions and beliefs, within the narrow confines of our language, which is generally insufficient for expressing what we really mean (the constant struggle of the poet and the thinker). That is, language makes the inherent but false assumption that sense can always be individuated; I say "inherent" because the very *raison d'être* of language is to arrest that which is in flux.

Whereas we still need these words for everyday practical living, we should be aware that they can be quite hollow (but see my discussion of the abuse of nominalism in the next chapter). Dissolving the sense of self and thereby banishing the ego-essence from the realm of perceived existence becomes one of the most salutary undertakings in which we can engage. There is nothing wrong with a healthy dose of "self"-promotion, but the narcissism inherent in the notion of the self, through which we view ourselves as absolute entities, leads to the mistaken belief that we might have acted in a morally pure way in past historical circumstances. That is, the belief in the self allows us to claim moral superiority vis-à-vis the past. This makes it easier for us to oikophobically reject our past, our history, and the figures who took part in it—to deface or tear down statues of the founding fathers, for instance—in the illusory belief that we would have done better than they. This is of course not to say that as a general matter we cannot distinguish between moral goodness and moral turpitude—that would be relativism—but it is to say that the drive toward moral purity is based on the narcissism that is inherent in the notion of the self, and that it feeds into oikophobia.

Were people truly interested in cultivating themselves, that bundle of characteristics that is properly theirs, they would strive to dissolve the moralistic ego and reject the erroneous notion that there is such a thing as their own true essence. This would help them achieve a measure of true liberation from enslaving self-engrossment and constant worries about appearances. Through that liberation, they would be better equipped to engage in true contemplation and to make the world around them, their communities, a bit more beautiful. And that in turn would help keep oikophobia at bay, as people would realize that their civilization is more important than their own selves.

None of this, incidentally, is to be interpreted as a rejection of that individualism that has contributed to vaulting Western civilization ahead of others, and America ahead of Europe. Even though the idea of a metaphysical self is an illusion, we retain bodily integrity. Individualism in the sense of personal rights, a person forging his own fate, and of the state's existence by consent is a crucial cornerstone of advanced and antiauthoritarian societies. But our individualism should not mean that we lose ourselves in false images. Our recognition of the importance of civilization and history, of the fact that there are things greater than ourselves, does not mean that we give in to some fascist superstructure that treats us like cogs in a machine. It simply means that we understand that our individualism is best served through association with others, with our communities. Others are those with whom love and creativity can be exchanged, with whom we grow richer, and in whom our egos can dissolve themselves in a joint development of our very finest characteristics. We give birth to beauty not in ourselves, but in others.

Some object that one ought to distinguish between those who hate their own cultures and those who do not hate them but are merely critical of certain aspects of them.[17] They maintain that such critique takes place out of love and not hate, since it is based on a desire that one's culture improve. I reply that constructive critique is of course very important, and that, as I have endeavored to show, there is usually a "midpoint" where the culture has abandoned its parochial tribalism and become more self-observing and scientific, which obviously includes self-critique, but has not yet degenerated into oikophobia. For the civilizations we have looked at together in this book, the peaks of these midpoints would be, very roughly, mid-fifth century BC (Athens/Greece), early first century BC (Rome), early eighteenth century (France), mid-Victorian era (Britain), and early twentieth century (the United States). Also in the declining phases of civilizations can critique be the result of love that one feels for the object of the critique. But I think it is a bit too easy to want to tear things up root and stem and say that one does it out of love. Americans can love a particular American food or their local birthplaces, and cheer for American sports teams in international competitions, but to truly love America in our context is, I think, to love her institutions, or rather the traditions upon which those institutions rest, because they—not foods and sports teams—are what makes America markedly different. Those traditions are, for example, Anglo-Saxon common law, federalism, free speech, and the individualist and equality ethic of Judeo-Christianity, especially Christianity. If one wants America to be like continental Europe—which does not share those traditions to the same extent—as many American oikophobes do, I do not believe that one loves America, but rather that one wants to change America into something different that it would be easier for one to love. But I do not wish more than necessary to label specific living persons as oikophobes, an effort that could easily degenerate into a sort of witch hunt, with all the excesses and abuses to which human nature shall always be prone. The main goal is merely to study the larger trends of cultures, hoping that the knowledge gained therefrom can help us understand our current state and make us better as individual human beings. On that note, let us once again leave American shores and look at all of the West.

Chapter 11

THE CONFLUENCE OF THE WEST

I have previously intimated that Western microcultures are fusing more and more into the overall Western macroculture. Oikophobia is now everywhere in Europe and North America, and so I should like to describe the present philosophical state of the West as a whole in this regard. Many strands of thought will come together here.

Of course, the West—and the world—have been gradually fusing together since their very inceptions. The moment a group of people became aware of the presence of a proximate group, which naturally happened already in prehistoric times, the fusing of cultures began. A grunting post-ape thinking that its neighbor's cave was nicer than its own, was the beginning of globalization. So to reprise a recurring theme, there is never anything truly new in the world, but only new and sometimes heightened manifestations of the same tragic patterns playing themselves out over and over again. But all the same, we can easily find some milestones within the West that led to differences among the microcultures becoming blurrier, and the whole macro-civilization hardening into something more monolithic, events that slowly shifted the smaller streams into a river's confluence. Obvious instances from antiquity are Alexander's Hellenization of the near East, Rome's conquest of most of the ancient world, the Hellenization of Rome through Greek culture, and the Christianization both of Rome and subsequently of barbarian-Germanic tribes.

In the modern era, since medieval times, other clear developments that brought disparate Western cultures closer to one another are the establishment of universities in the late Middle Ages and Renaissance, trade organizations such as the Hanseatic League, moveable type and the printing press, the Industrial Revolution, television, and the Internet. And so we increasingly find ourselves in a situation in which cultural progress in one western European country will have a direct bearing on that in the others, and developments on one side of the Atlantic on those on the other. Whereas each microculture had a more or less independent road to oikophobia, it is also the case that the Western macroculture has, as a whole, been influenced by those independent developments. Local differences persist, but it is with every passing day more and more the case that all of the West is tottering under the weight of its oikophobic malaise. In light of this coalescence, it is only natural that what was mostly microcivilizational oikophobia slowly becomes macrocivilizational, whereby people detest not only their own countries but all of Western civilization.

Philosophically, the modern confluence of the West can be seen in the ever broader cross-microcultural appeal of a certain set of ideas and hermeneutical fads that began in academic circles but whose way of thinking has since seeped out into the larger population. These philosophical roots of our current oikophobia are not difficult to find. Although one can trace all ideas back to antiquity in some form or other, I should like to focus here on newer manifestations. The two most important strains of these philosophical roots were planted by the so-called Frankfurt School, and by the French postmodernists of a few decades later.

Both these movements were influenced by Marx. Although there are many differences between him and them, especially the postmodernists, we can detect a thread of macro- and micro-monomania running from Marx through the Frankfurt School and the postmodernists up to the present day. Although it is true that this monomaniacal tendency is rooted in plain human nature, it is regrettably the case that philosophers of the last century and a half or so have been particularly prone to it. Hegel had only engaged in macro-monomania; Karl Marx was one of the first to fully combine both the macro and the micro level. For instance, in *The Communist Manifesto* he explicitly maintains that all politics, law, science, art, religion, and so forth is reducible to the means of production alone—how to produce sustenance. This is macro-monomania, that is, reducing all phenomena to one element. The Marxist position all too often does not recognize that a thought can retain its truth and beauty, all its other characteristics, even if it has material or economic causes.

Later, in for example 1.4.1 of his *Capital* ("The General Formula of Capital"), Marx believes that the fact that the capitalist is motivated by greed means that he is motivated by greed alone. This is micro-monomania, reducing one phenomenon, in this case the capitalist, to a single essence, greed. That is, Marx settles for the basic characteristic of each phenomenon that best serves his ideological purpose, rather than viewing the complexity in it, which would have complicated his goal of communist revolution—for example, it is perfectly possible to be motivated by pecuniary gain and at the very same time by a genuine desire to manufacture products that are beneficial to others as well.[1] Indeed, Max Weber, in *The Protestant Ethic and the Spirit of Capitalism* 1.2, calls it a "very obvious truth" that capitalists are motivated also to improve communal life and to make their cities flourish.

Several decades and a major conflagration after Marx, the Frankfurt School began, in the Weimar Republic. It consisted in the main of a group of rather anti-capitalist, Marxist-light, and quite oikophobic gentlemen understandably disillusioned by the carnage of World War I, but whose interest today is mainly historical; of its earlier members, such as Ernst Bloch, Walter Benjamin, Max Horkheimer, Herbert Marcuse, and Theodor Adorno, really only Adorno is still read with a measure of seriousness outside of academia. The Frankfurt School popularized historicism, to which I have previously made passing reference, the belief that reflection itself is a part of history, which is to say that earlier thoughts are historically conditioned by the circumstances in which the thinkers lived, and should be seen in that light, and that what passes for "knowledge" is marred by the historical time and place in which that knowledge appeared (this idea is present already in the second part of *The Communist Manifesto*). The insights that a more positivist outlook claims to be certain based on sensory data, historicism will consider uncertain and necessarily bound by subjective value judgments. A part of this view is the concern—and the French postmodernists will pick up this point—to identify, isolate, and thereby exorcise every sort of domination that any group might have exercised over any other group. They wanted to find the particular reasons why someone in the past had thought in a particular way, reasons that were to be found mainly in external factors. Essentially, the Frankfurt School endeavored to establish a "value-free" social science, that is, the erasure of any sort of prejudice among philosophers and sociologists. Since Western civilization was monomaniacally seen as the history of dominations by various groups over one another (macro-monomania)—which meant that individual actors had to be viewed as purely nefarious oppressors (micro-monomania)—it followed quite naturally that much of the West was ready for the garbage heap. Not only were the workers and the poor oppressed by the rich, but the rich in turn were, along with everyone else, oppressed psychologically by Christian sexual mores and by the overall familial hierarchy of Western civilization. This is why, to many of the school's members, not only smaller fixes had to be implemented here and there, but the whole edifice had to be brought down (which was itself ultimately a morally positivistic effort). With the rise of Nazism in Germany, many Frankfurt scholars moved to New York and thereby gained a broader audience of impressionable college students.

Herbert Marcuse's *Eros and Civilization* (1955) is quite a typical Frankfurt School work; let us therefore dwell upon it for a moment.[2] Marcuse feels that Western culture is inherently repressive and must be replaced. He refers to "surplus-repression" as that which goes beyond the normal inhibitions necessary for societies, but then he includes in such surplus-repression even things like the "corporealization of the ego, manifest in the frozen traits and gestures, produced at the appropriate occasions and hours . . . regulating the co-ordination of the individual with the whole" (chapter 4). But his discerning reader may wonder whether it was truly those dashed industrialists who brought about norms of how one ought to behave in public. Did such things not exist in preindustrial societies, too? (Of course they did.) That is, Marcuse's work commits the standard error of rejecting Nietzsche's and Freud's entirely correct understanding that a considerable measure of repression is required for all human civilization, no matter where or when it may arise. And so Marcuse, in discarding the possible for the impossible, thereby lets the perfect be the enemy of the good, rather than its inspirer. Several errors, such as when he says in chapter 2, with Marxist-Rousseauian atavism, that only in modern times has the state exercised mass control of entertainment for the sake of repression, facilitate this rejection of the West and reveal Marcuse's ignorance of antiquity, and it is always with antiquity that we must begin if we wish to understand modernity.

He has difficulty accepting the fact that we no longer live among the dark satanic mills of the early Industrial Revolution, since he feels the need to make up new problems instead. He says in the introduction that "intensified progress seems to be bound up with intensified unfreedom," which is the exact opposite of the truth. In fact, repression generally decreases as civilizations age, because they move away from the most extreme patriarchal forms, and because with increased strength they have more room for maneuver and for social deviants, as our view of oikophobic trajectories should have made clear. If we were to travel back even just seventy or eighty years, to say nothing of two hundred years, we would find a far greater number of repressive elements (blasphemy laws, sodomy laws, prohibition of certain books and films, various sedition acts, etc.). We are also not discussing smaller ups and downs in repression or social development in general, but larger civilizational trends from beginning to end.[3] Marxists first thought that capitalism leaves workers destitute; once it became clear that capitalism enriches all classes, the Marxists had to change their minds and decide that these riches are actually bad since, as Marcuse says in chapter 4, so much wealth and so many possessions distract people from the important things. Once one has decided, monomaniacally, that the West is all about repression, then such sleights of hand become necessary.

In order to replace the West as it is, Marcuse finds the key in—what else?—sexual liberation. He claims, contrary to all historical evidence, that sexual liberation could absorb the human instinct for destruction (chapter 6). Drawing on Freud he also maintains, similarly, that reproduction, and hence the familial structure, is a socially enforced by-product of sexuality, whose primary function is actually the attainment of pleasure (chapter 2). Here I can only bear witness to how far philosophy has fallen from Plato's *Symposium*, the text that truly understood what sex is; it is itself an expression of sexual repression to suggest that our desire for sexual pleasure is entirely unrelated to the drive toward self-replication. At the end of chapter 4 Marcuse celebrates the arts as a denunciation of repression and social reality, which again gets it backwards, for most instances: it is on the contrary the very decline of tradition and the decrease of repression that make the arts assume such an antagonistic role (compare the situation with the quite domesticated arts under the far more repressive reign of Louis XIV, for example). That is to say, modern arts are not rebelliously heroic, but rather spoiled elements that through a lack of repression are as frivolously antagonistic as they please. That in itself is fine, but it means that they do not stand against the social order at all, contrary to what their creators and Marcuse would like to believe, but are, precisely, a confirmation thereof. Modern art is what it is because society lets it, and has stopped caring about it. And so, both when it comes to sex and art, what Marcuse views as a fight against Western oppression is in fact a manifestation of Western permissiveness. Finally, he descends into messianic megalomania in the last chapters, joining the end-of-history types we have previously met, whose work lies in the shadow of the cross. Many modern oikophobes are plagued by all these errors even today.

Marcuse's Kantianly titled *A Critique of Pure Tolerance* (1965), which he coauthored with others, maintains that the intolerant should not be tolerated (and it is fallible humans who must then determine what is "intolerant" and what is not), and that the "correct" ideas will be repressed if all ideas are allowed a voice.[4] The repression of free speech and of those ideas that a small elite consider inappropriate, which has often been a hallmark of the right, has thus become part of the legacy of the modern left. Consequently, "hate speech" laws in Europe and Canada grow ever broader and include ever more speech in their ambit. The problem here is of course that full freedom of speech is necessary to arrive at "correct" conclusions, because no single person, or even group of persons, can come up with infallible thought, and so one must open oneself up to the full plethora of existing counter-ideas. The prepackaged opinions and talking points of political camps, both left and right, are not thought. True thought, rather, is a journey whose destination is unknown. Everything I write wills itself as a step on that journey, a journey that considers nothing too small, and nothing too great, as an object of our sightseeing, a journey where the posture of a statue or the detail in a façade makes us pause and look, just as much as do the demise of armies and the rise and fall of civilizations. If you refuse to look at certain sights you come across on that journey—no matter how ugly and hateful they may appear to your imperfect being—then you will quickly get lost on the road and dizzy yourself in a labyrinth of solipsism.

One can say about the Frankfurt School what is later to be said of the French postmodernists, namely that they are mostly wrong, and that in the instances where they are right they are really just belaboring the utterly obvious. That all human relations, both between individuals and between groups, involve power play is perfectly true. But it is even truer than the Frankfurters themselves realize: someone like Marcuse and his ilk understood only that domination has always dominated, but not that in fact it always will dominate, which is why any effort toward utopia is pointless and will only make matters worse. Precisely because power relationships are everywhere, it is misguided to think that the Frankfurters would stand ready with an emancipatory embrace once the institutions have crumbled. And if something is obviously true and always will be, then it is a trivial truth.

Their historicism, that ideas are to be viewed as products of their socio-historical environment, has been enormously influential, but can also be dispensed with. As I and others have never tired of pointing out to historicist colleagues in academia, this charge of historical conditioning that they level at previous eras is itself a child of its time, to be leveled at those who level it at others. Criticizing the Frankfurters is thus similar to the liar's paradox-critique of relativism as self-refuting. So if we wished to do to them what they do to others, we might say: It is not a coincidence that it was just after the horrendous World War I that German thinkers began to feel rather tepidly about the West, especially because their side lost, and to view history as group domination. Something similar could indeed be said about the French postmodernists who first arose in the 1950s, after France had been humiliated in World War II and was also gradually losing her empire—namely, the postmodernists are sore losers. You will not find too many postmodernists among the victorious hordes wiping the blood of the vanquished off their swords. In the twentieth century, whether the West might not be such a good idea after all was a question asked first by those who drew its shortest straw.

It is also not a coincidence that the Frankfurters lived at a time when practically everyone was influenced by Nietzsche, and it was Nietzsche who in a reaction against the exaggerated positivism of his day had championed historicist perspectivism, that is, personal interest. In this we also see, again, the danger of trying to construct a monomaniacal "total history," a view of the world where everything is to be seen through one particular lens—in this case domination, selfish interest—which renders the complex beauty of our species dull and monochromatic. Since the truth of domination is a trivial truth, and since the truth of historicism must be all-encompassing if it is to exist at all, we may disregard them as irrelevant. Even though there is some causal relation between historical events and the thoughts of philosophers—indeed this book is "historicist" insofar as it ties literature to developing civilizational trends from the point of view of oikophobia—establishing such a relation is not enough to discredit the thought, because then every single thought ever formulated and ever to be formulated in the future must be rejected; rather, the thought must be accepted or rejected on its own terms.

It is really quite embarrassing, since it is such an obvious error, that many historicists even today exclude themselves from the charge of historical prejudice which they level at earlier thinkers, even though their own attitude is so clearly in line with the general antiheroic, postmodern, and relativist adage of our own age. Today's Western academics are certain that earlier philosophers thought what they did for particular reasons (elitism, economic superiority, domination, oppression, etc.), but we are meant to believe that there are no external reasons for their own thinking, which is supposedly pure, free, and unconstrained by any economic, social, or historical factors. Insofar as they are oikophobic, they apply historicist methods only to Western thoughts and ideologies, while non-Western philosophies are granted a sort of immunity to social and economic constraints and appear to reside in a separate dimension as pure as that of Plato's forms. They believe they are establishing, as I mentioned, a "value-free" social science, even though such a science is neither possible nor desirable. They fail to see that behind any attempt to improve and to understand, there must always be some kind of normative position. They accuse everyone of bias because everyone has a norm, which is tantamount to rejecting someone simply for not being a tabula rasa.[5]

But why is a "value-free" social science or philosophy not even desirable? Is not the effort to erase philosophical prejudice at least a laudable effort? Not really, no. The problem is that since the complete erasure of prejudice is impossible—we are all products of our environments to a great degree—the final result of this effort among philosophers will simply be that they merely believe they have erased their prejudices, without actually having erased them. The prejudices thereby become even more dangerous than they previously were, because they will now operate under the illusion of being their own opposite: pure reason. And so, deleteriously, instead of simply stating what they think is true based on empirical observation, prejudices begin to state that they are not prejudices, and thus to take on the veneer of pure truth.[6]

Another way of putting it is that the Frankfurt School is profoundly German, positivistically claiming its prejudices to be science, and thereby illustrating yet again the influence of its own environment upon itself. The forefather of this kind of thinking is Kant, who in his first two *Critiques* goes out of his way to claim that he has stripped away everything from his thought that lies beyond the grasp of pure reason, but who still ends up with a map of reality that so thoroughly corresponds to what he would like it to be, that one might do well to ask whether a wee bit of personal prejudice did not creep in after all. Less influentially, because less subtly, Descartes is also like this: for all his self-congratulatory doubt and skepticism, he ends up precisely where he wanted to be all along. Just as Descartes uses reason to try to prove God, so too even Kant, over a hundred years later, while claiming in his *Critique of Pure Reason* the inadequacy of reason in proving such ideas as God, in fact bends himself into the most grotesque verbal contortions for the purpose of, all the same, arriving at God and free will, a goal to which someone like Bacon, a generation before Descartes, simply does not lend much relevance.

Even today this Kantian spirit reigns supreme in Germany, though it may at least be said, to the credit of that nation, that it produced some brave dissenters, the foremost of these being Nietzsche. Nietzsche, however, took things too far in the other extreme, as I have said, claiming that everything is the outcome of personal perspective and inclination. So I love Nietzsche not because he was right about everything—he most certainly was not—but because his prejudices were so purely his own rather than those of his society, and because he expressed them with such beauty, clarity, and sincerity, without any false pretense. Society and its popular opinions were thoroughly irrelevant to him and to how he formed his own worldview. He was like a young child that does not need to know what anyone else thinks in order to see beauty and miracles everywhere, and it is in this light that I embrace him as my kin.

But it is important to note, thus, that the Frankfurters ended up standing both in the shadow of Kant—in their positivist scientific posture—and in the shadow of Nietzsche—in their relativist emphasis on personal perspective and external factors. This is indicative of the philosophical problems plaguing the Frankfurt School, and of how relativism and positivism have come together in their oikophobia, for Kant and Nietzsche are mortal enemies. Indeed they belong on the opposite extremes of the rationalist-empiricist fault line that has always divided philosophers into two main camps: Kant stands with for example Plato and Descartes, Nietzsche with Aristotle and Hume; I place myself squarely among the latter.

Historicism as a means of rejecting intellectual tradition has been so influential that even many ordinary people share its attitude, even if they do

not possess the full range of terminology. But the historicists often lack the
courage of their convictions; they dare not go all the way. If they did, what
they treasure in today's society would have to be rejected as well. And as of
late, in fact, some remnants of the Frankfurt School appear to have come
around slightly. One of its proponents I came across once in Heidelberg, an
aging Jürgen Habermas, who seemed finally to acknowledge, with a hint of
regret and irony, that Western civilization is in fact not so bad after all, a posture that is echoed also in his earlier *Philosophical Discourse of Modernity*
(1985), in the last essays of which he even pokes gentle fun at the French postmodernists.[7] I was tempted to say that the rest of us could have told him so
from the beginning, and that he would then have saved himself the tiresome
burden of a long academic career, but, little stripling that I was, still in need
of my doctoral degree, I uncharacteristically held my peace. And perhaps it
was just as well: Habermas has many good things to say, and he is in fact
the Frankfurt School plus a sprinkle of sanity.

Nonetheless, the Frankfurters, as will the postmodernists, get lost in a sort
of anti-capitalist atavism—or Marxist-Rousseauian atavism, as I called it a
few pages ago—by which they think that we first had *homo faber,* "man the
maker," who was then corrupted into a *homo fabricatus,* a man fabricated by
the constraints of his class and condition.[8] Like Marx himself, they do not
understand that the impersonal laws of capitalism have existed since barter
was abandoned, and that there was never a pure golden age where the noble
worker plied his creative trade in freedom: *homo faber* was always *fabricatus.*
As so often, the Marxist liberators, in making the claim that capitalism has
chained us, make the mistake of assuming that we were free to begin with.
The Garden of Eden never existed, and it is very Judeo-Christian of the
Marxists—who think they scoff at religion—to believe that it did: just like
the messianically religious, they place paradise in the beginning, and hope
for an eschatological paradise again at the end. In actual fact, one of the first
things our caveman ancestor did when he realized he was a homo sapiens
was to use his newfound wisdom by employing a flint stone as a projectile
against his neighbor, whose grand grotto was much nicer than his own puny
little hole in the mountainside, and decorated with all the latest in ochre
painting and shell necklaces. Those who believe an original natural state of
delight did exist are often those who, *à la Gauguienne,* long for a sexual freedom that was never theirs, and proceed to structure their creative or intellectual work around their private paradise lost.[9] So when the Frankfurters

seek to tear down power structures, they do not realize that once these are gone, we shall immediately have to build up new power structures again, or stand bewildered in an empty, anarchic void, with nothing for which to live.

Let us now hop over the Rhine, have a final glass of late-harvest Riesling, leave Germany, and arrive in France and in rainy but stately Paris. Here we find the intellectual inheritors of the Frankfurters, that other strain of the philosophical roots of our current oikophobic state: the French postmodernists, many of them gathered around the École Normale Supérieure. Among them we find the continuation of the same Marxist and Frankfurt combination of macro- and micro-monomania.

Although postmodernism's first proponents or at least associates were indeed mainly French—Lacan, Althusser, Lyotard, Deleuze, Foucault, Baudrillard, Derrida, et al.—they then proceeded to influence the whole macrocivilization, especially as several of these gentlemen, such as Lyotard, Foucault, and Derrida, also traveled to and worked in the United States, as had many of the Frankfurters. I cannot do justice here to all the differences among them—but some of the basic postmodern claims are: thought systems qua systems are to be rejected, and we should look at history only "atomistically," or as little separate islands of discourse, and not as an overarching narrative; since language is unstable, the stability of the entities we describe with language must be called into question; "ideology" as a sort of primitive mythology and blind following is to be rejected, similar to the more general postmodern rejection of "narratives"; the "death of the author" opens up limitless interpretations of texts. There are other facets to postmodernism as well, but these are some of its basic assumptions. It continues in the spirit of the Frankfurters and their obsession with domination and oppression, such as when Foucault famously claims that "insanity" is defined by society, that is, is a social construct, and is a method of repressing those that are supposedly "insane" (*History of Madness*, 1972).[10]

Each of these points can be offered a brief retort, which makes no claim to completeness; indeed I am only looking at postmodernism within the context of oikophobia, and as we shall see, some postmodern claims are better than others. First, postmodernism itself is a thought system (the fact that many of its proponents did not want to be labeled as postmodernists does not make a difference), and so, once again in a repetition of the liar's paradox and the rejection of relativism, postmodernism is apt to reject itself. Postmodernism's rejection of "grand narratives" falls victim to its own condemnation, since viewing everything as domination, oppression, and exclusion is, precisely, a monomaniacal grand narrative of dominating and excluding contrary viewpoints. If the postmodernists were true to their own theory of discarding narratives and systems, they would approach every history individually and purely on its own merits—from the arch-narratives of Hegel to the atomistic analyses of Foucault—and criticize a history neither for its larger narrative nor for its lack thereof.

Second, the calling into question of stable entities due to a rejection of language as stable is part of the abuse of nominalism, which I shall shortly discuss a bit further. For now I shall content myself with pointing out that since the postmodernists had failed in subverting the political system with their version of Marxism, they trained their artillery on language instead and focused on power. This teasing out of power and domination in every phrase and word, and their condemnation of every system and structure for this reason, have become the vain pleasure of a defeated group. By decrying everything as oppressive, one automatically assumes the mantle of a liberator. This oppositional self-definition, by which one stands at the head of huddling masses cowering behind for protection, is part of what has rendered the postmodernists so attractive to so many people. They are the epitome of the "fight-the-power" type, the Byronesque revolutionary who spends more time in making sure that he is dashing and charismatic than in actually toppling the tyrant. The French of the twentieth century have been particularly susceptible to this sort of charlatanry; it can be found, in a milder form, among the German idealists of the late eighteenth and early nineteenth centuries.

Third, the rejection of "ideology" misunderstands the nature both of ideology and of human beings in general, for it assumes that people are capable of a nonideological approach—that is, of being clean slates of pure thought—but we are not. "Ideology" is sometimes used in the sense of blind partisanship, or as seeing everything through a particular lens. This, of course, is to be avoided, but the postmodernists tend to subsume any general philosophies or normative positions under the rubric of "ideology," which of course is highly ironic in view of their own ideological uni-lens of power and repression. Those who reject ideology do not realize that nonideology is impossible.

Fourth, the idea of the "death of the author" (from Roland Barthes's 1967 essay) maintains that the author's biography and own opinions do not have a monopoly on how his or her text is to be understood.[11] This notion is meant to subvert the "domination" of canonical interpretations. This postmodern claim is one of those points that are true but obvious and therefore trivial. That a text, or any creative work, brims with possibility beyond the original intentions of its creator is something that every child understands; a child has no need for canonical interpretations and will approach a work any which way it pleases, and that is a good thing. It took hordes of professors to deny hermeneutic liberty through stilted theory, and then even more professors to reaffirm it again through ever more interminable theory.

Now, although most postmodernists themselves would not hold that absolutely anything goes, the spirit of limitless interpretations has often been endorsed in too literal a way by modern oikophobes. To them one must say that although a text most certainly can be interpreted in a limitless number of ways, it is not true that all of these interpretations have the slightest use. Even if we were to discard all philological labor that stands as a bulwark against insane interpretation and say that everything is hermeneutically possible, we must still distinguish between the hermeneutically possible and the de facto possible. If I determine that the *Iliad* means that I should punch in the face every third person I meet, then I would soon find myself either beaten to death or locked up in the state penitentiary, and so even though I can say that my interpretation of the *Iliad* is not hermeneutically excluded by the text itself, it is still de facto pointless. And in the end we should in fact not discard all philological labor; doing so would be a convenient way of avoiding having to engage in the difficult work that reveals meaning—and this is part of what Foucault will criticize in Derrida, as we shall see in a moment. The fact that much philological work in the past has been too rigid is not an argument against philology per se.

Finally, as regards Foucault's insanity claim, it is true but obvious that society defines what is insane so as to protect its other members from those thus labeled. We are therefore dealing once more with a trivial truth. As among the Marxists and Frankfurters, Foucault's monomania expresses itself on both the macro and the micro level. On the macro level, across many of his works Foucault is focused on the idea of oppression. While Marx had been obsessed with power relationships because he hoped the proles would revolt, the postmodernists were obsessed with power relationships because the proles did not: the communist struggle was lost in the real world and thus became intellectualized. Foucault's teasing out of power and domination in every possible phenomenon is of a piece with that obsession: the only thing that is perennial is power and oppression, which rear themselves across time and space in ever new forms, in social actions and in the myths that a society tells of itself. On the micro level, if Foucault is able to point out a repressive element in a particular action, he all too often thinks that this excludes the presence of other elements that may also properly describe that action, and which may be opposed to the repressive element (his *History of Madness* is riddled with this error).

For instance, private philanthropy, in his view, was invented by the bourgeoisie for selfish purposes; and the birth of the insane asylum had nothing to do with care for the deranged, but was purely a new form of repression; and so on. Since power has risen to the level of independent actor and been given its own ontological status in their analyses, Foucault and his postmodern colleagues often seem to forget that power is not something that actually has independent existence, but rather is a way in which we describe certain actions and phenomena, which in turn possess other characteristics as well. A typical example is when Foucault's friend and colleague Paul Veyne argues, in *Foucault Revolutionizes History* (1978), that the abolition of gladiatorial games in Rome in the late fourth century AD actually had nothing to do with Christian charity or sensitivity to the suffering of others, but was in fact simply a paternalistic politics of domination meant to coddle the people into being more easily ruled.[12] It did not occur to the postmodernists, just as it had not occurred to the Frankfurters or to Marx, that such conclusions are a type of reductionist monomania that renders the world monochromatic. In fact, it is perfectly possible, and even quite likely, that the abolition of gladiatorial combat was the result both of paternalistic domination and, at the very same time, of post-Constantinian Christian-humanist sensibilities. But it bothers philosophers that human beings are so complex as to defy full characterization of their motivations, since this would mean that there are some things those philosophers do not understand. And when one is oikophobically obsessed with making Western civilization appear as awful as possible, then one monomaniacally discards any elements that might paint a rosier picture of things.

It is true that Foucault himself, in a couple of places early on in the second part of the *History of Madness*, and also in the essay "Madness, the Absence of an Œuvre" (1964), seems to recognize the triviality of his claim regarding insanity. But he nonetheless lapses much too often (especially in the chapter "Birth of the Asylum") into the default position of condemning any social phenomenon that contains any repressive element, as if he did not know that all norms, qua norms, must to some extent repress and exclude. He never properly explains what a society without repression might look like, how a social order without any "myths" about itself would function. In his article "Reply to Derrida" (1972), Foucault says that with the *History of Madness* he had also intended to show "that there are conditions and rules for the formation of knowledge to which philosophical discourse is subjected in every era"—to which, again, the best reply is: You don't say?[13] It is perfectly obvious to anyone with a clear philosophical mind that this is the case, and as I previously stated, a "value-free" social science, a tabula rasa, and an independence of philosophical thought from exterior circumstance are all impossible, which is why this truth is trivial. (There are echoes in all this of Marcuse, and Foucault's enormous influence on many scholars continues to implicate them in the same error to this very day.) Again, as already Freud, Nietzsche, and arguably Aristotle knew, societies are and always must be to some measure repressive, or they will not be functioning societies.[14] It is a tautology to state that our social behavior is socially determined. But that Foucault is celebrated for such discoveries is indicative of the current oikophobic trend in academia, where what seeks to question the established will be endorsed and lauded—unless it is the established contemporary oikophobic dogma that is being questioned.[15]

Indeed Foucault has been treated fairly by neither his admirers nor his detractors. To much of the left, he is the kin of God himself, the most quoted academic of the twentieth century, whom everyone imitates both in style and content; to much of the right, he is the catch-all boogeyman, the worst human being since Karl Marx. Both these views are quite silly. My own opinion of Foucault is tepid, but his contributions to the history of thought are still significant, and he is a far more serious thinker than many of his contemporary French colleagues.

In fact, Foucault, in his "Madness, the Absence of an Œuvre," does acknowledge the objection that prohibitions exist in every culture, and then answers it as follows: "But we still understand poorly the organization of prohibitions in language. The two systems of restriction are not superimposed on each other, as if one were simply the verbal version of the other; that which must not appear on the spoken level is not necessarily that which is proscribed within the order of action." He continues, "The Zuni, who prohibit it, still speak of incest between brother and sister, and the Greeks of the Oedipus legend. Inversely, the Code of 1808 abolished the old penal laws against sodomy, but the language of the 19th century was much more intolerant toward homosexuality (at least in its male expression) than the previous eras had been. And it is probable that the psychological concepts of compensation, of symbolic expression, cannot explain such a phenomenon."[16]

In this reply, Foucault confuses two different levels of discourse, that of myth and that of daily life. If Foucault thought that the Greeks spoke openly about sex with one's mother in daily life—though surely he did not—he would be very much mistaken. Similarly, though people in the nineteenth century did not wish to speak of incest, their myths (the Bible) are littered with a great many indecent acts. Foucault states in a perfunctory manner that compensation and symbolic expression might not explain such discrepancies, but in fact myth, as art in general, serves as an accepted outlet by which certain taboo subjects can be cordoned off from the quotidian sphere and thus be discussed in a respectable fashion without the risk of direct personal miasma. A boy making doodles of a naked woman might incur reprobation from his parents or teachers, but Botticelli's and Rubens's paintings of whole companies of naked women will (fortunately) be considered perfectly respectable. The point is that social repression both in act and in language is universal—the Greeks had a strong sense of blasphemy and the unsayable, even if their points of focus were somewhat different from those of nineteenth-century Frenchmen.[17] And so Foucault is unable to answer the charge that his claims are trivial, and that various forms of repression and interdiction will always exist in every society and are by no means peculiar to the modern bourgeois society he wishes to criticize. (Incidentally, the French penal laws against sodomy had been tacitly abolished already in the Code of 1791, at a time when the public stigma against sodomy and homosexuality was still not quite as strong as it was to become in the nineteenth century.)

The oikophobic fascination with anything that appears to undermine Western civilization we see in the popularity of Derrida as well, upon whom praise was heaped whenever he would painstakingly explain that everything in society is in some way an act or an artificial "structure." To his acolytes it was news that after the supposed state of nature, things are no longer "natural." The realization that there are logocentric structures is supposed to be liberating, but, again, any child already possesses this liberty instinctively by not yet having had those structures imposed upon its mind; Derrida declares with the most touching pomposity as fruits of a lifetime of research what all children in unadulterated sincerity know. He maintains that Western culture contains arbitrary hierarchies that can be "deconstructed," and that these hierarchies have always repressed and excluded. This is perfectly true, and it is also perfectly trivial, for it holds for every human civilization.[18] So instead of absorbing Derrida's theories, one ought simply to retain something of a child's naïveté—to remain awestruck by even the smallest of objects in nature, like a little stone polished by a thousand years, and to reach up in enthrallment toward the full moon though one has seen it a thousand times. If one is capable of that, one will take life as it is, with all its imperfections, one will see through the joke of social and linguistic hierarchies right away but also understand that they are a necessary part of how human beings make sense of the world and order their lives within it, which Derrida, in his more lucid moments, also acknowledges.

Derrida is popular among some academics mostly because he flatters their oikophobic prejudices.[19] Foucault, however, does become better with age, such as in his multivolume *History of Sexuality* (1976–84).[20] The univariable fixation with power and social construct appears here as well, but by and large there is, at least in the second and third volumes, a genuinely interesting pursuit of truth and understanding, an exemplary archaeology of thought. Foucault, who as opposed to Derrida at least deserves to be taken seriously, suggests in "Reply to Derrida" that Derrida criticizes knowledge qua knowledge but without bothering (or perhaps so as not to have to bother) with any real analysis of its content or form—which is exactly right.

And so it is Germany and France where the philosophical twin influences of modern-day macrocivilizational oikophobia arose. Today's oikophobes take over from the Marxists, Frankfurters, and postmodernists at this point, in thinking monomaniacally that everything must have some basic essence: society is unjust, or tradition is oppressive. A very recent and high-profile example is "The 1619 Project," which considers America simply racist and tyrannical, tying every conceivable thing to slavery and racism, from the capitalist and justice systems to medicine, music, traffic jams, and high-calorie diets. Many of the contributions appear to suggest that America's founding was all about oppression and enslavement, which is just as unserious a claim as that America's founding was all about freedom and liberation. The truth is of course that the founding involved both liberation and enslavement, and that it is possible to celebrate the former while condemning the latter.

This monomaniacal analysis of history and society that focuses only on oppression is a wasted opportunity, because part of the postmodern effort had been to try to dismantle precisely such static definitions that disregarded the hidden meanings of historical practice. That is, the postmodernists had tried to question old definitions by pointing to repressive elements that people did not want to talk about. But they replaced such older definitions with others, focused purely on power and oppression, that were just as static and simplistic: by "discovering" and insisting—correctly—that a lot of power relationships and manipulation underlay historical practices, the Frankfurters and postmodernists became exuberant and thought that these alone underlay historical practices. The truth, however, is much more complex. Again, the phenomena we observe are crowded with different characteristics, some of which are in tension with—but without excluding—others. Our society can not only be unjust, in some respects, but also just, in some respects; tradition can not only be oppressive, but also ennobling, at the very same time. Since the Frankfurters and postmodernists monomaniacally thought that everything is about power and oppression, the less intellectual sort of people they have influenced feel they can dispense with argument and simply shout their way to what they believe is liberation, a liberation in which discourse is silenced.[21] As it happens, however, such silencing of discourse is an indication that society is plunging into tribalism and barbarianism again, because the position of a civilization on its historical trajectory can always be measured by its degree of respect for the art of speech and argument.

We also see here the positivist and relativist positions that we have come to know well by now. Something of the spirit of each of these two approaches can be useful: from positivism we learn that there is in fact a higher truth, even if it may be very difficult to find it, and from relativism we learn that personal perspective and cultural mores constitute a large part of what sometimes passes for truth. But when taken to an extreme, they have noxious consequences. The positivists want to tear down tradition and custom in order to coerce their societies into an impossible utopia; the relativists want to tear down tradition and custom in order to admit—which is tantamount to rejecting—all truths. Part of this shared goal of tearing down is, as I have indicated, to monomaniacally reduce objects or phenomena to their bare scientific essentials, as it were. For example, if it can be found that Christianity started as resentment against Jews and Romans, then they maintain that resentment is the main property we must understand in order to understand Christianity; or if a civilization was partly built on the backs of slaves, then the exploitation of slaves is the most defining essence of that civilization; or if sex is simply built on carnal lust and pleasure (as Marcuse thinks), then sex between human beings is no different from sex between animals and may thus be treated and devalued as the basic and unremarkable phenomenon it supposedly is.

But we lose half of life if we view it through this purely "scientific" or essentialist lens, since such a lens hides from us the great beauty and potential that lie just beyond its horizon. This beauty must inform both our emotional and intellectual understanding of the world. In order to preserve whatever science can gain for us, but without yielding to positivist or relativist overzealousness, it is necessary to keep both a narrow and a broad view in mind at the same time. You will recall that there are two ways of looking at every single thing: one narrow and emotional, one broad and logical, and indeed both sensible and logical knowledge are crucial for a full understanding of the object.

I owe a little something here to Edmund Husserl and his distinction between the world of science and what he called the "life-world" (*Lebenswelt*, in *The Crisis of European Sciences and Transcendental Phenomenology*, 1936).[22] This concept is poorly developed in that book, in my view, but the basic idea is that the life-world contains that which impinges upon the senses; it is the world of lived experience. The scientific world, on the other hand, takes the objective and distant view in explaining phenomena. I believe that both worlds are usually necessary for a full understanding of a phenomenon, although I would say that this depends somewhat on what sort of object is discussed, what its "purpose" is. For an aesthetic object, in the regular sense of artistic, the life-world alone is no doubt able to provide more truth than the scientific world alone would. For example, I cannot imagine ever understanding Beethoven's Ninth Symphony any better than I did when I first heard it as a young boy without any particular musicological, "scientific" knowledge, and was overwhelmed by its beauty and nobility, with my ears tingling for days afterwards, as if heaven itself had decided to sing for me, as if the whole world was subsumed in that sound, as if each note was a star that shone but for me, a work that made me run through the universe and discover new planets everywhere. In such a case, the life-world is the closest we can get to actual transcendence.

But as a general matter, objects or phenomena require both worlds to be grasped. If we were to take the case of the sacred fire of an indigenous African tribe—to use yet an example from my own experience—to me, as a

Western outsider, this sacred fire is quite simply a fire, with its various chemical compounds (the science-world). To the tribesmen, however, the fire is the means by which they communicate with their deceased ancestors, and it thus reinforces the bond they feel toward their traditions (the life-world). These two viewpoints seem to exclude one another, but as a purely logical matter they are clearly not mutually exclusive. (If they are, the life-world must yield, lest one end up in a relativist universe.) If one is able to give each view its due, which is difficult for the tribesman who wishes to plead with his vengeful grandfather, and for the distant Westerner who scoffs at any sort of superstition, then one truly understands the sacred fire, both intellectually and emotionally. The long-waged quarrel between poetry and philosophy will then have come to an end, with the two media united under one banner, in the same spirit, one that understands that poetry and philosophy are both valid ways of describing the world, each complementing the knowledge gained by the other.[23] The life-world can also explain, incidentally, why it sometimes happens that a layman is able to solve a difficulty haunting the experts. The experts have been trained only in the scientific world of that field, while the layman comes equipped, naïvely, with only the life-world and suddenly sees the truth emerge at an innocent glance. The history of discovery is replete with examples.[24]

Whereas both views, through their interaction and mutual tempering, must be employed conjointly for phenomena to be properly understood, the positivists and some relativists would hold only the scientific view, while more extreme relativists would hold only the life-world view (that is, something is whatever you think it is). Those who embrace only the scientific view would, specifically, engage in an abuse of nominalism, which is very common nowadays. The old philosophical distinction between realism and nominalism is as follows: Realism, which basically goes back to Plato, states that concepts have a real separate existence, whereas nominalists believe that concepts do not have real existence but are only the names that we give to physical, material phenomena. When we call something beautiful, are we referring to actual beauty that really exists (realism), or is "beauty" just a name (nominalism) that we give to our own impression?[25]

I consider myself a moderate nominalist, which is to say that I do not believe that abstract things actually exist. Rather, I believe that they are simply words or names, or, if they do exist, that they are in fact physical, not abstract. By and large in the modern history of philosophy, nominalism has won out over realism, but in the philosophy of the last half century or so, this has led to an overreach, by which nominalism has come to be abused for very reductionist and destructive ends. Some of this abuse stems from Wittgenstein's philosophy of language and rejection of Cartesianism, by which many would insist that concepts are but linguistic constructs with no claim to truth.[26] The abusers of nominalism hold that if words are merely constructs of convention, or "signs," then the concepts to which the words refer must be treated with suspicion, and the signs must be decoded, revealing the dishonesty of the society that instituted them, because surely society chose its words for the purposes of its own power (we recognize some of Foucault here). Since language constructs new meanings, we cannot properly rely on the reality of the things to which language refers.

Against this abuse of nominalism one might say that things are still real, in spite of language's instability: If I say that "love" is only a word, as indeed it is, it does not follow that the physical phenomena for which "love" serves as a shorthand, like heart palpitations and warmth, are not real and important. So whereas I can say with some legitimacy that love does not exist—because it is only a word under which an enormous palette of the most diverse phenomena is subsumed—the things to which we can plausibly refer when we say "love" do exist. This existence is real, even though love is simply a word that, for convenience's sake, we use as a rubric under which to gather a broad variety of sensations. Realism is still false, and Plato's mistake was to begin with the words—"love," "justice," and so on—and then to try to define what they are, whereas the truth is that the words came afterwards, as shorthand descriptions of a huge number of various phenomena in the physical world. We cannot describe satisfactorily or exhaustively what love is; "love," rather, is itself the description. (In fairness to Plato, he like most ancient Greeks knew only one language and therefore did not possess a system of checks on his own thoughts and on his attachment to his words that a knowledge of other languages can provide.) But while we reject the reality of abstract concepts, this rejection does not affect the basic substratum of underlying reality. Similarly, while we reject essences in the Platonic sense we do not deny the reality of the underlying bundles of characteristics, which are real and important, albeit constantly in flux.

But more to the point, the abuse of nominalism has become one of the main tools for oikophobia. For example, nominalism-abusers would say that Western civilization is just a verbal construct and thus nothing we ought to take seriously. The following quotes are salient and representative. Those defending the idea of the West "take 'Western Civ' as a fact (rather than a construct) and the correct starting point for all educational endeavors," and "The concept of 'Western Civilization' is premised on a clear distinction between the 'West' and everyone else, a distinction that is clear to no one but those ideologues who insist upon it. If we accept the notion of 'Western Civilization' with a straight face, we must acknowledge that this puts us, not necessarily on the same footing as white nationalists claiming Greco-Roman antiquity as their past, but certainly on the same spectrum."[27]

We might reply: That Western civilization is a construct—that it is not real in the sense that for example my hand is real—is merely a trivial truth; the construct still has usefulness and meaning because it refers to a number of physical particulars (Shakespeare, ballot boxes, the Parthenon, etc.) that do exist or have existed in the real world. By rejecting concepts as mere constructs and therefore devoid of reality, the nominalism-abusers forget that concepts, even though they do not have real, physical existence, nonetheless contain meaning by dint of their physical particulars. The oikophobic nominalism-abusers would level the same charge against the concept of oikophobia, insisting that it, or an idea like cyclicality in history, is a mere cognitive tapestry, woven only in the heads of those who advance such theories. But again, this is a trivial truth. In fact, stating that there are no discernible concepts or patterns to be gleaned from history is as much of a cognitive construct as the statement that there are.[28] One does not need to be a full-fledged realist to recognize that concepts, constructs, and categories can still be useful tools as we set out to navigate the world, and that these tools aid us in our empirical investigations. This does not mean that all constructs or categories are of equal value or usefulness, but to reject a construct qua construct is extremely short-sighted. In the previous chapter I said that "language makes the inherent but false assumption that sense can always be individuated," and I made the Heraclitean point that language seeks "to arrest that which is in flux." But although words can therefore be quite hollow, this does not mean that we should discard them all in our attempts to understand and describe the world.

The oikophobic nominalism-abusers themselves in fact often recognize the usefulness of concepts and constructs, but only those that they find politically congenial (such as "racism," "xenophobia," etc.), while their ultranominalism kicks into high gear only when they encounter concepts (such as "oikophobia") that do not look quite as pretty within their oikophobic world-view. This is why one hears them protest against concepts like "the West" as a fiction, while they at the same time insist that the West is plagued by "racism," "white supremacy," and any other concept they find convenient. A more intellectually honest attitude would recognize that for example "racism" is a useful concept because there are physical events that can plausibly be described as racist, and, at the very same time, that "the West" and "oikophobia" are also useful concepts because there are physical events that can plausibly be described as Western or oikophobic. (And, incidentally, the claim that the West as a distinction is clear only to Western ideologues is plainly false: many people in the developing world recognize and speak of that distinction, too.)

The tragedy here is that in the development of civilizations, as people become more cultivated and educated, they try to leave behind that which is physical and immediate—home, hearth, and the plough—and to arrive at abstract concepts. If nominalism then conquers, as it has, they then realize the putative emptiness of these abstract concepts. They have already rejected the physical and now end up rejecting the metaphysical, and are consequently left with: nothing.

In sum, therefore, the life-world and the scientific world ultimately refer to and describe the same world, and both verbal constructs and physical particulars have their uses. So if we wish to understand the world, we must open our minds and realize the multiple valid ways of describing it. We must let physical particulars impinge upon our senses, while also employing concepts and categories wherever they may be useful. It is this open approach, without preconceived strictures, that enables us to pursue multiple strands of thought at once. And it is then that we understand that our civilization, for all its violence, cruelty, and oppression, contains so much beauty and goodness, and that its traditions merit our proper care. A rejection of the life-world of human experience, and an ultranominalist attack on concepts, are part of what has made the contemporary manifestation of Western oikophobia possible and reduced our ideas to empty shells devoid of meaning.

One sees this in action all the time. Sex is always a pleasant example. Sex is biological, which is precisely what the scientific world will tell us, reducing the union of bodies to sexual organs. Kant, in *The Metaphysics of Morals* (1797), infamously referred to marriage as a pact for the reciprocal use of the genitals and said that sexual desire is a desire for the genitals of another person (it probably should not surprise anyone that he died a bachelor). But the life-world of sex is what for instance the arts can illustrate through poetry, music, sculpture, and the like, and what we ourselves, if we are lucky, may experience in the act of union, that is to say, what sex can actually mean: tenderness, spiritual unity, a desire for the other's happiness—in a word, love. Now, this is a construct, to be sure, but it is nonetheless based on real and meaningful particulars. When the life-world is stripped away, and when concepts like the sacred union of two persons are ridiculed or treated like a quaint relic of the past, it becomes possible for modern oikophobes to reject the foundation upon which rests so much of the beauty that is disseminated in our institutions and in our art.

Oikophobes have forgotten that the world can and ought to be viewed in more than one way, that the biological coupling of genitals is also, at the very same time, a part of a tradition, of a force, namely the force that lived in Keats as he wrote his final love letter from his deathbed in Rome, his perspiring face already immortal; that lived in Michelangelo as he carved his statues, his chiseling hands and fingers full of love and care; that lived in the Lyonnaise Labé as she composed her love poems by her window; that lived in the Theban men who fought and died in pairs at Chaeronea. So the abuse of nominalism leads to a debasement of some of the world's most wonderful things: our love, our art, our civilization. And so we see again how contemporary oikophobes, inheriting the mantle from the Frankfurters and the postmodernists, monomaniacally simplify the world by thinking either that concepts are empty, or that everything has its own basic essence rather than a bundle of characteristics.

Similarly, monomaniacally, many philosophers of the last century and a half or so have erroneously assumed that if the genealogy of a particular phenomenon or institution can be discredited, then the phenomenon itself must also fall. Not only Marx but also Nietzsche, with his focus on genealogy in his otherwise perceptive critiques, are among the main culprits, and they are followed by the Frankfurters and the postmodernists in this respect. These latter like to think that if, for instance, it can be established that the laws of justice were set down by aristocrats in order to control the lower classes (an idea appearing already in Plato's *Republic* 338e and *Laws* 714c–d, and also in part 2 of Rousseau's *Origin and Basis of Inequality*), if the outlawing of theft represents the interest of the rich in protecting their own property, then the laws of justice should be rejected or at least radically reformed. But there are two problems here. First, all human activity is interest-based, and the conclusion that laws or ideas are power structures is therefore a trivial truth. It should consequently not be considered a special case if a particular action represents a particular interest vis-à-vis opposing interests. Some interests are more dangerous than others, but the mere fact that something represents an interest and a structure is in and of itself unremarkable, even though the postmodernists view their observation as the second coming of Copernicus. Second, even though it is true that the laws of justice reflect a particular interest, we can nonetheless consider the laws of justice just; and even though theft may have been made illegal by someone merely wishing to protect his own property, the illegalization of theft may still be just. That is to say that the quality of a phenomenon is not beholden to that phenomenon's genealogy. The belief—typical in Foucault—that sordid genealogy serves as an equalizer among thoughts and ideas is one of the greatest philosophical blunders in history.

Indeed it is a common point among oikophobes that even when their countries do something good, they do it in their own interest and should therefore not receive any credit for it. But everything we do is interest-based, even if sometimes others' interests are also involved, and everything is subsumed under the pleasure principle (even when we are altruistic, we derive pleasure from our altruism), which means that there is no such thing as pure selflessness. And so because we do everything also for our own sakes, the critique of the morality of an action by establishing that pleasure or benefit was conferred upon the agent is never a sufficient reason for rejecting the morality of that action. For the same reason, the oikophobic critique that one's country acts in its own interest is a trivial, pointless critique, because there are many additional ways of describing the action beyond pointing out the obvious fact that it is self-interested.

We may of course question the laws of justice, but when we do, we must question them on their own terms, which is intellectually far more difficult than to dismiss them as part of a nefarious power structure. The eschatological positivists and relativist postmodernists have thus made us here in the West oikophobically attack our heritage for the wrong reasons, or for reasons that are true but trivial. The eschatological notion that history proceeds toward a goal, that this goal can be scientifically established, and that it is our duty to hurry it along, and, further, the notion that Western society is a power structure intent on domination, these have been the great philosophical calamities of the nineteenth and twentieth centuries, and they continue to haunt us into the twenty-first.

So in the nexus of oikophobia and modern civilizational decline we find a confluence not only of Western microcultures, but also of opposing Western philosophies. While it is technically possible for a positivist outlook to maintain that conflicts will be solved by the imposition of a dominant Western culture—a more Hegelian flavor of positivism—it is nowadays more often the case that it entails an egalitarian paradise. And if everything must be made equal, then this positivist internationalism becomes so international and so certain that all cultures are morally the same, that there ends up being no such thing as superiority or, by extension, superior truth. In the cauldron of oikophobia, positivism thus finally becomes its opposite, relativism. Oikophobes in ancient Greece were generally relativists; it is only in modern times that many oikophobes have become both positivist and relativist at the same time. This, ultimately, is the most modern manifestation of the ancient and recurring phenomenon that is oikophobia.

Because of all this, Westerners might do well to try to find again the goodness in their heritage, without being blind to its shortcomings. In chapter 5 I referred to Napoleon's grave in Paris, in the Invalides, as an "obscene" cupola, but the French should still keep their identity and monuments as best they can. So too Americans would do well to hold on to such things as Columbus Day and other customs. Many oikophobes, by pointing out that this American holiday, as well as numerous American figures and events, do not have quite the noble background they are sometimes purported to have had, demonstrate how much they understand of the very small (like Christopher Columbus), and how little they understand of the very large (like the rise and fall of civilizations).[29] This preservation of identity is useful in the face of both external and internal threats to a civilization.

One of the problems here is that the positivist spirit of Rousseau, Kant, and Popper has lulled us into the misapprehension that order and a desire for peacefulness are somehow part of the underlying substratum of reality. But in fact Hobbes and Hegel—and indeed the postmodernists—are right insofar as chaos, power, and domination are the rule. When power play appears to be absent, it is only because your hope for a better world blinds you. Power play is always there, right under your nose, in every word, in every gesture, in every passing glance, and it can be painful to be clear-sighted enough to always see it. But the advantage of seeing it is of course that once we openly acknowledge the grim cruelty of our reality, we are actually better equipped to do something about it and to establish a semblance of order within our own proximity. It is when we think that being is fundamentally luminous and good that we yield to the forces of darkness and welcome them into our homes. Making the world better must always begin with the realization of how cruel and violent it is. If you deny this cruelty, you will be fighting against flies while the dragons fly by.

But the decline of religion will make the preservation of identity exceedingly difficult. It is not an endorsement of mysticism or tribalism to acknowledge the historical fact that a people still capable of being religiously enthralled by the moon will fight more fiercely for what they believe. When the world has been reduced to only the science-world, there is nothing anymore in which to put one's faith. And since diversity weakens the cohesiveness of religious and political structures, the more cultures we try to incorporate under one umbrella and the more faiths we want to render compatible with one another, the weaker the macrocivilization will grow. This is why, for instance, the European Union had failure built into it from the very beginning.

There has now started to awake an awareness of some of this. Books have begun to appear that, with their own particular points of focus, try to muster a defense based on cultural integrity, like Pascal Bruckner's *La tyrannie de la pénitence* (The tyranny of guilt), where what he calls "Western masochism" is precisely oikophobia; Thilo Sarrazin's *Deutschland schafft sich ab* (Germany abolishes itself), especially the last three chapters; and Douglas Murray's *The Strange Death of Europe*.[30] But the trajectories of civilizations indicate that such efforts cannot, in the long run, make much of a difference.

Nonetheless, I wish to end on a more constructive note. As I have said, my goal is more to understand than to condemn oikophobia; declining civilizations will also have their cultural beauty, often even more than those that are in their infancy, with so little to build upon. The repetitive patterns of history never exclude the creation of individual beauty and purpose. Indeed, if one had gained the impression that there is a measure of atavism to be read in these pages, that I am woefully complaining that things used to be better in the good old days and desiring to turn the clock back to some supposed golden age, one would have read rather superficially, since I have repeatedly stressed the cultural achievements of later stages of civilizations, as well as the importance of viewing both the good and the bad together. I in fact do not wish to go back, because there has never been a golden age, nor will there ever be one. We have made enormous strides in medicine and technology, and may in many ways consider ourselves lucky to be alive at the present time—and in this, at least, the positivists are right, even if it is a fairly obvious point. You can read Hippocratic treatises on how one used to cure certain diseases to appreciate how good it is to live in the present age rather than even in ancient Greece.

When it comes to philosophy and intellectual life, we are not much worse off today either. We live in an oikophobic era, which I think is a pity, but it would be delusional to believe that we would be individually better off in the early tribal days of jingoistic brutality and conquest. For the most part in the philosophical regard, the old days were neither much better nor much worse than the present ones. They had their ups and downs, as do ours. When one is ready to take all the world and all its stories in one's grasp, one finds that history is ebb and flow—ebb, and flow. I simply look with a certain melancholia—but also acceptance—at its perennial repetition. This acceptance stems from the fact that a sufficient familiarity with the overarching story of our species enables me to take us less seriously, and to understand that the world is not as dramatic as it sometimes appears. When I am able to rise high enough and soar with my mind through the skies, then I see that the laboring peasant with mud on his shoes, the charging knight with blood-stained armor, the roaring helmsman with brine-splattered face, the incanting preacher in a cathedral's grey light, and even the quiet writer in self-indulgent isolation, all have something faintly comical about them. And so, as I land again on the earth, rather than wishing for a golden age, or for my oikophobic society to finally listen and learn, I choose neither to turn the clock back nor to rush forward toward an end of history, but merely, while waiting for my own personal end, to seek out some minor moments of happiness and rejoicing in the small acts of love and creation with whose potential we have all been blessed.

EPILOGUE

On Personal Freedom

Why the seeming inevitability of history, suggesting a lack of freedom, why living in an oikophobic civilization where tradition qua tradition is ridiculed, does not hinder us from great endeavors, is the question to which we now turn, and with which our journey together through time, space, and thought will end.

A risk in examining historical trends is always that one will be accused of taking away from people their freedom to act, of being a Marxist-Hegelian end-of-history preacher, someone who believes that history will and must turn out a particular way. As we saw in chapter 9, it was precisely the emphasis on eschatology and teleology, the insistence that history has an immutable end that made me reject such preachers. Once we settle for the more modest goal of recognizing cycles in history, cycles that will continue to exist with no ultimate end station, then historical trends and patterns, as opposed to Popperian haphazardness on the one side and immutable Marxist progressivism on the other, become evident.

We have already seen how the danger of robbing people of their individualities lies close at hand. Hegel has played a part in the popularization of such notions as fate and historical destiny. And Marx, especially, reduces people to cogs, in the social machinery of production. He thinks that it is the capitalists who have destroyed human will and individuality, but in denouncing them for this it is he himself who does so, in that he belittles the workers he wants to save and takes away any capacity for independent influence they may have. Marx and Engels explain that the communists are the ones who best understand the proles' movement—and this written by men still in their twenties and knowing so little of the world; to them, the human being does not have will, but capital itself actually does (part 2 of *The Communist Manifesto*), as it apparently controls the actions both of the capitalists who wield it and of the workers who suffer from it. So human beings do not have will, but inanimate concepts do.[1] This sort of thing tends to happen when history is viewed within too narrow confines.

So one may now ask: What is this freedom of which we can make use in shaping our destinies and in influencing positively our oikophobic societies, and does it even exist? There has been a very great tendency among philosophers over the centuries to want to defend at any price the concept of free will, which is usually understood as meaning that one could have chosen differently under identical circumstances. Philosophy overall has been able to break free from that nonsensical notion (most philosophers who peddle it today are of the cloth), but even when systems of philosophy were devised that aimed to demonstrate how we are all victims of larger social or physical forces, there was almost always a considerable squeamishness on the part of philosophers toward the logical conclusion that we are not free. They would refuse to say it explicitly, as if it were the task of philosophers to tell people what sounds comfortable and reassuring rather than the truth, as if they were political propagandists rather than independent thinkers. On the contrary, I think that we philosophers should be proud of the fact that society has shown an obstinate tendency of executing, banishing, or at least silencing us. When determinist bondage is called freedom, when forcing oneself to adapt to what will necessarily happen is called freedom, then one would do well to suspect that the philosophers are not being entirely forthright with their audiences or with themselves.

Even Hume, one of my darlings, appears almost to feel obliged to confirm the existence of free will, even though everything he has said about it indicates that it is not free (mainly *A Treatise of Human Nature* 2.3.1–2), namely that a human being could only have made a different decision if he had had different convictions and characteristics than the ones he actually does have, which is to say, if he had been a different person. So too the otherwise reasonably clever young Wittgenstein, in the *Tractatus Logico-Philosophicus* 5.1362, yields to the same temptation: "Free will consists in the fact that future actions cannot be known now," which is not dissimilar to what a famous contemporary philosopher on the subject, Daniel Dennett, would say.[2] Well then please have the courtesy not to call it free will, because what you are describing is clearly not free; you are changing the definition so as to be able to defend it.

And so I shall state it plainly: free will, the idea that there is an independent faculty of the will which in turn acts freely, is an illusion. The will is considered metaphysically free by not operating under necessitating natural or physical laws, by being self-regulating, and thus by allowing a person to make a different decision under identical circumstances; the processes of natural causality in the world may incline but do not force the free will in one direction or the other. This is the most common definition. But the notion of free will is a Judeo-Christian illusion that exists mainly because, to many, the structure of that religious complex will collapse if it is not possible to ascribe bad events to the free agency of human beings rather than to an omnipotent and benevolent God. Many people today who insist on free will—who even take it for granted that we are free—do not know that they are propagating Christianity.

People seem to take personally the notion that they might be unfree, since no one wants to call himself a slave. They think that justice and retributive judgment are impossible without it, but this too is a notion that was developed mainly as a defense of Christian theology. It is worthwhile in the present context to rehearse the development of the notion of free will in history in order to see how theology played a part in crystallizing it, and what the Christians borrowed from pagan Greekdom. In this way, we may better understand why free will is not something that should be taken for granted, especially not by those who think of themselves as rational by dint of being anti-religious. But most importantly in our context, we may come to better understand why the oikophobic trajectory of civilizations, and the concomitant lack of free will, do in fact not weaken the force of our actions.

We can isolate three basic phases in the history of free will: (1) Philosophers have no conception of free will either way, and so this is strictly speaking a "prehistory" (early to mid-antiquity); (2) most philosophers defend free will (late antiquity, Middle Ages, early modern period); and (3) most philosophers deny, or redefine, free will (late modern and present times). In the Homeric, Archaic, and at least early Classical Greek world, there is no need for an independent faculty of the will. When a person performs an action, he simply performs it. Greek actions are hormetic (from the Greek *horme*, "impulse," whence "hormone"). If someone changes his mind or decides upon some course of action, Homer simply explains formulaically that "(s)he then thought other things" (*enth' aut' all' enoese*). This does not require a separate part of the human organism called will, to say nothing of a free will.[3]

As intimated, free will exists out of a need to view the cosmos as just, as shall become clearer by and by. Now, there are some scattered ideas here and there in early Greek thought that might, with considerable generosity, be considered as precursors of the notion of a broader cosmic justice, such as possibly Heraclitus's *logos*, or all-encompassing reason, and Anaxagoras's *nous*, or cosmic "mind"; or maybe even Anaximander's *apeiron*, the "unlimited," and Xenophanes's nascent pantheist or pandeist monotheism, though his theological skepticism would not become widespread until the fourth century BC, when Greek society had become fully ready to oikophobically tear down its own traditions. But the earliest more substantial textual passages regarding a just world, and with it the first seeds of a free will, begin, as might be expected, with Plato and Aristotle, but with Aristotle as so often being a bit more typically Greek and pagan than his proto-Christian teacher.

The most significant passage in Plato in this regard is his famous "Myth of Er," in book 10 of the *Republic*, which describes the reincarnation of the soul and how various dead figures have the opportunity of choosing what their next lives will be like. We find here the two crucial words *theos anaitios* (617e): "God is not responsible" for (or more literally "God is not the cause" of) the souls' choice when they choose their next lives, but only the souls themselves are; this is echoed in *Laws* 904b–c. There is also some material in Plato's *Timaeus* (e.g., 29e–30b), above all in the treatment of the demiurge, where we perceive a certain flavor of the notion of a just world and that there will be an imposition of justice for human beings after death. Aristotle, for his part, in 3.1–5 of the *Nicomachean Ethics*, speaks of choice, preference, and will, and he explicitly connects responsibility with the freedom of the agent in choosing his course of action.

But freedom here, as well as words like "choice" and "will," mean something else than when they will later be expressed by Christian and certainly Kantian thinkers. In the *Republic* passage we learn that the souls who had exciting and eventful lives now choose simplicity and calm for their next lives. That is to say that their choices are dependent on their previous experiences. It is also significant that the souls during the process of reincarnation pass under the throne of Necessity (*ananke*), and that the cosmos itself is represented as a spindle controlled by Necessity's three daughters, the Fates. Since Plato goes on to speak about the orbits of the planets, there are also hints of astrology in the passage. There is choice and responsibility here, but no clear freedom.

As for Aristotle, he denies the immortality of the soul and must therefore withdraw from Plato's position of reincarnation, and consequently considers the question of reward and punishment after death to be moot.[4] Further, his discussion of freedom involves merely physical freedom: you are responsible for your action if no one compelled you to do it, but this does not say anything about a metaphysical-mental freedom to act. The Greek word for "will" (*boulesis*) in itself contains no individual freedom, and its etymology in fact has the flavor of "counsel" and "advice," of a plan of action mapped out in concourse with others. In any case, the existence of some unusual ideas among the Greeks regarding cosmic justice and such does not mean that there was no general Greek mentality of which we may speak, and which indeed was very pagan in outlook.

Some scholars argue that Epicurus takes another step in formulating non-deterministic ideas toward individual freedom, which he supposedly does by arguing that there is no necessity in the mind, due to the swerve of atoms (Lucretius's *On the Nature of Things* 2.281–93). But it is questionable how much Lucretius, who lived in the first century BC, is editorializing Epicurus's (late fourth / early third century BC) opinions. In any case, some translators, who possess the concept of "free will" that still did not exist in Lucretius's day, somewhat modernize the Latin in what is a rather murky passage. But it is at least possible that Epicurus was a bit ahead of his time in this regard.

The early Stoics, shortly after Epicurus, are more deterministically minded yet again, in that they believe God, in the form of *pneuma*, or divine breath, controls everything in a pantheistic fashion. They think everything is fate, that is, determined through a chain or network of causes, with no gaps in it.

But the Stoics nonetheless consider us responsible for our actions, and when the word freedom (*eleutheria*) is used in their writings, they are not thinking of the same sort of metaphysical freedom that we have in mind today. They are thinking, rather, of that which is on a physical level dependent on us, and which therefore falls within our bailiwick, as it were. That is to say, there is no necessary link between metaphysical freedom and moral responsibility. Not even in the later, adulterated version of Stoicism that we find in the Roman Empire, whose foremost proponents are Seneca (first century AD) and the Greek slave Epictetus (late first / early second century AD), do we find free will. They speak much of responsibility and proper action, but they never say that we are metaphysically free, that our minds are independent of physical causality. That thought does not yet appear to exist.

That free will and moral responsibility must be carefully distinguished merits emphasis, since the two are so closely linked in the popular consciousness. Historically, we see that the idea of moral responsibility existed—naturally—well before the idea of free will; philosophically, if one takes the materialist view of the universe there must as a matter of practical necessity be room for moral responsibility even while the existence of metaphysical, immaterial freedom is denied. This is not a novel point. David Hume, after his initial squeamishness, begins to scratch the surface when he states in *A Treatise of Human Nature* 3.1.1 that "as liberty and choice are not necessary to make an action produce in us an erroneous conclusion, they can be, in no respect, essential to morality . . ."[5]

We now leave the prehistory of free will, and enter into the second phase. In late Aristotelian exegesis, around 200 AD, which also happens to be the time when the first major crop of Greek and Latin church fathers arises, there is a change in how freedom is understood. The Aristotelian exegete and philosopher Alexander of Aphrodisias, the last of the significant Peripatetics, and also his younger contemporary Plotinus, founder of Neoplatonism, criticize the early Stoics for, as they see it, abandoning Aristotle's freedom as a cause of moral responsibility. Alexander, especially, is under the impression that Aristotle had introduced a free human faculty of will that guides action and thus ensures moral responsibility, and wonders why the Stoics would reject it. But the Stoics never did reject it, because it had never been suggested in the first place. Alexander misconstrues Aristotle's conception of freedom by understanding it in a way that had not started to develop until after Aristotle, during the five hundred years that separate Aristotle and Alexander.

Various terms are often identical, but their meanings change over time, misleading some people into assuming that we are dealing with the same things in different eras if the same words are used for them. So, as very often in philosophy, much comes down to shifting semantic fields. The Greek term *to eph' hemin*, "that which depends on us," when Alexander uses it leads to a free-will problem, because Alexander understands something "dependent on us" to mean that we could freely choose what to do. But the same idea is unproblematic in Aristotle, who simply sees it as a physical dependence regardless of any metaphysical considerations of free choice on our part. These differences can be discovered by carefully juxtaposing various passages from Alexander's *On Fate* (12, and passim) with the aforementioned *Nicomachean Ethics* 3.1–5 of Aristotle. To Aristotle it is evident that nature has gifted different people differently, and that our possible courses of action—our self-determination—are limited by the degrees of necessity that nature has imposed upon us. To Alexander, on the other hand, this notion is completely unacceptable, since it would mean that nature, which is divine, is unjust in treating people differently, and such a claim would be tantamount to blasphemy. And so a measure of theology has now entered into the question.

Alexander, using the classic "lazy argument" (*argos logos*) against the Stoic theory of fate, asks: If everything is determined by fate, why should we bother to do anything at all? Our powers of reflection would be in vain, and we could spend our lives in sloth and laziness—hence the name of the argument—since in any case everything is predetermined. If I am destined to win an athletic trophy, then I will win it regardless of whether I train or not, and therefore, I do not need to train; similarly, if I am destined not to win the trophy, then no training in the world will make me win it, and so, again, I do not need to train. The same argument has often been used in favor of the more modern conception of free will.

But in fact there is no contradiction between reflecting on a course of action and at the same time realizing that what one ultimately decides will not stem from a metaphysically free choice. The Stoic Chrysippus, who lived in the third century BC, several hundred years before Alexander, had already refuted the "lazy argument"; he did so in a deterministic rather than free-will context, since he had no conception of free will, but the logic of the answer is the same regardless. He maintains that even if an outcome is fated, the reflection, thought, and effort that lead to it are concomitantly fated. That is to say, Alexander, as well as modern critics who employ the "lazy argument" in favor of free will, and thereby display their ignorance of the fact that it was answered over two thousand years ago, erroneously place the "goal-action" (winning the trophy) in a category separate from that of the actions that lead to the goal-action, such as training, dieting, concentrating mentally on the goal, and so on.

But that separate categorization is an illusion, and Chrysippus's point is that all actions are in the same category. By placing the goal-action in a different category, the proponents of the "lazy argument" assume that the intermediate actions (training, dieting, concentrating) are up to us; that is to say, they assume in the premise that which they wish to prove, namely that action is free, and so their error of categorization is also an error of circularity.[6] And not only are our efforts concomitantly fated with their goal, but also reward or punishment is fated along with the action that is rewarded or punished. In an anecdote handed down to us by Diogenes Laertius (7.23), the Stoic philosopher Zeno was beating his slave for stealing. When the slave, who had probably listened in on his master's philosophical conversations, whelped in his defense: "I was fated to steal," Zeno replied: "And to be beaten!"[7]

So in ascribing freedom to human beings independently of the necessity of physical causality, and independently of nature, Alexander of Aphrodisias takes a long step away from Aristotle and the more pagan-physical outlook, and toward a real concept of free will. He is eventually, in fact, forced to draw the conclusion (*On Fate* 38) that the earlier Stoics may have used words like "that which depends on us" in a very different sense than what he himself is used to.[8]

To the Christians, on the whole, or at least to the Latin if not the Greek church fathers, freedom is finally "free will": *liberum arbitrium*, as Augustine calls it. It is only with them that we have the concept in its full development. *Liberum arbitrium* is of course a Latin term, and indeed the notion of free will was codified more fully by the Latin than the Greek church fathers. There is no exact ancient Greek equivalent of the Latin phrase; a close word is *exousia*, the power or ability to do something, which however is more like Latin *potestas*. The Greek *to eph' hemin*, that which depends on us, as well as its Latin variations like *in nobis* and the somewhat more advanced *in nostra potestate*, do not signify freedom before circa 200 AD. But nonetheless there were, in addition to Augustine and the early Latin Christian writers, such as Arnobius, also some Greek men of the church who contributed to the development of the concept of free will, such as Origen and Victorinus, and perhaps Nemesius. The Neoplatonist (i.e., pagan) Porphyry also contributed, but by this time (late third century AD), Neoplatonism and Christianity had intermingled to such a degree that the distinction, in the present context, was not very significant.

Some argue that the idea of original sin, formulated by Augustine but with inspiration from, among others, the more materialist Tertullian, who believed that the soul is inherited from one generation to the next, limits free will, if it does not abolish it outright (which much later became the attitude of for example the Calvinists, and to a considerable extent even of Martin Luther himself). In light of what Augustine says elsewhere, I do not find this particularly convincing: the fall of man places our field of action in a world of sin and suffering, but within that field we are nonetheless, to Augustine, free to act as we desire—Augustine's entire effort around the *liberum arbitrium* would be pointless if this were not so. It should nonetheless be stressed that some Christians have managed without free will, but they were drowned out by the majority voices over time.

So freedom now comes to mean more or less what it will be to Kant, namely metaphysical freedom, a freedom insisting that there is a justice to the world insofar as responsibility can finally be connected to metaphysically free agency, and insofar as human beings are said to be in full control of their choices.[9] The Christian attitude considers a freedom that is not tied to an independent and free faculty of the will—a mere physical freedom, as in Aristotle—to be unfree. It is not that Aristotle or the other Greeks rejected a notion of metaphysical freedom, but rather that it did not even occur to them in the first place, because the pagan universe does not require it. That universe takes a tragic, nonutopian view of life, with pleasure and pain repeating themselves in eternal recurrence. Nature is unfair, having endowed some people with nobility, weighed others down with turpitude, rewarded the criminal, punished the righteous—Heracles, in the moment of saving his family from the clutches of an evil tyrant, is struck down by madness; Hector, also fighting for his family, is killed and ignobly dragged on the ground by a chariot, while a selfish Achilles, caring for almost nothing but booty, lives on in immortal fame.

There is no cosmic fairness assuring that just deserts are received, and history is not seen as its own judge. The mourner weeping over the funeral pyre cannot take solace at meeting the beloved again in a paradise afterlife. It is most certainly not a coincidence that Plato, who took the first little step

toward free will in the Myth of Er, was also philosophy's first political uto-
pianist. The insistence on free will is the insistence on an underlying fairness to the world—you receive what you deserve, for you choose freely—and
the fairness that is thought to underlie the world is then to be implemented
in human society as well, where everything must become perfect. And so, as
always, the insistence on total fairness is the insistence on tyranny.

The Christian universe has metaphysical freedom and a human faculty
of the will so that all bad actions can be properly grounded therein, rather
than be placed within the responsibility of a supposedly benevolent deity. The
Christian attitude is thus not simply a popularization of Plato—although to
some extent it is also that—but in fact adds a new metaphysical element to
the notion of freedom. It is ultimately not Plato or Aristotle but the Christians who, with some help from the late Peripatetics and from the Neopla-
tonists, create the concept of free will and tie it to moral responsibility; they
need free will in order to save the messianic and utopian worldview they have
just dreamed up in their North African brothels and Cappadocian grottoes.
And this, very briefly, is how the idea of free will came about and why we
should not take it for granted, or even very seriously; its tradition is younger
and less venerable than many think. As philosophers started to shuffle off
their theological coil and become more materialist-minded in the modern
era, it is natural that they would finally see through the illusion of free will,
in the third and final phase of this history, even if they were sometimes reluctant to admit it, as we have seen.

But earlier in this chapter I asked: What is this freedom of which we can
make use in shaping our destinies and in influencing positively our oikophobic societies, and does it even exist? If it does not exist, does this not mean,
then, that Marx was right in his straitjacket view of history, that the proletariat will ultimately rebel no matter what we do? Not really, no, because our
common feeling that this lack of free will would lessen the worth of our actions and our influence upon our surroundings has been ingrained in us by
thousands of years of Judeo-Christianity. And this is the point at which many
irreligious oikophobes go wrong, and where more Judeo-Christian-minded
people who do believe in free will go right: we are still always responsible for
our actions, and our influence on the course of things is very real.

So the fact that no one has free will does not mean that one is not a responsible and impactful agent. Many oikophobes, through a sort of popularized Marxism, tend to believe that impersonal social forces remove people's

agency and responsibility, which is why they begin to defend criminality, violence, and generally low standards as the legitimate outcome of such forces. They thereby dehumanize humanity, like Marx himself had done when he ascribed will to capital but not to actual flesh-and-blood people. And so those who believe in free will may be wrong about the metaphysics, but are right about the physics: We must all be held accountable for what we do. We must understand, with the pre-Platonic and to a great extent post-Platonic Greeks—and to some degree even with Plato himself—that the larger social and historical forces that are constantly at work must never be allowed to remove agency and responsibility from human beings, or to reduce us to the instinctual beasts. Western individualism is not excluded by our lack of free will—that is to say, this lack is not dehumanizing in any way—because free will is irrelevant to the question of good and bad action, to the distinction between nobility and turpitude. And so we always hold humans responsible for their actions, which in turn means that we do not view them through the lens of "hard determinism," according to which strict physical causality and the lack of free will are incompatible with responsibility.

This hard determinism, also known as incompatibilism, is opposed to compatibilism, or "soft determinism." Soft determinism or compatibilism holds that responsibility can coexist with determinism. But one must distinguish here between antiquity and modern times. Ancient compatibilism considers determinism to be compatible with responsibility, while modern compatibilism (like that of Kant) considers determinism to be compatible with free will, not merely responsibility, since by modern times there is a clear notion of free will. Ancient compatibilism is correct: responsibility is a must, with or without externally determined action or physical causality. But modern compatibilism is a waste of breath. The mere fact that philosophers have tried to uphold modern compatibilism presupposes, incorrectly, that there is an almost a priori connection between responsibility and free will, that these must in some way or other go together: they feel that if responsibility can coexist with determinism, then free will must coexist with determinism.

The terms "hard" and "soft" determinism were popularized through William James's otherwise forgettable essay *The Dilemma of Determinism* (1884), a title that shows perfectly the extent to which Christian theology has influenced our thinking: because why should it be a "dilemma"? It can only be a dilemma when we assume, desperately, that there must be a natural link between responsibility and free will, which then causes the "dilemma" or "problem" of how to combine free will with physical causality. But there is no ground for this assumption. Indeed, people desire free will to be the outcome, but see no way of arriving there, which is why they call the whole issue the "free will problem" and thereby betray their bias.

In fact, we should not view the human being as responsible for his actions metaphysically, because of free choice, but physically: moral turpitude is punished not because it is "evil" in and of itself, but because of its actual, physical consequences, and so physics comes before and guides ethics, because the agent is the physical field from which an action emanates. In Greek, in fact, there is an expression for this: something is not necessarily done "by us," but rather *di' hemon*, "through / by means of us." When the Greek hoplites hold firm against the Persians at Thermopylae, their bravery is not lessened by the fact that they did not freely choose to be brave, just as the beauty of the rose is no less beautiful because the rose did not will its own beauty and wondrous fragrance into existence. Ultimately, therefore, the difference on a purely moral level between a person who commits murder out of insanity and a person who commits murder out of selfishness and greed is not very great. (And as Michel Captain Obvious Foucault might ask: who is to decide what is insane? The murderer was abnormal, whether by insanity or moral vice, and his abnormality made him kill.) So there should be no question of a "problem" of free will, or a "dilemma," because all this assumes that responsibility and freedom must be two sides of the same coin of human agency. But they are not.

If one were to interject that denying free will and still holding people responsible for their actions would render the world unjust, there is a twofold reply. First, again, why must the world be just? It is precisely the Judeo-Christian conviction that an omniscient, omnipotent, transcendent, self-aware, and benevolent force rules all that leads to the necessity of a just world, and thus to the philosophical branch of theodicy (the justice of God, or why bad things happen to good people). If we do not believe in such a god, there is no need to hold on to cosmic justice. Second, the mere assumption that just deserts depend on the freedom of the agent is Christian or proto-Christian. Again, why do we assume that responsibility must have this dependence on freedom? And why, really, is justice tied to freedom? Why? But for God, there is absolutely no ground for this assumption. Anyone who does not understand that, cannot understand pre-Christian antiquity, the era of the greatest philosophy the world has yet produced.

The desperate effort to defend metaphysical freedom is based on an equally desperate desire to view our world as essentially—metaphysically— just. People feel almost morally obliged to defend free will, and they cannot handle John Keats's "negative capability," to which I referred in chapter 9. They cannot get through their day without telling themselves, as they look into the mirror in the morning, that the good will be rewarded and the evil will get their comeuppance. But the world is not particularly just—it simply is, and the understanding of this fact brings us closer to the tragic Greek out- look and its rather dour view of the world and of humanity. In a way, how- ever, this more pessimistic attitude turns us into optimists, for we accept the world as it is, in all its simple, physical beauty, without sprucing it up super- naturally, and we love it in its unadulterated sublimity. Life is rather miser- able and absurd, and so the art of living consists in recognizing those peaks of pleasurable and beautiful experience as soon as they occur and in tying them together into a string, a flowery garland that becomes the higher level upon which one looks back, as the valleys below are outshadowed.

In the modern era, after the French Enlightenment had ensured that Greekdom was irretrievably lost under Christianity, Kant made himself the philosophical father of the comfortable and self-satisfied bourgeoisie by throw- ing out much of the faith and trappings of religion while in fact preserving a great deal of what is important about Christianity, such as its moral under- pinnings. Less educated secularists could thus come to believe that they are beyond Christianity and to array themselves against those who openly embrace faith. A liberal but ultimately quite religiously minded thinker, Kant contrib- uted to the anchoring of free will in the popular consciousness. By preserving some of Christianity's metaphysical absolutism even in the process of ostensibly rejecting absolutist Christian dogma, he rendered that absolutism acceptable and palatable even to the non-religious. A more logical result would have been for people who rejected religion to also reject any pretension to a higher meta- physical understanding. But as things are, most people who pride themselves on "rationally" rejecting religion unwittingly preserve in their thought and mentality much of what is at its core religious metaphysics. As I said, they would not know how to face the world without it, and they have merely re- placed one metaphysical belief—God—with another—free will—but still have the gall to criticize the putative irrationality of religious people.

And so to apply all of this to the main subject of this book, it ought to be established that the understanding of parts of history as cyclical or helical in no way implies that anyone is liberated from agency and responsibility. We dwell on the issue of freedom in order to emphasize that the civilizational trajectories and unfree developments that take place in the world must never be taken as an excuse for irresponsibility, or as meaning that we cannot influence the course of our cultures, or as a way for people to avoid the consequences of their economic and socio-moral decisions. If we did take them as an excuse, as many Marxist oikophobes do, then our civilization would go under even quicker. This is why religion remains the most practical bulwark against civilizational collapse, because religion comes with the entire set of metaphysical norms and feelings of membership that are best at assuring social cohesion. And therefore, even though I am an atheist, I greet Jews and Christians as fellows in our love of our civilization. Their love letter to the West would no doubt read differently from mine, but love is not to be argued with.[10]

This is also why the division between ethics and political philosophy is important. The former answers the question of how the individual should behave, the latter the question of how the group should behave. When we look at ourselves as a group in our current civilizational phase in the West, we can find the answer in tradition and the Judeo-Christian religions, that is, in Jerusalem, as long as it is balanced by the rationalist-scientific ethic of Athens, and as long as neither city gains total dominance over the other. Religion as a basic phenomenon will never disappear, and so it is better for the group to keep a religion that is not entirely unfriendly to rational argument, instead of a religiously oikophobic cult that seeks to tear everything down, both God and reason. The state cannot do much for religion itself, but it can, and should, enact policies that encourage marriage and reproduction— families—because families are what will provide a sense of civilizational rootedness and thereby create an environment more conducive to religion.

But when it comes to ethics, to the single individual, my answer is sometimes different, because not all of us believe in God or the illusion of free will. So what about those people—perhaps a diminishing number—who do not follow any religion or accompanying metaphysics but who nonetheless reject the condition into which the fall of God would cast our society? What about those who love their home, but are at the same time faced with the lack of free will and the onslaught of oikophobia? What about those who wish to be strong, independent, open-minded, and freethinking individuals, who nonetheless are devoted to the great beauty that their civilization has bequeathed unto them? It is to you that I address the final pages of this book, and it is here that Athens reigns supreme.

When we eject all this metaphysical ballast, we come to view ourselves as body only, which is why we cannot escape physical causality. The fact that we are mere bodies, the lack of freedom, and the force of our moral responsibilities in spite of that lack, are not only not a problem; they are in fact salutary, and to be welcomed with open arms. In the acknowledgment that we exercise no "free" control over our actions, many would be inclined to feel powerless, some even to despair. The world and its vicissitudes might appear to us even grimmer than before. But we can easily resist this despondence if we embrace something of the Greek spirit, and thereby train ourselves to see the advantages of this surrender of our idea of freedom (the freedom itself we need not surrender, for we never possessed it).

When we look upon wrongdoers, we come to see not only perpetrators, but also victims, victims of their own criminal deeds insofar as they were unlucky enough to have the composition, background, and natural influence on their volition that led them to those deeds. We do not believe that this state of affairs excuses the wrongdoers in any way. But when we inflict punishment for the crime, as of course we must in order for society to function, we do so without hatred or fury, but simply because it is necessary, to stop the criminal and to offer a future deterrent. That is to say that ethics to us becomes more pragmatic and less judgmental, for all feeling of vengeance within us has disappeared. If we stop hating the criminal and the evildoers because of their lack of free will, we can elevate ourselves above resentment and scorn. We will be able to refrain from rejoicing at our enemies' demise, although their defeat is necessary to us; rather than selfishly exult in victory, we view with melancholia that we had to fight at all. For all hatred disappears from us, and only love remains.

And when we love, our love will be no less passionate simply because the objects of our love had no say in their own creation, in their own loveliness. We do not love beauty because it chose to be beautiful; we love beauty because it is beauty—we appreciate things for what they are, whether they chose to be as they are or not, and so false reflection and judgment evaporate. Since we are all but bodies, we understand that we are of one substance with all. Indeed when we finally understand, truly understand and internalize, that we are only body, without metaphysical free will, it becomes impossible to hate.

Someone will ask, perhaps, why the love does not disappear for the same reason as the hatred. One might object that if we do not hate criminals because of their lack of free will, why should we love those who perform good deeds in spite of their lack of the same? But it is already a quite common thought that immaterial souls with their free-will scaffolding often divide us—I am one separate entity and you are another; I am one metaphysical essence with a self, and you are another. If all is body, on the other hand, there is only one substance. If the world is not divided into disparate essences, a detachment from rage and wrath becomes so much easier, while we continue to love our own substance.

This emphasis on unity is a choice we can deliberately train ourselves to make, with the aid of the self-love that we all possess naturally to some degree. (And that deliberately training oneself does not imply free will, we have already seen, in connection with the "lazy argument.") We become human beings who absorb and are together with all the beauty in the world, who can see the beautiful in everything, as artists and lovers of worlds and words do. It will make us more creative, more artistic, because artistic creation is a process of pure affirmation, of understanding the presence of beauty in all things, even those things that would repel others. This posture does not grant us our freedom in a nonmaterialist, metaphysical sense, but it makes us as whole and free as we can ever hope to be, because we see ourselves in the Other.

And this is where the Greek spirit fully enters. To be neither xenophobic nor oikophobic, we must imitate to some degree that portion of Greek civilization where a balance between those two vices first appeared, filled with those individuals who looked at themselves in the mirror, with neither self-exultation nor self-hatred. The Greek represents the highest cultural achievement so far, and its Classical era offers us a combination of wholesome self-confidence and sound self-critique and self-correction. If we want what is best for mankind, then it is natural that we should emulate its highest expression and attempt to perpetuate in ourselves everything this expression got right, and to avoid what it got wrong. It is thus that Greekdom lays claim to universality. This type of universality is not the absolutist one of the conservative early-culture man, who instinctively believes his own culture to be superior to all else, and certainly it is far removed from late-culture relativist universality, a concept alien to the typical, Classical Greek. It is rather that which appears between these two, and is the best universality there is, and the only one toward which we ought to grasp if we want to make any claim at all to a common human bond. Though this universality rejects progressivist utopianism, there are also limits to its conservatism: one is aware and proud of one's worth, but looks at oneself with a critical eye. Just as openness and a desire to learn from other cultures should not yield to oikophobia, so too conservatism should not yield to jingoism or xenophobia.

Some may indeed have gained the impression that a study of oikophobia might lead to a haughty rejection of everything that is foreign, and to a new tribalism or nationalism. But since we have embraced only love and banished hatred from our beings, we do what we must to preserve the beauty and greatness of our own civilization, but always greet the stranger with love and kindness when we cross paths. I myself have been a stranger in numerous countries and civilizations, and recall with fondness and gratitude the many times I was treated kindly; I would pay forward that kindness to any stranger who came to my own door, while at the same time not compromising the integrity of my civilization.

There is another way in which the lack of a soul helps us be more creative. If we believe in a soul and in life after death for that soul, then it is easier to come to terms with death. But if we do not, then we find ourselves, like the Greeks, in the constant shadow of death and permanent termination—and it is, perhaps counterintuitively, salutary to view ourselves in that way.[11] This is not only because it makes us more grateful for what we have now, but also because it pushes us toward more production. If death holds absolute sway over us—absolute extinction, with no continuation—then the goods we acquire during life should be those over which death holds no sway, things that will remain once we are gone, such as the fruits of artistic and intellectual labor. That is to say, death becomes useful if we adjust our desires in accordance with it. We become more productive if we realize that this life is the only one we have. Without a glorious afterlife or metaphysical refuge of the soul to look forward to, we treasure all the more the actual here and now. And that is the value of death, and one of the values of being only body: We are most open to others, and embrace most passionately them and the goodness they offer us, if we know that they one day will permanently disappear.

And so we act well not because of metaphysics, but because of materialist ontology. Good works are sometimes related to a faith that is geared toward a person's salvation. We, on the other hand, do not assume that the world in which we live functions according to just metaphysical principles, according to some system devised but for us, that there is a God who puts us above all. We do not assume that we are the *sine qua non* of everything, the beginning and the end, and that there is a separate realm of morality that prescribes to us how to act. There is no cosmic justice, but only individual just deeds. Even in the best of all possible worlds, which is not necessarily the fairest of all possible worlds or the best of all imaginable worlds, punishment for the criminal is the best of all possible decisions, even though the criminal did not freely choose to act.[12]

The Archaic and early Classical Greeks did what was necessary in a given situation, without worrying about whether their action was compatible with a man-made metaphysical system imposed upon nature. They did have notions of just behavior, of course, but these were limited to human interaction and were not transcendent; that is to say, they asked, "What is it just to do now?"—not "What is justice?," a very different question. The latter question turns us into vain busybodies interfering in the lives of others; the former simply answers how to treat in a given circumstance our fellow human being, with whom we are materially connected. And learning to connect must always begin with the family, which is why the state must encourage families, since they are the means by which we learn to relate to others, to the community as a whole. Someone who wants to save humanity but cannot treat his family right, like Rousseau, has already disqualified himself.

The immediacy of the earlier Greeks' approach to their physical surroundings dispensed with the notion of transcendent justice. With Heraclitus's *logos*, Anaxagoras's *nous*, and even Aristotle's unmoved mover, we are really only dealing with a type of natural and perhaps logical force: Especially Heraclitus's unity of opposites is not a normative principle of morality, and Aristotle's unmoved mover is posited as a logical necessity, not as a benevolent power whose existence obliges us to devise a larger justice system that will justify or render possible that existence. In Anaximander and his *apeiron*, injustice is *sensu stricto* no moral injustice. It is, rather, a natural inequality that is evened out by the equally natural order of the world which eliminates disturbing forces and, like all bodies, strives toward equilibrium. That is to say, we distinguish between elemental-physical justice and metaphysical-normative justice. The latter is an illusion.[13]

Philosophy began as the philosophy of nature, and nature served the first philosophers, the pre-Socratics, as an object of science that was based on ethically neutral elements. It was with the Platonic turn in philosophy that metaphysical-normative justice gained center stage, but even then in a relatively limited way. It is only Judeo-Christian ethics, and today specifically oikophobic positivism, which grasp at everything that can possibly happen and seek to place it in the cell of cosmic justice. The justice that stands outside of such systems is that which has physically developed from the natural urge to strive for life and to avoid death and which existed prior to convention. We avoided killing lest we be killed ourselves, and so a reciprocity developed very early on that was useful to everyone.[14] Some arbitrariness still remains, for whereas certain norms did develop in a biological-utilitarian way, we can still decide to abide by them or not; that is to say, even an original organic convention cannot lose every single trace of arbitrariness in its final outcome. But the remaining arbitrariness is generally sorted out, historically speaking, by the nonarbitrary experimentation of what works best in real life for personal thriving, which is usually the reciprocity that comes to include our well-being in the well-being of others. To look back at Aristotle and his *Nicomachean Ethics* again: if one considers the sort of activities that he identifies with *eudaimonia*—happiness—and those he identifies with *hedone*—a lower pleasure—the moral criterion of pleasure through giving pleasure, that is, of including our well-being in the well-being of others, fits quite well into his model, even if we do not desire happiness because it is happiness—a rather vague term—but because it is pleasurable.

In this process of establishing reciprocity, in tying our moral criteria to sociobiological utility, reason is merely our maid, our surgeon's assistant who hands us the tools and instruments that we then use as we see fit. And reason can never be more than this, for although the truth of the syllogism, for example, is an absolute or necessary truth, it does not bring us morally very far. But understanding reason's proper and limited role is not to disrespect her; on the contrary, we love her more than do those who abuse her for their own arbitrary ends.

Although religion can serve a very salutary function for society, and although I have great respect for religion, we who remain strong, spiritual, and patriotic without its aid, we who wish to embrace something of the Greek spirit, we look at nature purely as an aesthetic object. The fact that nature is indifferent, merciless, unjust, that it contains fruitful forests and desolate deserts, does not mean that it is not a great work of art. And if nature is a work of art, we draw the conclusion that everything in it is beautiful. We follow the Stoic hero Heracles, who does what he must even though he knows he is a victim of the capriciousness of the gods and of cruel fate. We do not require a just world, and see clearly that nature is inherently unjust, or rather utterly indifferent to the question of justice, which in a way is even worse. We accept the lack of justice as part of our map of reality and carry it as best we can, which we do by growing to understand and accept the force of nature, and the natural interconnection and *agon*—competition—among all things, the weighing of everything on the same set of scales, which leads us to excel and to try, as Homer says, *aien aristeuein*, always to be the best.

The Greeks are sometimes reduced to mere occupational tools to advance academic careers, and one forgets to ask more personal questions of them. One then comes to laugh condescendingly at those who do, at the student who might want to write plays as great as those of Euripides, at the one who reads Pindar's odes to the Olympic champions and consequently wants to become a great athlete himself, at the one who converses in his mind with Aristotle about the veracity of his opinions, at the one who reads Sappho's despondent love poems and throws himself in tears to the feet of his beloved and grasps her knees. We may be content to let such academics busy themselves with the latest postmodern or oikophobic fads, while we ourselves choose to approach the Greeks not first as scholars but as plain human beings.

So the Greeks do not belong to the professors; they belong to all of us, if we are but willing to open ourselves up to them. If you are a scientist who labors from dawn to dusk in the laboratory in pursuit of the discovery, if you are an athlete who trains hard every day and denies every decadent impulse in order one day to be a champion, if you are a musician who beautifies everything around you with your sonic waves, if you are a young girl who writes a love poem to the object of your passion, then you are the one in whom the Greek spirit lives, you are the one in whom the great spirit of human endeavor lives, and you are the one in whom lives the love that will unite peoples, the love that will build civilizations.

NOTES

Introduction

1. Ronald Doctor, Ada Kahn, and Christine Adamec, *The Encyclopedia of Phobias, Fears, and Anxieties* (New York: Infobase Publishing, 2008), 210, 281, 286.

2. Robert Southey, *Letters from England: By Don Manuel Alvarez Espriella* (London: Longman, 1814), vol. 1, 346 (Letter 30). This is a book of letters Southey wrote in the persona of a traveling Spaniard who comments on English society and mores, a bit like Montesquieu's *Persian Letters*. A new edition is Carol Bolton, ed., *Letters from England by Don Manuel Alvarez Espriella* (New York: Routledge, 2016).

3. Roger Scruton, "Oikophobia," *Journal of Education* 175, no. 2 (April 1993): 93–98.

4. Roger Scruton, *England and the Need for Nations*, 2nd ed. (London: Civitas, 2006), 36–38. See also his "Oikophobia and Xenophilia," in *Stereotypes and Nations*, ed. Teresa Walas (Cracow: International Cultural Centre, 1995), 287–92; and Mark Dooley, *Roger Scruton: The Philosopher on Dover Beach* (London: Continuum, 2009), mainly 78–83 and 149ff.

5. James Taranto, "Oikophobia: Why the Liberal Elite Finds Americans Revolting," *Wall Street Journal*, August 27, 2010, https://www.wsj.com/articles/SB1000142405274870 4147804575455523068802824.

6. Thierry Baudet, *Oikofobie: De angst voor het eigene* (Amsterdam: Prometheus, 2013). To the best of my knowledge, no English translation has been published, though I have come across a German one. On page 11 he writes that the cause of oikophobia remains unresolved. May he read on.

7. Exceptions may be Spartaco Pupo, "Oikophobic Prejudice Against Nation," *Notizie di POLITELA* 31, no. 118 (2015): 3–22; Michael Walsh, *The Devil's Pleasure Palace: The Cult of Critical Theory and the Subversion of the West* (New York: Encounter Books, 2015), which contains a chapter titled "Oikophobes and Xenophiles," dealing with cultural self-hatred especially in the context of twentieth-century geopolitics; and Bill Whittle's video "Walking into Mordor" (YouTube, July 1, 2011, https://www.youtube.com/watch?v=mq NVpACRLaI), which correctly states that oikophobia recurs cyclically in history and which draws a connection between oikophobia and the Frankfurt School (discussed in chapter 11 of this book). I also mention my own article "'Oikophobia': Our Western Self-Hatred," *Quillette*, October 7, 2019, https://quillette.com/2019/10/07/oikophobia-our-western-self -hatred/, and its expanded version, in German, "Obacht, Oikophobie" [Caution, oikopho-bia], *Schweizer Monat* 1073 (February 2020): 24–29, the former of which has in turn inspired a number of YouTube videos. See also the *Quillette* podcast with me, "PODCAST 65: Bene-dict Beckeld on Oikophobia—Fashionable Disdain for Your Own Culture," December 1, 2019, https://quillette.com/2019/12/01/podcast-65-benedict-beckeld-on-oikophobia-fashion able-disdain-for-your-own-culture/.

8. When I first wrote this I meant it figuratively, but recent developments, of, for ex-ample, white Americans kneeling before black Americans to ask forgiveness for their ancestors' sins, have shown that it is sometimes also literally true.

9. Nietzsche's remarks on master and slave moralities are to be found most system-atically in the First Essay (sections 5–11) of *On the Genealogy of Morality*, and—to cor-rect a common misconception—although he criticizes slave morality more severely, Nietzsche does not consider master morality beyond reproach either. He draws partly on Hegel's master-slave dialectic, described in the *Phenomenology of Spirit* (the "Self-Consciousness" [*Selbstbewußtsein*] section; see also the *Encyclopedia* of 1830, sec. 430–35), which according to Hegel lies at the beginning of societies: two autonomous human beings encounter one another and engage in combat for the sake of receiving recogni-tion from the other; the weaker finally submits and becomes a slave. It is a variation of Hobbes's brief discussion of the theme at *Leviathan* 20.10.

10. The correct view of the theory is simply that the state takes the form of an under-standing between ruler and ruled, and Locke himself explains this clearly in the *Second Treatise of Government* 8 (especially paragraphs 99–106; see also Rousseau's *On the Social Contract* 1.6, and Kant's *On the Common Saying* 2, beginning of the Conclusion). Locke's description of a more or less consensual community has been erroneously understood by careless later readers, who think of consensual communities in the modern sense, with open, democratic elections, which is not what Locke has in mind with the contract the-ory, as he explains in paragraph 105. The social contract theory has been contrasted with what in Plato amounts to a theory of the state originating with conquest (*Laws* 683c–e), an idea to be found in Machiavelli (*The Prince*, passim in the first several chapters, and *Discourses on the First Decade of Titus Livy*, early in book 2, with book 1.1–2 including both contract and conquest language); Hume (*Essays, Moral, Political, and Literary* 2.12, although he also uses, precisely, the contract language in the very same passage); and

Nietzsche (*On the Genealogy of Morality* 2.17). But these two notions, of conquest and of social contract, are actually not incompatible, for they merely refer to different stages in civilizational development, the conquest coming before one contract and after another: after a conquest, a contract is established with the newly conquered population, and before a conquest, a contract will have to have been established in order to create a cohesive group around a leader that can carry out the conquest. In fact, even though he supports the conquest theory, Plato also offers pieces of a social contract theory (*Republic* 358e–359a and 369b–c; *Laws* 681b–d, 690c, and especially 684a–c), thereby further underlining that the two positions are not mutually exclusive; indeed we find that same juxtaposition of conquest and contract states in Hobbes's *Leviathan* 17.15 as well (he calls them commonwealths by "acquisition" and by "institution"; see also 20.1–2). Plato may have been partly inspired by Protagoras, as seen in his *Protagoras* 322a–323a and perhaps by Lycophron, according to what Aristotle mentions of the latter's views at *Politics* 1280b, a passage that also contains a very early version of what I call Anglo-Saxon freedom of conscience, namely that it is not the task of the state to render the citizens virtuous but merely to allow them free interaction. And Rousseau in establishing the contract theory is indeed indebted to Plato. In any case, it is probably true that no one model can account for the creation or subsistence of every single state in history.

11. The division between the narrow/emotional and the broad/logical is similar to the aesthetic distinction drawn by Alexander Baumgarten between sensible and logical knowledge in his *Metaphysics* (1739) and also in his *Aesthetics* (1750). Both sensible and logical knowledge—both sensation and reason—are crucial for a full understanding of the object (see also my discussion of Husserl's *Lebenswelt* in chapter 11). This is not to say that Baumgarten's aesthetic principles as a whole, through which he endeavored to establish certain rules for a critical judgment of beauty, are to be endorsed. Kant rightly criticizes them in a footnote of section 1 of the Transcendental Aesthetic of the *Critique of Pure Reason*.

1. Oikophobia in Ancient Greece

1. A classic study of this world is Moses Finley, *The World of Odysseus* (New York: Viking Press, 1978); see especially chap. 4.

2. The relative youth of Greek civilization will later be held against it, such as when Plato, in the *Timaeus* 21e–22b, has an Egyptian priest chide Solon for there supposedly not being a single ancient belief or old science among the Greeks, and thereby say that the Greeks are children. As for the slow movement of Greek thinking from myth to rationalism and science, this was a popular idea especially in the first half of the previous century, and especially in Germany, before Allied carpet bombing took the Hegelian spirit out of that country. See such classic studies as Wilhelm Nestle, *Vom Mythos zum Logos* [From myth to logos] (Stuttgart: Alfred Kröner, 1940); Bruno Snell, *Die Entdeckung des Geistes* [The discovery of mind] (Hamburg: Claassen & Goverts, 1946); and to a lesser extent the first volume of Werner Jaeger, *Paideia: The Ideals of Greek Culture* (Oxford: Oxford University Press, 1939). This idea subsequently went out of vogue—in no small part due to the aforementioned bombing, and consequent postmodern disgust with

the idea of grand civilizational narratives—though some continued to insist on it, such as Marcel Detienne, *Les maîtres de vérité dans la Grèce archaïque* [The masters of truth in Archaic Greece] (Paris: Maspero, 1967). One of many theses I am setting down in this book is not only the truth of this idea, but also that this civilizational trajectory from myth toward rationalism holds, *mutatis mutandis*, for other civilizations as well.

3. Due to metrical irregularities toward the end of the play, some question the claim that Euripides's deviation in the Iphigenia myth is actually by him. It may be readily agreed that the passage as we have it was not written by Euripides, but it seems likely that the general content of the story at this point is in fact by him. The reasons for this are well summarized by Martin Hose, *Euripides, Der Dichter der Leidenschaften* [The poet of the passions] (Munich: C. H. Beck, 2008), 231–32.

4. My opinion of Nietzsche here is shared by the magisterial Eduard Zeller, *Die Philosophie der Griechen in ihrer geschichtlichen Entwicklung* [translated as: Outlines of the history of Greek philosophy], 1.2 (Leipzig: O. R. Reisland, 1920), 1442–43.

5. Nietzsche's remarks on the enfeeblement of a people through awareness of its own history are to be found in his essay "On the Use and Disadvantage of History for Life" of the *Untimely Meditations*, and in section 4 of his later self-critical preface to *The Birth of Tragedy*. In the latter passage, he suggests that the Greeks became more scientific and more devoted to a logical view (*Logisierung*) as they became weaker (compare sections 18 and 23 of *The Birth of Tragedy*). Also relevant is the approximately twenty-page bit from Nietzsche's *Nachlass* called *Wissenschaft und Weisheit im Kampfe* ("The Struggle between Science and Wisdom"). Nietzsche's disparaging comments on his fellow Germans are legion. His last work, *Ecce Homo*, is a veritable goldmine in this regard, and my personal favorite there is "Even the proximity of a German delays my digestion" ("Why I am so clever," section 5). How some of Nietzsche's philosophy of history pertains to oikophobia I have outlined in my talk "Nietzsche and the Disadvantage of History: The Rise of Western Oikophobia" (presented at New York University, March 28, 2019), available online as "Nietzsche and Oikophobia," YouTube, April 4, 2019, https://youtu.be/WNAOi94nQbU.

6. On the question of Antiphon's identity, see the introduction in Gerard Pendrick, *Antiphon the Sophist: The Fragments* (Cambridge: Cambridge University Press, 2002), 1–26.

7. Thomas Hobbes, *Leviathan*, ed. Edwin Curley (Indianapolis/Cambridge: Hackett, 1994), 221.

2. Oikophobia as Relativism

1. One of the pithiest encapsulations of the former attitude will come later, in Voltaire, who will rebel against his culture. In the *Notes on Pascal's Pensées* he writes, "Morality is the same everywhere, in the emperor Marcus Aurelius, in the emperor Julian, in the slave Epictetus, and as you yourself admire it in Saint-Louis, and in his conqueror Baibars, in the Chinese emperor Qianlong, and in the king of Morocco." See also Rousseau, *Emile*, book 4: "Among this prodigious variety of manners and customs, you will find everywhere the same ideas of justice and righteousness, everywhere the same principles of morality, everywhere the same notions of good and evil."

2. Moral relativism (there is no absolute moral truth) and cultural relativism (truth is culture-based and should be evaluated on the terms of the culture in which it arises) are related but not exactly the same. I am discussing mainly moral relativism, but in a historical-cultural context, which may make it sound as if I were conflating the two, although the distinction is not so crucial for my present purposes. The distinction can be traced in, for example, John Cook, *Morality and Cultural Differences* (New York: Oxford University Press, 1999); and Steven Hales, ed., *A Companion to Relativism* (Oxford: Blackwell, 2011). A glimpse of how the distinction can play itself out in the world is Elvin Hatch, *Culture and Morality: The Relativity of Values in Anthropology* (New York: Columbia University Press, 1983). A decent defense of moral relativism in the sense that morality presupposes general agreement is Gilbert Harman, "Moral Relativism Defended," *Philosophical Review* 84, no. 1 (January 1975): 3–22; a reply to him is Loren Lomasky, "Harman's Moral Relativism," *Journal of Libertarian Studies* 3, no. 3 (Fall 1979): 279–91.

3. Among a host of overviews and examples, see Grégor Puppinck, "The Council of Europe Is 'Greatly Concerned' by the Application of Sharia in Europe," *European Centre for Law & Justice*, 2019, https://eclj.org/religious-freedom/pace/le-conseil-de-leurope -sinquite-grandement-de-lapplication-de-la-charia-en-europe; Dominic McGoldrick, "Accommodating Muslims in Europe: From Adopting Sharia Law to Religiously Based Opt Outs from Generally Applicable Laws," *Human Rights Law Review* 9, no. 4 (December 1, 2009): 603–45.

4. Thomas Nagel calls "Cartesian" the opposite attitude, that of the universalist who appeals to his reason as something universal: *The Last Word* (New York: Oxford University Press, 1997), 3–4. This is not incorrect, but the difference is that Nagel likes Descartes, whereas I do not and consider his *Cogito* ("I think . . .") to be a logical error, and so I find that the relativist here commits the very error that he imputes to the universalist.

5. A recent study linking narcissism with the exaggerated political correctness that is connected to oikophobia (and also linking narcissism with the far right) is Jordan Moss and Peter O'Connor, "The Dark Triad Traits Predict Authoritarian Political Correctness and Alt-Right Attitudes," *Heliyon* 6, no. 7 (July 2020), https://doi.org/10.1016/j.heliyon .2020.e04453. A more classic study is Christopher Lasch, *The Culture of Narcissism* (New York: W. W. Norton, 1979).

6. Karl Popper has a useful discussion of the convention-arbitrariness contrast in chap. 5, sec. 3, of *The Open Society and Its Enemies* (London: Routledge Classics, 2011), first published in 1945.

7. Regarding multiculturalism, some useful literature: Mancur Olson, *The Rise and Decline of Nations: Economic Growth, Stagflation, and Social Rigidities* (New Haven, CT: Yale University Press, 1982), explains, from a mainly economic but still quite interdisciplinary perspective, how success and stability will lead to an increase in lobby groups— diverse interests—that will hurt the collective in the long run, and that homogenous groups have (almost tautologically) greater social cohesion than heterogenous groups. A more recent critique of multiculturalism is Brian Barry, *Culture and Equality: An Egalitarian Critique of Multiculturalism* (Cambridge, UK: Polity, 2001), who maintains that multiculturalism as an endorsement of group rights destroys individual rights, which lie at the very core of liberalism, and is thus actually illiberal. A more neutral volume is Amy

Gutmann, ed., *Multiculturalism: Examining the Politics of Recognition* (Princeton, NJ: Princeton University Press, 1994), with contributions by Jürgen Habermas and others, who, however, are only able to find the most academically tortured way of making their fairly simple points. Paradigmatic for the pro-multiculturalism position is Will Kymlicka, *Multicultural Citizenship: A Liberal Theory of Minority Rights* (Oxford: Oxford University Press, 1995).

3. Oikophobia in Rome

1. A useful case study of the complex way in which an empire usually begins is Nicholas Canny, ed., *The Origins of Empire: British Overseas Enterprise to the Close of the Seventeenth Century* (Oxford: Oxford University Press, 1998); for the philosophical side of things, see David Armitage, *The Ideological Origins of the British Empire* (Cambridge: Cambridge University Press, 2000).

2. *The History of the Decline and Fall of the Roman Empire*, chapter 4, although elsewhere he enters more into root causes.

3. More extreme than Gibbon is Guglielmo Ferrero, who paints a rosy picture of the inner state of the empire up to Commodus, in *La rovina della civiltà antica* [The ruin of ancient civilization] (Milan: Edizioni Athena, 1926).

4. See more generally the still useful anthology Arthur Lovejoy and George Boas, *Primitivism and Related Ideas in Antiquity* (Baltimore: Johns Hopkins Press, 1935).

5. The etymology of "religion" (Latin *religio*) is controversial, but it is probably *religare*, "to bind/obligate," as the early Christian writer Lactantius has it in *Divine Institutes* 4.28. Cicero's claim in *On the Nature of the Gods* 2.72 that it stems from *re-legere*, "to read/consider again," is probably false, just as the ancients in general tended to have rather a poor understanding of the etymology of their own words.

6. Some of the many studies on risk-taking as typically male are: Jon Rosenblitt, Hosanna Soler, Stacey Johnson, and David Quadagno, "Sensation Seeking and Hormones in Men and Women: Exploring the Link," *Hormones and Behavior* 40, no. 3 (November 2001): 396–402; Christine Harris, Michael Jenkins, and Dale Glaser, "Gender Differences in Risk Assessment: Why Do Women Take Fewer Risks than Men?" *Judgment and Decision Making* 1, no. 1 (July 2006): 48–63; Tatia Lee, Chetwyn Chan, Ada Leung, Peter Fox, and Jia-Hong Gao, "Sex-Related Differences in Neural Activity during Risk-Taking: An fMRI Study," *Cerebral Cortex* 19, no. 6 (June 2009): 1303–12.

7. See also Bari Weiss, "Camille Paglia: A Feminist Defense of Masculine Virtues," *Wall Street Journal*, December 28, 2013, https://www.wsj.com/articles/a-feminist-defense -of-masculine-virtuesa-feminist-defense-of-masculine-virtues-1388181961?tesla=y.

4. The Role of Religion

1. See Arinze Agbanusi, "Conflict of Cultures and the Need to Check Negative Cultural Dynamism in Nigeria," *African Research Review* 12, no. 49 (January, 2018): 132–39; and Precious Obioha, "Globalization and the Future of African Culture," *Philosophical*

Papers and Reviews 2, no. 1 (April, 2010): 1–8, the latter of which also includes a good overview of some of the literature on the subject.

2. The United States might seem to be a counterexample, since it never had an established church and assimilated many different religious groups at an early stage, but it was still far more religious (and Christian) than it was to become, and it also began at a more advanced cultural stage; see the beginning of chapter 8.

3. We can dispense with the common canard that the fact that the least religious societies (such as the Netherlands and Scandinavia) are also among the most peaceful is an argument against the social power of religion. These societies seem cohesive and peaceful because they are small and ethnically fairly homogenous (though becoming less so, with concomitant decrease in cohesiveness and peacefulness), and because they do not face serious foreign dangers. It is not a coincidence that it is a more religious people—the Americans—who are, heavily armed, patrolling the world's waterways, something a less religious society benefits from but does not have the stomach to do itself; if it had to, the incapacity for rallying in unity behind such a cause is a fact that the lack of religion would immediately reveal.

4. See, for example, Machiavelli, *Discourses on the First Decade of Titus Livy* 1.11–15, 1.55, 3.1; Hobbes, *Leviathan* 38.5; Voltaire, *Treatise on Toleration* 20; Rousseau, *On the Social Contract* 2.7 and *Emile* 4; Hegel, sec. B of the introduction to *Lectures on the Philosophy of History*; Schopenhauer, *The World as Will and Representation*, Supplements 17, and Arthur Hübscher, ed., *Der handschriftliche Nachlass* [The handwritten *Nachlass*] (Frankfurt: W. Kramer, 1966–75), 3:279; Nietzsche, passages in many works to the effect that the rejection of traditional myth and religion will sap a people of its energy (for example, *The Birth of Tragedy* and *Untimely Meditations*: see note 5 of chapter 1 above for some of the passages), and that the death of God will cause nihilism (for example, *The Gay Science*, famously sec. 125); and Durkheim, *The Elementary Forms of Religious Life*, passim. Mention should be made also of Oswald Spengler's seminal but no longer as influential *The Decline of the West*. Spengler correctly individuates religion as one of the core elements that bind a society together, and maintains, also correctly, that a society moves away from religion and toward rationalism as it approaches its decline. But the problem with Spengler is that he tries to accomplish too much: by linking every phenomenon of any given civilization with a specific phenomenon in every other civilization, he glosses over unique differences, so that the reader is left with the impression that absolutely everything is explainable by his models. This, in my opinion, is closer to mysticism than empirical observation. Spengler has a "cultural" explanation for everything: for example, in his first main chapter, "On the Meaning of Numbers," he says that it was a Greek fear of the irrational that kept them locked up in city-states rather than expanded into larger political entities, to which one might reply that a brief look at Greek topography could offer an even better explanation. In chapter 9 I shall discuss the problem with theories that try to explain everything.

5. This is the main thesis, and *mutatis mutandis* for other Western civilizations as well, of Victor Hanson, *Carnage and Culture* (New York: Anchor Books, 2002). A more nuanced view—though I agree with Hanson—of a supposed Western way of war is offered by Azar Gat, *A History of Military Thought* (Oxford: Oxford University Press, 2001).

6. A classic study here is René Girard, *La violence et le sacré* [Violence and the sacred] (Paris: Grasset, 1972), though a fair bit of the main idea goes back to Nietzsche. Notable here is also Durkheim's *The Elementary Forms of Religious Life*, 2.6 and passim.

7. My remarks on Dawkins are based mostly on Richard Dawkins, *The God Delusion* (Boston: Mariner, 2008), and a number of his tweets and public interviews. In this case, see *The God Delusion*, 270–72.

8. Dawkins, *The God Delusion*, 20. He has also said it in public appearances.

9. Richard Dawkins, "Why I Want All Our Children to Read the King James Bible," *Guardian*, May 19, 2012, https://www.theguardian.com/science/2012/may/19/richard -dawkins-king-james-bible.

10. Even the claim that religion has not always been a friend to science is to be further qualified, since the positing of an absolute monotheistic and discoverable truth is amenable to scientific and empirical exploration. See, for example, Rodney Stark, *For the Glory of God: How Monotheism Led to Reformations, Science, Witch-Hunts, and the End of Slavery* (Princeton, NJ: Princeton University Press, 2003).

11. Nietzsche is well known for the critique that modern atheism, and bourgeois morality in general, are in fact Christian. The idea is one of the central themes in *On the Genealogy of Morality*; see also *The Gay Science*, sec. 344–47. Dawkins in *The God Delusion* defends himself against the critique that he is as fundamentalist as the religious people he criticizes (see, for example, 18–19, 319), but his defense claims that he is not a fundamentalist about *science*, where he is open to new evidence. But this is not the point of the critique, which is, rather, that Dawkins is a fundamentalist in his attitude to *religion*. This is one reason why his effort in this regard is rather like a crusade.

12. This point, and Aquinas's statement, are reinforced by the fact that the Catholic idea of doctrinal development, as articulated by John Henry Newman (see John Henry Cardinal Newman, *An Essay on the Development of Christian Doctrine*, ed. Ian Ker [Notre Dame, IN: University of Notre Dame Press, 1989], originally published in 1845), requires a commitment to the authority of inherited tradition that would make temptations to oikophobia less likely, while at the same time not insulating a culture from legitimate change.

13. See Dominic Erdozain, ed., *The Dangerous God: Christianity and the Soviet Experiment* (DeKalb: Northern Illinois University Press, 2017).

14. See note 11 above. The matter is even more extreme now than it was in Nietzsche's day.

15. A version of a part of this paragraph first appeared in my article "Why Those Who Claim to 'Follow the Science' Are More Likely to Ignore It," *Federalist*, January 4, 2021, https://thefederalist.com/2021/01/04/why-those-who-claim-to-follow-the-science -are-more-likely-to-ignore-it/. The *Federalist* editors without my permission rewrote and thereby worsened my prose, but the basic ideas are mine.

5. Oikophobia in France

1. Sigmund Freud, *Das Unbehagen in der Kultur* (Frankfurt: Fischer Taschenbuch, 1994), originally published in 1930.

2. Fairly typical is Arthur Herman, *The Idea of Decline in Western History* (New York: Free Press, 1997), but at least he engages constructively with his subject matter. More problematic—because more perfunctorily dismissive—are Karl Popper and Steven Pinker (see my discussion in chapter 9).

3. A good older study on the later consequences of this is in Paul Hazard, *La crise de la conscience européenne, 1680–1715* (Paris: Boivin & Cie, 1935). An English translation is *The Crisis of the European Mind* (New York: NYRB Classics, 2013).

4. The *Emile* also contains some material that is friendlier toward the idea of private property, and Rousseau's treatment of the subject across his oeuvre is not entirely consistent. Two fairly recent studies that try to work out this issue are Chris Pierson, "Rousseau and the Paradoxes of Property," *European Journal of Political Theory* 12, no. 4 (October 2013): 409–24; and David Siroky and Hans-Jörg Sigwart, "Principle and Prudence: Rousseau on Private Property and Inequality," *Polity* 46, no. 3 (July 2014): 381–406.

5. Moral vegetarianism and at least traces of oikophobia very often go hand in hand throughout history. Contemporary examples would include Gloria Steinem, Peter Singer, and Ibram X. Kendi, all vegans or vegetarians, and all oikophobic to varying degrees. This is not to say that moral vegetarians cannot be motivated by a genuine love of animals, but genuinely loving animals and therefore not wanting to eat them, and also being moved toward vegetarianism through a subconscious or latent oikophobia, are by no means mutually exclusive.

6. These trends we are witnessing are indeed repetitive in nature. If one looks at modern astrological practices, it is clear that women are overrepresented. See the results of a 2017 poll for the Pew Research Center in Claire Gecewicz, *"New Age" Beliefs Common among Both Religious and Nonreligious Americans*, October 1, 2018, https://www.pewresearch.org/fact-tank/2018/10/01/new-age-beliefs-common-among-both-religious-and-nonreligious-americans/; and a 2005 Gallup poll in Linda Lyons, *Paranormal Beliefs Come (Super)Naturally to Some*, November 1, 2005, https://news.gallup.com/poll/19558/paranormal-beliefs-come-supernaturally-some.aspx.

7. Some holistic studies on vegetarianism, which do not explicitly seek to plot the phenomenon on a civilizational trajectory but in which can be seen when in fact vegetarianism tends to occur, are Colin Spencer, *The Heretic's Feast: A History of Vegetarianism* (Hanover, NH: University Press of New England, 1995); and Rod Preece, *Sins of the Flesh: A History of Ethical Vegetarian Thought* (Vancouver: University of British Columbia Press, 2008).

8. One can compare the respective indigenous reactions to the various European empires. See, for example, John Hargreaves, *Decolonization in Africa* (New York: Routledge, 2014); and Henri Grimal, *Decolonization: The British, French, Dutch, and Belgian Empires, 1919–1963* (Boulder, CO: Westview Press, 1978).

9. Edmund Burke, *Reflections on the Revolution in France*, ed. Leslie Mitchell (New York: Oxford University Press, 1999), 36.

10. The idea that civilizations begin to focus more on victimhood as they progress may seem odd in light of the fact that hospitals, orphanages, and other charitable organizations grew out of Christianity in its ascendancy (see Robert Wilken, *The First Thousand Years: A Global History of Christianity* [New Haven, CT: Yale University Press, 2012]). But this rather confirms the point, since Christianity began in the Roman Empire as it was progressing and declining, with the Christians' focus on charity and caring for the weak as a departure from earlier pagan ways. As for the civilizations that followed the Roman Empire in western Europe, the fact that they formally converted to Christianity does not mean that they were not in many ways fundamentally barbarian and violent in their early days. The mere fact that a society or its leadership is officially Christian should not be

taken to mean that there are not other factors that may play a greater determinative role in the prevailing morality of that society—while there was a general charitable Christian practice across many separate societies, those societies were many other things in addition to Christian; they were also brutal and violent in many ways, and became softer only over considerable time. (See my remarks toward the end of chapter 4 on the growth of "implicit Christianity" and the fulfillment of the Sermon on the Mount; see also chapter 9, note 23.)

11. A volume on the beginnings of the city-countryside dichotomy in antiquity is Ralph Rosen and Ineke Sluiter, eds., *City, Countryside, and the Spatial Organization of Value in Classical Antiquity* (Leiden: Brill, 2006). A case study for modern times is Robert Wuthnow, *The Left Behind: Decline and Rage in Small-Town America* (Princeton, NJ: Princeton University Press, 2018).

6. Oikophobia in Britain

1. The issue of the Catholic attitude to English rule is a complicated one. A useful study within the present context is Albert Loomie, "The Armadas and the Catholics of England," *Catholic Historical Review* 59, no. 3 (October 1973): 385–403. More general primers are Edward Watkin, *Roman Catholicism in England, from the Reformation to 1950* (Oxford: Oxford University Press, 1958); and Edward Norman, *Roman Catholicism in England from the Elizabethan Settlement to the Second Vatican Council* (Oxford: Oxford University Press, 1985).

2. The newest study of this is Greg Lukianoff and Jonathan Haidt, *The Coddling of the American Mind* (New York: Penguin, 2018). But see also chapter 11, note 3, below and its accompanying main text.

3. Walter Bate, ed., *Selected Writings of Edmund Burke* (New York: Random House, 1960), 283 and 286.

4. George Orwell, *Burmese Days* (New York: Harcourt, 1962), 40–42.

5. George Orwell, *Notes on Nationalism* (London: Penguin Random House, 2018), 23 and 20–21. A word for what Orwell is describing in the last quote is "ethnomasochism": see Patrick Buchanan, *Suicide of a Superpower* (New York: St. Martin's Press, 2011). This term has a more racial angle than does oikophobia. While it is true that hostility to one's own ethnicity can be a part of the oikophobic process—more so in modern than in ancient times—oikophobia is more useful as a general term for the repudiation of home.

6. For the point regarding increasing sensitivity, see Bradley Campbell and Jason Manning, "Microaggression and Moral Cultures," *Comparative Sociology* 13, no. 6 (January 2014): 692–726. Useful literature on the history and impact of feminism includes the following: Neil Lyndon, *No More Sex War: The Failures of Feminism* (London: Sinclair-Stevenson, 1992), argues that already second-wave feminism went too far in its flirtations with Marxism and focus on society itself as antagonist; Janet Richards, *The Sceptical Feminist: A Philosophical Inquiry* (New York: Routledge, 1980), while defending many feminist positions, also attacks those parts of feminist dogma that according to her have positioned themselves against the feminine and against science; and Christina Hoff Sommers, *Who Stole Feminism: How Women Have Betrayed Women* (New York: Touchstone, 1995), criticizes the scholarship of some feminist work and highlights

the social consequences of gender partisanship. A more positive examination of the interaction between feminism and society in history is Annelise Orleck, *Rethinking American Women's Activism* (New York: Routledge, 2015). Two historical and philosophical surveys are, respectively, Christine Stansell, *The Feminist Promise: 1792 to the Present* (New York: Random House, 2011), with a focus on the United States; and Rosemarie Tong and Tina Botts, *Feminist Thought* (New York: Routledge, 2018).

7. Figures from UKPublicSpending.co.uk, accessed February 23, 2021, https://www.ukpublicspending.co.uk/past_spending.

8. It should be pointed out that a society's inward turn and the power of interest groups as causes of increased social spending do not exclude but rather complement the reasons for increased spending as proffered by Wagner's law, according to which public spending as a share of GDP increases over time: Adolph Wagner, *Grundlegung der politischen Ökonomie* [Foundation of political economy] (Leipzig: C. F. Winter, 1893), 892–908. A summary is the "Wagner's Law" entry in John Black, Nigar Hashimzade, and Gareth Myles, *A Dictionary of Economics* (Oxford: Oxford University Press, 2017).

7. Oikophobia as Positivism

1. While it does not really matter for the overall point at hand, which seeks to understand positivist oikophobia, it is indeed debated among scholars whether More meant his *Utopia* seriously or not. See for example the editors' introductions in Thomas More, *Utopia*, ed. Mildred Campbell (Roslyn, NY: Walter J. Black, 1947); and Thomas More, *Utopia*, ed. George Logan (Cambridge: Cambridge University Press, 2016); as well as Jack Hexter, *More's Utopia: The Biography of an Idea* (Princeton, NJ: Princeton University Press, 1952); and George Logan, *The Meaning of More's Utopia* (Princeton, NJ: Princeton University Press, 1983).

2. For the former, see, for example, *Lectures on the Philosophy of History* 4.1.1, "the migration period" (*die Völkerwanderungen*); for the latter, see, for example, the section called "The abstract definitions of the nature of spirit," in the introduction of the same work.

3. I discuss this, as well as the general problem of applying scientific methods to the humanities, in section 3 of Benedict Beckeld, *Art and Aesthetics* (La Seyne-sur-Mer: Lux Classic, 2016), especially 153–78.

8. Oikophobia in the United States: The Past

1. This has become a bit controversial among modern-day revisionists—for example, Steven Green, *Inventing a Christian America: The Myth of the Religious Founding* (New York: Oxford University Press, 2015)—but it should not be, and among revisionists much of it comes down to a question of emphasis and to hair-splitting definitions of terms. There is truth in both the religious and the secular narrative, but that early America was far more religious than modern-day America, and that American development thus fits within the common oikophobic trajectory in this regard, is indisputable. See, for example, James Hutson, *Religion and the Founding of the American Republic* (Washington, DC:

Library of Congress, 1998); Thomas Kidd, *God of Liberty: A Religious History of the American Revolution* (New York: Basic Books, 2010); Matthew Harris and Thomas Kidd, eds., *The Founding Fathers and the Debate over Religion in Revolutionary America* (New York: Oxford University Press, 2012). An attempt at balance between the two sides is John Fea, *Was America Founded as a Christian Nation?* (Louisville, KY: John Knox Press, 2011).

2. That religion has continued to decline in the United States should be uncontroversial, and is indeed confirmed by many polls. See, for example, Pew Research Center, *In U.S., Decline of Christianity Continues at Rapid Pace*, October 17, 2019, https://www.pewforum.org/2019/10/17/in-u-s-decline-of-christianity-continues-at-rapid-pace/; and Gallup, *Religion*, https://news.gallup.com/poll/1690/religion.aspx.

3. See *Federalist* nos. 9 and 10, in which Hamilton and Madison, respectively, attempt to answer Anti-Federalist arguments that a large nation with many diverse interests cannot survive. For those arguments, see, for example, the pseudonymous *Cato* no. 3. For an overview of the debate, see Saul Cornell, *The Other Founders: Anti-Federalism & the Dissenting Tradition in America, 1788–1828* (Chapel Hill: University of North Carolina Press, 1999).

4. I trust it is clear that this statement should not be interpreted as an endorsement of slavery: the United States is of course a better place for having abolished it; we are simply trying to understand how a nation progresses along a particular trajectory and why this path leads to the results that it does.

5. Allen Ginsberg, *The Fall of America: Poems of These States* (San Francisco: City Lights, 1973). The poem *America* is from Allen Ginsberg, *Howl and Other Poems* (San Francisco: City Lights, 1956).

6. I refer again to the Lasch study (see chapter 2, note 5), which focuses also on the 1960s.

7. See also note 3 of chapter 4.

8. See, for example, Jimmy Carter and Mary Robinson, "How to Fix It," *Foreign Policy*, August 4, 2014, https://foreignpolicy.com/2014/08/04/how-to-fix-it/.

9. A selection of apologies, which includes the quote, is Nile Gardiner and Morgan Roach, "Barack Obama's Top 10 Apologies: How the President Has Humiliated a Superpower," Heritage Foundation, June 2, 2009, https://www.heritage.org/europe/report/barack-obamas-top-10-apologies-how-the-president-has-humiliated-superpower.

10. "Barack Obama's Small Town Guns and Religion Comments," YouTube, April 12, 2008, https://www.youtube.com/watch?v=DTxXUufI3jA.

11. Office of the Press Secretary, "'Islam Is Peace' Says President," George W. Bush White House (archived website), September 17, 2001, https://georgewbush-whitehouse.archives.gov/news/releases/2001/09/20010917-11.html.

12. This topic is fraught with historical revisionism, and both sides of the issue tend to cherry-pick their evidence. While the founding fathers did make general provisions for freedom of religion, including Islam, what they publicly said and wrote about that religion is a different matter. For a representative sample of each viewpoint, see Akbar Ahmed, "'Burn Quran Day' an Outrage to Muslims," *CNN*, August 20, 2010, https://www.cnn.com/2010/OPINION/08/20/ahmed.quran.burning/index.html; Laura Rubenfeld, "No, Professor Ahmed, the Founders Were Not So Fond of Islam," *Middle East Forum*, September 10, 2010, https://www.meforum.org/campus-watch/17803/no-professor-ahmed-the-founders-were-not-so-fond.

13. This is part of the thesis, with which I agree, of Samuel Huntington, *The Clash of Civilizations* (New York: Simon & Schuster, 1996).

9. Cyclical and Progressive Theory

1. *The Open Society and Its Enemies* (London: Routledge Classics, 2011), chap. 10, n. 19, and passim.

2. Karl Popper, *The Poverty of Historicism* (London: Routledge Classics, 2002), first published in 1957.

3. Steven Pinker, *Enlightenment Now: The Case for Reason, Science, Humanism, and Progress* (New York: Penguin, 2018).

4. The opposite extreme, perhaps also not entirely correct but certainly very charming, is offered by Leibniz: "It sounds fantastical, but I approve of almost everything I read, for I know well how differently things can be understood," in Ludwig Grote, *Leibniz und seine Zeit* [Leibniz and his time] (Hannover: Carl Brandes, 1869), 411.

5. Pinker indeed uses the concept of progress as if it covered every aspect of life (*Enlightenment Now*, 165, 191, 386–87, 394–95, and 403). One of the best examples, by dint of its conciseness, of the muddiness of Pinker's thinking in this regard, of the fact that he is not equipped to handle philosophical-cultural issues, is his statement that scientific achievements like the curing of smallpox "put the lie to any moaning that we live in an age of decline, disenchantment, meaninglessness, shallowness, or the absurd" (386–87)—as if the wonderful medical eradication of smallpox had anything to do with sociocultural feelings of shallowness and such.

6. For example, Pinker writes, "To take something on faith means to believe it without good reason, so by definition a faith in the existence of supernatural entities clashes with reason" (*Enlightenment Now*, 30). This is a surprisingly egregious bit of sophistry. By Pinker's own logic, his faith in the sacredness of human beings clashes with reason. The truth is actually that reason militates neither for nor against these things.

7. Francis Fukuyama, *The End of History and the Last Man* (New York: Free Press, 2006), 330 (Fukuyama's italics).

8. The same error can of course be made in the opposite direction too, where cultural considerations are allowed to crowd out everything else. I would for example consider Oswald Spengler to be guilty of this, on whom see note 4 of chapter 4 above.

9. One may have the impression from my theses that history "must" proceed the way it does, but I am not endorsing any sort of inexorable law of history. It is true for human action that when a certain set of circumstances is given, the outcome is given also. But since we do not know the future, we still must strive to act judiciously, and we therefore reject the straitjacket of eschatological progress that some philosophers would put on history. To draw from my *Die Notwendigkeit der Notwendigkeit* [The necessity of necessity] (Frankfurt: Peter Lang, 2013), 129–31, there are different ways of understanding concepts like necessity and possibility. They can be understood within either a physical or a modal logical context. Logically, an event is "necessary" when the proposition corresponding to it is necessary; so too, an event that will never happen is still "possible" if the proposition corresponding to it is possible. This type of possibility concerns, for example, the inherent

characteristics of objects (like the brittleness of glass) and of human beings (like "I walk on the Brooklyn Bridge", which I can, but not "I walk on water," which I cannot), as long as no exterior circumstance would necessarily prevent it (like "I walk on the Brooklyn Bridge although my legs have just been cut off"). The last two propositions are impossible, while the first, "I walk on the Brooklyn Bridge," is still possible, even if in actuality it will never come to pass that I am in New York; so too, in the logical sense, it is possible for the glass to break, even if it never actually breaks. Physically, however, the matter is different. Since a given set of circumstances must produce a particular result, "I walk on the Brooklyn Bridge" is just as impossible as "I walk on water," if it never happens that I walk on the Brooklyn Bridge, just as it is necessary that I do walk on it when it comes to pass that I do; and it is impossible for the glass to break if it does not, and necessary for it to break if it does. This is because the networks of physical causes have brought about the event of me walking on the Brooklyn Bridge or of the glass breaking. And if these things do not happen, it is because the causal networks led in another direction, and so my walking on the Brooklyn Bridge and that particular glass breaking remained beyond the realm of the possible. And so in the physical sense, we only say that something is "possible" because we are ignorant of the eventual outcome. In physical fact, something cannot be "possible"—it is either necessary or impossible. But when we are discussing historical forces and historical determinism, even though we should be aware of the stricter physical sense it is a good idea in general to err in the direction of the logical sense, lest we descend into the Hegelian-Marxist totalitarianism that would force us all to accept a certain conclusion as given. One might accuse the logical sense of being a fight over words rather than facts, just as one might accuse the physical sense of being that straitjacket of history against which I have warned. But both senses have something to teach us: The physical sense teaches us a certain acceptance of things as they are, of the limits to our capacities, and the ridiculousness of our hubris that wishes to save the world when we cannot even take care of ourselves; the logical sense teaches us the potential of our volition, that the seemingly impossible is possible if we make it so. (For those who are not satisfied with the resolution to this seeming contradiction, which in fact is not a contradiction since we are operating at two different levels of discourse, the theme will be discussed further in the epilogue.)

10. I fondly recall Locke's remark in the preface to his *Two Treatises of Government* that "Cavilling here and there, at some Expression, or little incident of my Discourse, is not an answer to my Book." (John Locke, *Two Treatises of Government*, ed. Peter Laslett [New York: Cambridge University Press, 1988], 138.)

11. Paul Feyerabend, *Against Method* (London: Verso, 2010), first published in 1975. I say I agree with it in a limited way because it is an uneven work, containing both preposterously false statements and wise insights.

12. Feyerabend, *Against Method*, 22 (my ellipsis; Feyerabend's italics); compare the first paragraph of his chap. 4.

13. Lest one accuse me of inconsistency: What I criticize in Pinker's book is not per se that he encroaches upon my field, philosophy (although the gulf between philosophy and socio-technological progress, his book's area, is far greater than that between the areas that I mix), but that his overzealousness for a particular cause leads him into serious reasoning errors within areas that he knows nothing about, and that his overly confident posture leads him to dismiss and even belittle experts in those areas. As I said in

chapter 4: "one branch of knowledge should not be forced to conform to another—when that happens, we are dealing not with philosophy but with a political agenda."

14. This view is not unique to me. See Victor Hanson and John Heath, *Who Killed Homer? The Demise of Classical Education and the Recovery of Greek Wisdom* (New York: Encounter Books, 2001), 21–28.

15. The totalitarian practical consequences of this sort of thinking have been described, for Marx's and Engel's case, by Miklós Molnár, *Marx, Engels et la politique internationale* [Marx, Engels, and international politics] (Paris: Gallimard, 1975), who examines their endorsement of Western colonization as a means of speeding up industrialization and ultimately communism in third-world countries.

16. See also J. S. Mill, *On Liberty*, chap. 2: "I acknowledge that the tendency of all opinions to become sectarian is not cured by the freest discussion, but is often heightened and exacerbated thereby; the truth which ought to have been, but was not, seen, being rejected all the more violently because proclaimed by persons regarded as opponents." (John Stuart Mill, *Utilitarianism* and *On Liberty*, ed. Mary Warnock [Oxford: Blackwell, 2003], 127.)

17. In an 1817 letter to his brothers George and Thomas: John Keats, *The Complete Poetical Works and Letters of John Keats*, ed. Horace Scudder (Boston: Houghton Mifflin, 1899), 277.

18. It is, in any case, an ancient sentiment. Cassius Dio, *Roman History* 58.23, says that Tiberius used to exclaim something similar: "When I am dead, let the world meet with fire," and here only the imperative (corresponding to the jussive) is possible. Already Cassius calls it an old expression. See also Suetonius, *Life of Nero* 38; it may originally be from a lost play by Euripides.

19. For example *Ecce Homo*, section 1 of "Why I Am a Destiny"; and the posthumous collection *The Will to Power*, section 125 (there are disparate numbering systems of the fragments across German and English editions; I refer to the edition that is probably most accessible to anglophone readers: Friedrich Nietzsche, *The Will to Power*, trans. Walter Kaufmann and Reginald Hollingdale [New York: Vintage Books, 1968]).

20. Indeed "law" (*Gesetz*) is one of the most overused words of *Capital*.

21. That historical development by itself does not imply teleology was understood also by Michael Foster, *The Political Philosophies of Plato and Hegel* (New York: Garland, 1984), originally published in 1935.

22. In-depth study of Aristotelian teleology is offered by the monograph Monte Johnson, *Aristotle on Teleology* (Oxford: Oxford University Press, 2005) and by Allan Gotthelf, "Aristotle's Conception of Final Causality," in *Philosophical Issues in Aristotle's Biology*, eds. Allan Gotthelf and James Lennox (Cambridge: Cambridge University Press, 1987), 204–242; David Charles, "Teleological Causation in the *Physics*," in *Aristotle's Physics: A Collection of Essays*, ed. Lindsay Judson (Oxford: Oxford University Press, 1991), 101–128; Susan Meyer, "Aristotle, Teleology, and Reduction," *Philosophical Review* 101, no. 4 (October, 1992): 791–825; and David Furley, "What Kind of Cause Is Aristotle's Final Cause?," in *Rationality in Greek Thought*, eds. Michael Frede and Gisela Striker (Oxford: Oxford University Press, 1996), 59–79.

23. One might argue that this is false because the rise of Christianity led to an improved status for women; see Rodney Stark, "Reconstructing the Rise of Christianity: The Role

of Women," *Sociology of Religion* 56, no. 3 (Autumn 1995): 229–244. But the same logic as in chapter 5, note 10, above applies here as well: the rise of Christianity strengthened further the role of women (which incidentally had also grown gradually stronger in the pagan era as well) in the late Roman Empire, as it was declining. And again, general Christian practice is one thing, and the way a specific society develops internally is another. The European societies that replaced the Roman Empire were many things in addition to Christian and contained other cultural influences as well, such as the patriarchal barbarism that had helped them overthrow Rome in the first place.

24. In book 3 of *Emile*, Rousseau does not quite hit the mark but still reveals a truth when he urges: "Remember, remember without fail that ignorance never caused any harm, that error alone is fatal, and that we do not go astray by what we do not know, but by what we believe we know." The same idea appears throughout in that work. (A version of a part of this paragraph in the main text first appeared in my article "Why Those Who Claim to 'Follow the Science' Are More Likely to Ignore It," *Federalist*, January 4, 2021, https://thefederalist.com/2021/01/04/why-those-who-claim-to-follow-the-science-are-more-likely-to-ignore-it/.)

25. We have already seen some of the effects of wealth on the oikophobic trajectory. The most essential has been summarized by Thomas Paine in his famous pamphlet *Common Sense* (1776)—which intellectually is quite worthless but contains some nuggets here and there—where he writes, "We are sufficiently numerous, and were we more so, we might be less united . . . for trade being the consequence of population, men become too much absorbed thereby to attend to any thing else. Commerce diminishes the spirit, both of patriotism and military defence. And history sufficiently informs us, that the bravest achievements were always accomplished in the non-age of a nation. With the increase of commerce, England hath lost its spirit. . . . The more men have to lose, the less willing are they to venture. The rich are in general slaves to fear." (Thomas Paine, *Common Sense* [Mineola, NY: Dover Publications, 1997], 40.) See also Adam Ferguson's *An Essay on the History of Civil Society* (1767), which makes some similar points.

26. On the subject of intellectual and artistic subversiveness, see also André Reszler, *L'Intellectuel contre l'Europe* [The intellectual against Europe] (Paris: Archives Karéline, 2010), which is a good book though it goes a bit too far in some of its conclusions.

10. Oikophobia in the United States: The Present

1. This episode took place in Namibia in 2012. One of the disgruntled volunteers later became the author of this book.

2. Human rights are here defined negatively: one has the right not to be robbed, not to be killed, etc. (genuine freedoms), rather than the right to own a house, have health insurance, go to college, etc. (claims toward others). Those who define human rights positively typically insist on the importance of equality of rights, even though equality is far more difficult to achieve in the positive case, and even though an ever-expanding list of positive rights will eventually contradict the negative rights. Once rights are defined positively there is no limit to how many entitlements can be added, which eventually leads to absurd results as well as to the complete impossibility of achieving equality. For more

on the nexus of human rights, Westernization, and Americanization: Stephen Shute and Susan Hurley, eds., *On Human Rights* (New York: Basic Books, 1993), includes essays by philosophers Rawls, Rorty, Lyotard, and others; the dynamic between religious and secular foundations of human rights is outlined in Ari Kohen, *In Defense of Human Rights* (New York: Routledge, 2007); quite interdisciplinary in its links between Westernization and democratization in modernity is Daniele Archibugi, David Held, and Martin Köhler, eds., *Re-Imagining Political Community: Studies in Cosmopolitan Democracy* (Stanford, CA: Stanford University Press, 1998); and a bit off the beaten path, with an interesting overview of the early phase of Americanization in the world, is Robert Rydell and Rob Kroes, *Buffalo Bill in Bologna: The Americanization of the World, 1869–1922* (Chicago: University of Chicago Press, 2005).

3. To Hegel's charge may more justly be laid the fact that he brings to its scandalous extreme the period, inaugurated by Kant, of the most awfully bad writing the German language has ever produced, which also included plenty of German idealists, like Fichte and Schelling. Their writing, as well as some of the French postmodern prose of especially the post-structuralists, are the two highest summits of pseudo-intellectual posturing that European pomposity has ever been able to scale.

4. Allan Bloom, *The Closing of the American Mind* (New York: Simon & Schuster, 1988).

5. A halfhearted answer one sometimes hears is that the culture in which, for example, homosexuals are killed is actually fine, only that there are some individual extremists at the top of society who as demagogues whip up the people into committing atrocities they would not otherwise condone. There should hardly be any need to point out that this answer is not to be taken seriously: those who offer it understand little of the underlying cruelty and tribalism of earlier-stage human culture (and of our human species). In some cultures, millions and millions of otherwise seemingly decent and ordinary people would support the death penalty for homosexual acts.

6. For the positive view immigrants to the United States have of their new home, see Alex Nowrasteh and Andrew Forrester, "Immigrants Recognize American Greatness," *Cato Institute*, February 4, 2019, https://www.cato.org/publications/immigration-research -policy-brief/immigrants-recognize-american-greatness-immigrants.

7. Noam Chomsky, *Terrorizing the Neighborhood: American Foreign Policy in the Post– Cold War Era* (Chico, CA: AK Press, 1991); *What Uncle Sam Really Wants* (Berkeley, CA: Odonian, 1992); with Andre Vltchek, *On Western Terrorism: From Hiroshima to Drone Warfare* (London: Pluto Press, 2013); and *Requiem for the American Dream* (New York: Seven Stories Press, 2017). Other emblematic examples are Howard Zinn, *A People's History of the United States* (New York: HarperCollins, 2005); and "The 1619 Project," *New York Times*, August 14, 2019, https://nyti.ms/37JLWkZ.

8. John Meroney, "A Conversation with Gore Vidal," *Atlantic*, October 2009, https:// www.theatlantic.com/magazine/archive/2009/10/a-conversation-with-gore-vidal/307767/.

9. Pascal Bruckner makes a similar point in the first chapter of *Le sanglot de l'homme blanc* [The tears of the white man] (Paris: Éditions du Seuil, 1983), using the older term "third-worldism" (*le tiers-mondisme*) to describe it.

10. Duncan Fairgrieve, ed., *The Influence of the French Civil Code on the Common Law and Beyond* (London: British Institute of International and Comparative Law, 2007),

contains several contributions on the dynamic between the two systems; and Mary Ann Glendon, Paolo Carozza, and Colin Picker, *Comparative Legal Traditions in a Nutshell* (Saint Paul, MN: West Academic Publishing, 2008), also analyzes them; while Martin Shapiro, *Courts: A Comparative and Political Analysis* (Chicago: University of Chicago Press, 1981), looks at law systems beyond Europe.

11. Mill in *On Liberty*, passim, especially chap. 4; de Tocqueville, *Democracy in America*, passim, especially 1.2.7, and see also for example 2.1.2: "In the United States, the majority undertakes to provide individuals with a host of already prepared opinions, and thus relieves them of the obligation to form their own."

12. Roger Scruton, *England and the Need for Nations* (London: Civitas, 2006), 38 (quoted in the introduction to this book).

13. A good overview of some of the problems is Jonathan Haidt and Tobias Rose-Stockwell, "The Dark Psychology of Social Networks," *Atlantic*, December 2019, https://www.theatlantic.com/magazine/archive/2019/12/social-media-democracy/600763/.

14. The coinage "ghost in the machine" is Gilbert Ryle's, in *The Concept of Mind* (London: Hutchinson's University Library, 1949), chap. 1, sec. 2, one of many good refutations of Cartesianism.

15. Platonic essentialism and Humean bundle theory do not exhaust all the possibilities of viewing the human being that exist in philosophical anthropology. A useful recent volume on some of the possibilities is Jonathan Loose, Angus Menuge, and James Moreland, eds., *The Blackwell Companion to Substance Dualism* (Oxford: Wiley-Blackwell, 2018).

16. Essentialists would argue in the opposite direction: since in their view human beings have an essence and are not mere bundles of parts, they can replace all their parts over time and still remain the same substance; see, for example, James Moreland, "Substance Dualism and the Unity of Consciousness," in Loose et al., *The Blackwell Companion to Substance Dualism*, 184–207.

17. Personal communications from a few readers.

11. The Confluence of the West

1. Other examples of micro-monomania in *Capital*: 1.13.1 ("Development of machinery"), where the capitalist can only be interested in extending his productive capacity, not in also improving the labor condition for workers (there may indeed have been capitalists who did not care about their workers, but one cannot assume from the start that a whole class of persons is fully defined by one essence alone); 1.22.3 ("Division of surplus value in capital and revenue. The abstinence theory"), where greed is the "absolute" passion of a capitalist starting out with his business; 3.15.1 ("General"), where the expansion of capital is the only goal of capitalist production; 3.48 ("The trinitarian formula") and 3.50 ("The appearance of competition"), where, respectively, the capitalist "is indeed nothing but personified capital" whose thoughts are "determined exclusively by his own interest and self-interested motives." See also 2.21.3 ("Schematic presentation of accumulation"), where Marx makes fun of the notion that the capitalist might also be motivated by philanthropy; and 3.18 ("The turnover of merchant's capital. Prices"), where

Marx insists that only a changing mode of production, not also common sense and humanitarian concerns, could have caused a change in sale prices.

2. Herbert Marcuse, *Eros and Civilization* (Boston: Beacon Press, 1955).

3. I am referring here mainly to repression by the state, not by individuals or corporations. Still, the idea might seem inconsistent with so-called cancel culture, in which "woke" oikophobes publicly shame and destroy the livelihoods of those who, like me, wish to think and express themselves more freely. It is certainly true that new forms of repression always arise, and that old taboos are replaced by new ones. But although our complaints about new taboos may be perfectly justified, it is still a relatively free and nonrepressive space—historically speaking—that allows us to be so disturbed by such taboos. A glimpse of this can be caught in Robert Goldstein, *Political Repression in Modern America: 1870 to 1976* (Urbana: University of Illinois Press, 2011); useful for the European context is Pieter Spierenburg, *The Spectacle of Suffering: Executions and the Evolution of Repression* (Cambridge: Cambridge University Press, 1984), which rightly criticizes some of Foucault's work on the topic. In Rome, the empire was more repressive than the republic, but within each, social developments tended toward less repression, albeit with sharp ups and downs depending on the relative sanity of the person holding the highest office. Plato's view that democracy degenerates into tyranny (*Republic*, book 8) does have some truth to it, however, and the decrease in repression is a tendency, not an absolute rule.

4. Robert Wolff, Barrington Moore Jr., and Herbert Marcuse, *A Critique of Pure Tolerance* (Boston: Beacon Press, 1965).

5. This paragraph contains material that first appeared in my article "Degrees of Diversity," *Salisbury Review* 34, no. 2 (Winter 2015): 23–26.

6. This is part of what I criticized about Popper in chapter 9. A version of a part of this paragraph first appeared in the *Federalist* (Benedict Beckeld, "Why Those Who Claim to 'Follow the Science' Are More Likely to Ignore It," January 4, 2021, https://thefederalist.com /2021/01/04/why-those-who-claim-to-follow-the-science-are-more-likely-to-ignore-it/).

7. Jürgen Habermas, *Der philosophische Diskurs der Moderne* (Frankfurt: Suhrkamp, 1985).

8. The term *homo fabricatus* has begun to be used in the context of the genetic manipulation of the human genome, which is not what I mean here. Habermas deals with this issue in *Die Zukunft der menschlichen Natur* [The future of human nature] (Frankfurt: Suhrkamp, 2001).

9. André Reszler, *L'Intellectuel contre l'Europe* [The intellectual against Europe] (Paris: Archives Karéline, 2010), 76–79, analyses the oikophobia of Gauguin as a case study.

10. Michel Foucault, *Histoire de la folie à l'âge classique* [History of madness in the Classical age] (Paris: Gallimard, 1972), published in English simply as *History of Madness*.

11. Roland Barthes, "The Death of the Author," *Aspen: The Magazine in a Box* 5 + 6 (1967).

12. Paul Veyne, *Comment on écrit l'histoire; (suivi de) Foucault révolutionne l'histoire* [How to write history; (followed by) Foucault revolutionizes history] (Paris: Éditions du Seuil, 1978).

13. The two essays "La folie: l'absence d'œuvre" [Madness, the absence of an œuvre] and "Réponse à Derrida" [Reply to Derrida] are collected in, respectively, Michel Foucault, *Dits et Écrits I*, no. 25, and *Dits et Écrits II*, no. 104 (Paris: Gallimard, 1994).

14. Even on the left there were some people who understood this and who resisted the more extreme conclusions of the postmodernists in this regard. See for example Jacques Ellul, *La trahison de l'Occident* [The betrayal of the West] (Paris: Calmann-Lévy, 1975).

15. This has been the case now for several decades. For a relatively early diagnosis by a distinguished philosopher, see Richard Rorty, "The Unpatriotic Academy," *New York Times*, February 13, 1994.

16. "La folie: l'absence d'œuvre" [Madness, the absence of an œuvre], in Michel Foucault, *Dits et Écrits I*, no. 25 (Paris: Gallimard, 1994).

17. See Susanne Gödde, *Euphêmia: Die Gute Rede in Kult und Literatur der griechischen Antike* [Euphêmia: Good speech in cult and literature in Ancient Greece] (Heidelberg: Universitätsverlag Winter, 2011).

18. For the triviality claim, see Barry Smith et al., "From Professor Barry Smith and Others," *Times* (London), May 9, 1992, http://ontology.buffalo.edu/smith/varia/Derrida_Letter.htm, which perhaps is a bit self-serving but makes the general point: "where coherent assertions are being made at all, these are either false or trivial."

19. See the excellent Michèle Lamont, "How to Become a Dominant French Philosopher: The Case of Jacques Derrida," *American Journal of Sociology* 97, no. 3 (November 1997): 584–622.

20. Michel Foucault, *Histoire de la sexualité*, 3 vols. (Paris: Gallimard, 1976–84).

21. See for example Tom Nichols, "Don't Let Students Run the University," *Atlantic*, May 7, 2019, https://www.theatlantic.com/ideas/archive/2019/05/camille-paglia-protests-represent-dangerous-trend/588859/; and Stephen Wermiel and Josh Blackman, "Thwarting Speech on College Campuses," *Human Rights Magazine—American Bar Association* 43, no. 4 (October 20, 2018), https://www.americanbar.org/groups/crsj/publications/human_rights_magazine_home/the-ongoing-challenge-to-define-free-speech/thwarting-speech-on-college-campuses/.

22. Edmund Husserl, *Die Krisis der europäischen Wissenschaften und die transzendentale Phänomenologie* (Hamburg: Felix Meiner, 2012).

23. The trope of the quarrel between poetry and philosophy goes back to book 10 of Plato's *Republic*, where it is related to the banishment of most kinds of poetry from the ideal state. Since poetry only represents objects instead of showing them as they are, poetry and philosophy become, to Plato, mutually exclusive. There is a connection in Plato's *Apology* 22b–c, where Socrates rejects the poets because they are not able to explain their own work but ascribe it to inspiration (I never understood why the *Apology*—Plato's most obnoxious work—is the first piece of literature with which almost all beginner students of Greek around the world are confronted, as if we were really trying to repel them from the discipline). The issue gains deeper intricacy by the fact that Plato himself was a poet and a fabulator, the *Symposium* being his greatest work in that regard.

24. A tiny selection: Goethe discovered that the incisive bone is common to all mammals; Michael Faraday was trained to be a bookbinder but achieved numerous discoveries within electromagnetics; Vincenz Priessnitz was a farm boy who invented hydrotherapy; the joule unit of energy derives from James Joule, who was really a beer brewer; that I have taught Mycenaean Greek I owe to the decipherment of Linear B in the 1950s by Michael Ventris, who was not a classicist, but an architect.

25. The are other forms of nominalism and realism that are more moderate, such as conceptualism, Aristotelian realism, Thomistic realism, and so on, and realism and nominalism can also be applied to different areas, such as those of material objects, ethics, mathematics, and others yet. But the plain realism-nominalism distinction is sufficient for my present purpose, which is to explain how certain philosophical ideas feed into oikophobia. ˙

26. Already in the *Tractatus Logico-Philosophicus* (1921) there are some remarks that made it easier for people to abuse nominalism: 4.002 ("Language dresses thought in such a way that one cannot determine the shape of the dressed thought from the shape of the dress"); 5.6 ("*The limits of my language* entail the limits of my world"); 5.62 ("That the world is *my* world is shown in the fact that the limits of *the* language (the language that I alone understand) entail the limits of *my* world"); and 6.41–42 ("The meaning of the world must lie outside it. In the world, everything is as it is and everything happens as it happens; there is no value *in* it. . . . Therefore there can also not exist any ethical propositions") (all emphases in the original). But there are also some statements that could be interpreted as being against the excesses of this abuse, such as 6.373 ("The world is independent of my will"). Compare also for the nominalism-abuse 1.1: "The world is the totality of facts, not of things," which goes back to Heraclitus's philosophy of becoming, as opposed to being (Ludwig Wittgenstein, *Tractatus Logico-Philosophicus* [Frankfurt: Suhrkamp, 2003]). Later (*Philosophical Investigations*, 1953, posthumously), Wittgenstein tries to solve some of the difficulties that arose from these statements. That early Wittgenstein easily lends himself to a number of divergent interpretations became exceedingly clear to me when a pianist acquaintance in Paris told me with charmingly naïve sincerity that he was composing a musical adaptation of the *Tractatus Logico-Philosophicus*. I had a good laugh at both his and Wittgenstein's expense as I imagined my acquaintance's terse hammering of the piano keys in some interminable scale, but secretly I was a wee bit curious about it.

27. Sarah Bond, "Blog: What Is 'The West'?" *Society for Classical Studies*, May 11, 2018, https://classicalstudies.org/scs-blog/sarah-bond/blog-what-west-addressing-controversy-over-hum110-reed-college, quoting Arum Park. A countering viewpoint I recommend is James Kierstead, "Is Western Civilization a Thing?" *Quillette*, January 11, 2019, https://quillette.com/2019/01/11/is-western-civilization-a-thing/; and Kierstead, "No, Classics Shouldn't 'Burn,'" *Chronicle of Higher Education*, February 23, 2021, https://www.chronicle.com/article/no-classics-shouldnt-burn.

28. To recall my statement earlier in this chapter: "If the postmodernists were true to their own theory of discarding narratives and systems, they would approach every history individually and purely on its own merits—from the arch-narratives of Hegel to the atomistic analyses of Foucault—and criticize a history neither for its larger narrative nor for its lack thereof." An early version of these attacks on patterns or concepts in history is Herbert Butterfield, *The Whig Interpretation of History* (London: G. Bell, 1931). That book contains some good points—such as its critique of teleological, progressive history—but it is focused more on original historical research than on the philosophy of history, and is also somewhat facile in its critique, since it does not realize that if the view of a pattern in history is an imposition, then the insistence that there can be no pattern is also an imposition; Butterfield seems to think that history has a basic bare-bones meaning independent of our active interpretation, which of course is incorrect.

29. See for example Michael Arnold, "Protesters Stop Mock Landing of Columbus," *Los Angeles Times*, October 12, 1992, https://www.latimes.com/archives/la-xpm-1992-10 -12-mn-160-story.html; Hannah Leone, "Goodbye, Columbus Day," *Chicago Tribune*, February 28, 2020, https://www.chicagotribune.com/news/breaking/ct-columbus-day -chicago-public-schools-indigenous-peoples-20200227-q65n2prm3rewrapk54zir7i7qm -story.html; and Royce Dunmore, "'Cancel Columbus Day' Has Twitter Mocking the Colonizer as Statues Come Tumbling Down," *NewsOne*, June 10, 2020, https://newsone .com/playlist/cancel-columbus-day-twitter-statues/item/1.

30. Pascal Bruckner, *La tyrannie de la pénitence* (Paris: Grasset, 2006); Thilo Sarrazin, *Deutschland schafft sich ab* (Munich: Verlagsgruppe Random House, 2010); and Douglas Murray, *The Strange Death of Europe* (London: Bloomsbury Continuum, 2017).

Epilogue

1. See also, in *Capital*, that capitalists do not have will: 1.8.5, "The struggle for a normal working day"; 1.22.3, "Division of surplus value in capital and revenue. The abstinence theory" (and here capital itself has both will and consciousness [*Bewußtsein*]); and passim.

2. Ludwig Wittgenstein, *Tractatus Logico-Philosophicus* (Frankfurt: Suhrkamp, 2003); Daniel Dennett, *Freedom Evolves* (New York: Viking Penguin, 2003).

3. I borrow this phrasing from Max Pohlenz, *Die Stoa: Geschichte einer geistigen Bewegung* [The Stoa: The history of an intellectual movement] (Göttingen: Vandenhoeck & Ruprecht, 1959), 1:124.

4. While Aristotle accepts the mortality of the soul (*psyche*), there is some evidence that he believes the intellect (*nous*) is not subject thereto (*On the Soul* 3.4), although he is not entirely unequivocal on the matter.

5. David Hume, *A Treatise of Human Nature*, ed. Ernest Mossner (London: Penguin, 1969).

6. The "lazy argument" continued to creep up in philosophy long after Chrysippus and Alexander of Aphrodisias; for example Thomas Aquinas resorts to it in *Summa Theologica* 1.83, a passage in which he also defends free will by referring to it as a power (*potentia*). But philosophers have lately realized that the argument is indeed inadequate, and those who advance it today are mostly laymen.

7. Alexander also argues (*On Fate* 30–31) that determinism would render prophecy pointless, since the same thing will come about regardless, but one can quite easily argue the opposite: prophecy implies not contingency, but, on the contrary, some form of predetermination; knowledge of the future can exist only if there is some form of providence or historical tendency that we can trace from the past.

8. Probably the most seminal work of classical scholarship on this issue is Susanne Bobzien, *Determinism and Freedom in Stoic Philosophy* (Oxford: Oxford University Press, 1998). Bobzien's philosophical output in general has done much to dispel modernizing misconceptions about ancient views on free will.

9. Kant's view of freedom is complex, and I am of course not doing it full justice here. For an analysis of this topic I recommend Henry Allison, *Kant's Theory of Freedom* (Cambridge: Cambridge University Press, 1990).

10. Some have been confused by the fact that I switch back and forth between defending and criticizing Christianity (and other things). But as I have stated repeatedly, the very same phenomenon can appear worthy of both praise and blame depending on the context and the area of knowledge within which one views it. We have become so accustomed to always side for or against something, a situation exacerbated by the polarity of contemporary politics, that we find it difficult to adopt, in at least some cases, a more disinterested view. It is in this vein that I quoted Leibniz (chapter 9, note 4).

11. The Greeks did have some notion of an afterlife, of course, mainly Hades, but this was not a pleasant place that anyone looked forward to; the more paradisiacal Elysium was not for normal people.

12. The famous phrase "the best of all possible worlds," as it is commonly translated, derives from Leibniz's *Theodicy*. When I say that the best of all possible worlds should not be confused with (1) the fairest of all possible worlds, or (2) the best of all imaginable worlds, what I mean is: (1) outside the Judeo-Christian belief nexus, the world will become worse if it is rendered perfectly fair, since fairness in the most common sense requires tyranny; and (2) inside the Judeo-Christian belief nexus, one may imagine a world in which there were no sinners, which might be better than our current world, but a world without sinners is not possible, since in Christianity we have free will, and therefore the world we currently inhabit remains the best of all possible worlds (outside that belief nexus, in a deterministic universe, the only possible world is the one we have; see chapter 9, note 9).

13. To what more specific unchristian ethical behavior this distinction leads in the real world is a worthwhile topic, but not one I shall explore any further here.

14. This is not to imply, of course, that practical reciprocity has never been a factor in Christian thinking. For example, Aquinas's understanding of natural law rests on certain inclinations that correspond to those of practical reciprocity (*Summa Theologica* 1-2.94, article 2).

Index